Italian Food

Part 1-2-3-4

Charles Thompson

Copyright© 2023 by Charles Thompson
All rights reserved.

This document is geared towards providing exact and reliable information with regards to the topic and issue covered. The publication is sold with the idea that the publisher is not required to render accounting, officially permitted, or otherwise, qualified services. If advice is necessary, legal or professional, a practiced individual in the profession should be ordered. -From a Declaration of Principles which was accepted and approved equally by a Committee of the American Bar Association and a Committee of Publishers and Associations. In no way is it legal to reproduce, duplicate, or transmit any part of this document in either electronic means or in printed format. Recording of this publication is strictly prohibited and any storage of this document is not allowed unless with written permission from the publisher. All rights reserved. The information provided herein is stated to be truthful and consistent, in that any liability, in terms of inattention or otherwise, by any usage or abuse of any policies, processes, or directions contained within is the solitary and utter responsibility of the recipient reader. Under no circumstances will any legal responsibility or blame be held against the publisher for any reparation, damages, or monetary loss due to the information herein, either directly or indirectly. Respective authors own all copyrights not held by the publisher. The information herein is offered for informational purposes solely, and is universal as so. The presentation of the information is without contract or any type of guarantee assurance. The trademarks that are used are without any consent, and the publication of the trademark is without permission or backing by the trademark owner. All trademarks and brands within this book are for clarifying purposes only and are the owned by the owners themselves, not affiliated with this document.

Contents

Introduction.....5

    Basic foods.....5

Appetizer, snack, side dish.....8

Main Course.....30

Pasta.....54

Fish and Seafood.....73

Meat.....94

Dessert.....114

Part 2.....141

Appetizers, side and snacks.....141

Pasta.....159

Main Course.....178

Meat.....201

Fish and SeaFood.....221

Dessert.....240

Appetizer, snack and side.....262

Pasta.....288

Main Course.....305

Fish and Seafood.....329

Meat.....349

Dessert…..368

Part 4…..387

Appetizers, sides and snacks…..387

Pasta…..403

Main Course…..421

Meat…..444

Fish…..465

Dessert…..485

Italian comfort food
Part 1
Introduction

Italian cuisine is the expression of the culinary art developed in Italy, comprising strongly rooted traditions common to the whole country, as well as all the regional gastronomies, in a continuous exchange: many Italian dishes that were once only known in the regions of origin over time they spread throughout the country.
It is known as a classic example of the Mediterranean diet, recognized as an intangible heritage of humanity by UNESCO in 2010. Furthermore, it is one of the best known and most appreciated gastronomies on a global level; Italy is also renowned for the production of cheeses, olive oil, cured meats, wines, fruit and desserts, which are among the more than 5,000 products of regional traditions.

Basic foods

The basic foods of Italian cuisine are olive oil, condiment par excellence, fresh wheat bread of the day, pasta, vegetables, wine; as regards protein foods, compared to the cuisines of other countries, a characteristic of the Italian gastronomic culture is to consider, in the preparation of a meal, meat of the same importance as other foods, including vegetable ones; moreover, its presence at the table is typically replaced, on certain days of the week, by other protein foods: fish, cheeses and eggs. Fresh meat alternates, in use, even choosing from the vast range of sausages and cured meats.
Coffee, espresso, is considered an indispensable element in the Italian food tradition, both by using it to end the meal, and by consuming it alone, at other times of the day.
The pasta
A fundamental component of Italian cuisine, pasta is divided into two broad categories: dry pasta (100% durum wheat flour mixed with water) and fresh pasta (also with soft wheat flour and almost always mixed with eggs). Characteristic of the pasta is the presence of numerous shapes and varieties: there are 300 different shapes.

Both dry and fresh pasta are used to prepare the first course, in three different ways:
- pasta with sauces: pasta is cooked and then served with a sauce or other condiment;
- soup: pasta is cooked and served in meat or vegetable broth, even together with chopped vegetables;
- baked pasta: the pasta is first cooked and seasoned, and then passed back to the oven.

The condiments for pasta are also very numerous and vary in taste, color and consistency. Sauces are common, but raw condiments are also common. Since the beginning of the nineteenth century, the typical sauce for pasta has been based on tomatoes.

The cheeses
Cheeses and dairy products are foods of which Italy can boast the greatest diversity of existing types. Cheeses are used as a second course, either eaten alone or as an ingredient. They are also used as an ingredient to dress pasta and soup; moreover, cheese is often served in appetizers.

Wine
Wine is a drink almost always present on the typically Italian lunch and dinner table. Italy is the world's largest producer of wine, as well as a country with the widest variety of indigenous vines in the world; there are numerous types of wine produced in the various Italian regions.

The olive oil
Extra virgin olive oil is the condiment par excellence of Italian cuisine, replaced only in some recipes and in some geographical areas by butter. Italy is the largest consumer of olive oil, with 30% of the world total, and is the second largest producer and exporter in the world.

Pizza and similar foods
Pizza is the best known and most consumed Italian food in the world. Furthermore, the traditional art of the Neapolitan pizza maker was recognized as an intangible heritage of humanity by UNESCO in 2017.

In Italy, it is consumed as a single dish (pizza to the plate) or as a snack for a snack, even on the go (pizza by the slice). In the various regions, pizza is accompanied by very similar foods such as focaccia or piadina.

Sausages and cured meats

Italian cuisine can boast a great variety of sausages and cured meats. They are served as a main course or as an appetizer, or used in snacks.

Meat
Meat, especially beef, pork and poultry, is very present and appreciated in Italian cuisine, in a very wide range of preparations and recipes for main courses, although its presence in the meal is not considered fundamental, as it can be replaced by cheese. eggs or fish. It is also important as an ingredient in the preparation of sauces for first courses.
In addition to the varieties mentioned, albeit less commonly, sheep, goat and horse meat is also consumed in Italy.

Fish and seafood
Since Italy is surrounded for more than three quarters by the sea, therefore having a great coastal development and being rich in lakes, fish (both marine and freshwater), as well as crustaceans, molluscs and other seafood , like meat, they enjoy a prominent place in Italian cuisine, as in general in the Mediterranean diet.

Fish is the second course in meals and is also an ingredient in the preparation of seasonings for the first course. It is also widely used in appetizers.

Desserts and ice cream
Italian pastry is full of numerous preparations spread throughout the country and typically regional specialties. Sweets are often present in breakfast and can be the main food of the mid-morning or mid-afternoon snack. In the Italian food tradition, the dessert is used at the end of lunch or dinner only on festive occasions or special occasions.

Appetizer, snack, side dish

Rice arancini
Ingredients:
- Saffron 1 sachet
- Butter 30 g
- Rice 500 g
- Salt up to 1 pinch
- Water 1.2 l
- Seasoned Caciocavallo to grate 100 g

FOR THE RAGU FILLING
- Salt up to taste
- Black pepper to taste
- Onions ½
- Butter 25 g
- Ground pork 100 g
- Extra virgin olive oil to taste
- Tomato puree 200 ml
- Peas 80 g
- Fresh Caciocavallo 50 g
- Red wine 50 ml

FOR THE HAM FILLING
- Cooked ham in a single slice 30 g
- Mozzarella 60 g

FOR THE BATTER
- 00 flour 200 g
- Salt up to 1 pinch
- Water 300 ml

TO BREAD AND FRY
- Breadcrumbs to taste
- Seed oil to taste

Start by boiling the rice in 1 liter of boiling salted water. Cook for about 15 minutes, then dissolve the saffron in very little hot water and add it to the cooked rice. Also add the butter into small pieces.

Add the grated cheese, mix well to mix everything, then pour and level the rice on a large and low tray and cover it with cling film, to make it cool completely. Let the rice rest for a couple of hours out of the refrigerator. In the meantime, dedicate yourself to the ragù filling: peel and finely slice the onion.

Stew the chopped onion in a pan with 2 tablespoons of oil and the butter, then add the minced meat; brown it over high heat, then add the wine and let it evaporate. At this point add the tomato puree, season with salt and pepper to taste and cook over low heat, covered for at least 20 minutes. Halfway through cooking, add the peas. While the peas are cooking, cut the caciocavallo, cooked ham and mozzarella into cubes. You will have all the fillings ready. Once the rice has cooled completely, you can form the arancini, to help you in the formation, keep a bowl full of water nearby so that you can moisten your hands. Take a couple of tablespoons of rice at a time (about 120 grams of rice), flatten the pile in the center of the hand forming a basin and pour in a teaspoon of ragù filling, add a few cubes of caciocavallo. Then close the base of the arancino with the rice and shape it giving it a round shape: you can give this shape to all the arancini stuffed with the ragù. While for the ham filling, stuff each arancino (about 130 grams of rice) with diced ham and mozzarella and shape them into a round shape. Now that you have all the arancini ready, prepare the batter: in a bowl pour the sifted flour, a pinch of salt and the water. Mix thoroughly with a whisk to prevent lumps from forming.

Then dip the arancini, one by one, into the batter, taking care to cover them entirely and roll them in breadcrumbs. In a saucepan, heat the oil and bring it to a temperature of 170 °, at which point fry one arancino at a time or at most two in order not to lower the temperature of the oil: when they are golden brown you can drain them by placing them on a tray lined with absorbent paper. I recommend: enjoy the very hot Sicilian rice arancini!

Peperonata (pepper and onion stew)
Ingredients:
- **Bell peppers 1 kg**
- **Red onions 400 g**
- **Tomato puree 400 g**
- **Extra virgin olive oil 3 tbsp**
- **Garlic 2 cloves**
- **Fine salt to taste**
- **Black pepper to taste**

To prepare peperonata, wash and dry the peppers. Then slice them lengthwise, all around the core , remove the white filaments and reduce them to thin layers. Peel and slice the onions. Pour a drizzle of oil and the whole garlic cloves into a large pan. Heat and add the onions. Stew the onions over medium-low heat for about 15 minutes, stirring occasionally. When they are softened and have released their water, pour in the peppers. Add salt and pepper, then stir and cover with a lid : cook the peppers for another 15 minutes over medium heat. The peppers will be softened, remove the cloves of garlic, and pour in the tomato puree, stir and cook for another 15 minutes with the lid on. Once cooked, your peperonata is ready to be enjoyed hot, warm or even cold to accompany meat, fish or cheese dishes!

Mozzarella in carrozza (Fried mozzarella)
Ingredients:
- **White bread loaf 12 slices 600 g**
- **Buffalo mozzarella cheese 500 g**
- **Fine salt to taste**
- **Eggs 5 -**
- **Flour 00 1 100g**
- **Breadcrumbs 300 g**
- **TO FRY**
- **Sunflower seed oil 1 l**

To prepare the fried mozzarella, start by cutting the buffalo mozzarella into 1/2 "(1 cm) thick slices. Place them gradually on a tray lined with blotting paper and cover with more blotting paper.

Press gently with your hands to blot the mozzarella and remove excess water. If necessary, use paper towels until it is completely dry. At this point, go ahead and stuff the bread. Put the slices of bread on a cutting board. Place the slices of mozzarella on top, so as to cover the entire surface, but without letting it stick out, salt and cover each slice with another slice of bread. Continue like this for all the other slices of bread, until you finish the mozzarella. Then trim the slices of stuffed bread using a knife, to remove the outer crust. At this point you can cut the mozzarella in the bread in two different ways. By cutting a cross you will get 4 squares from each slice.

For a triangular cut you have to cut the bread first in half on the diagonal and then in half on the other diagonal. This way you will get 4 triangles. Continue this way until all the pieces are finished. Now switch to the breading. Break the eggs into an oven dish and beat them with a whisk for a few minutes. Then in two other baking dishes place the breadcrumbs in one and the sifted flour in the other. At this point dip each piece of stuffed bread first into the flour and then using 2 forks into the egg, to coat them completely. Then set them on a plate for a few seconds, to remove the excess egg part. and avoid lumps when you dip it in the breadcrumbs. Transfer to a cutting board and with the blade of a knife lightly press the edges and the surface in order to even out the breadcrumbs and make a more precise shape. If necessary, dip it in the breadcrumbs again and press again with the knife blade. Continue in this way for all the other pieces and transfer them gradually to a tray lined with baking paper. Then place in the fridge for about 30 minutes.
After the breaded mozzarella has set, you can start with the second breading, first dip into the egg, then set in the saucer to remove the excess and finally dip in the breadcrumbs. As previously, then transfer the pieces of breaded mozzarella onto a cutting board and with the blade of a knife even out the breadcrumbs. Continue this way for all the others by placing them on a tray lined with baking paper. Store in the fridge to set for another 30 minutes. Pour the oil into a frying pan and bring it to a temperature of 340-350 ° F (170-180 ° C) maximum. Put in a few pieces at a time and cook the fried mozzarellas for 1-2 minutes, turning them from time to time with a skimmer. When they are well browned, drain them from the oil and put them on a tray lined with absorbent paper to remove the excess oil. Fry the others and serve.

Potato croquettes
Ingredients:
- Red potatoes 1 kg
- Egg yolks 2
- Nutmeg to taste
- Black pepper to taste
- Fine salt to taste
- Parmigiano Reggiano DOP cheese (100 g) - grated
- **FOR THE BREADING**
- Eggs 2)
- Breadcrumbs to taste

TO FRY
- **Peanut seed oil to taste**

To prepare potato croquettes, wash the potatoes under running water to remove soil residue, place them unpeeled in a large saucepan, cover with water and bring to a boil: to cook them evenly, use similar sized potatoes as much as possible. It will take about 40 minutes if you boil them or about half that time with a pressure cooker. Once ready, let them cool down slightly (just enough to be able to handle them) and peel them. Pass them through a potato masher to obtain a puree while they are still hot; in a separate bowl, beat the yolks with pepper and salt then add them to the potato puree flavor with grated nutmeg and season with grated cheese, stir with a spoon to mix the ingredients to obtain a soft and dry mixture. Take about 1/4 cup of mixture and shape into a croquette, giving it a cylindrical shape, slightly pressing both ends. As you make the croquettes, place them on a tray covered with baking paper. This recipe will yield about 30 croquettes. Once you've used up the mixture, proceed to bread the croquettes: beat the two eggs in one bowl and place the breadcrumbs in another. Pass the croquettes first in the egg, then in the breadcrumbs.

Place the croquettes on a tray covered with baking paper. Once all the croquettes are finished, heat plenty of peanut oil in a medium size pan until it reaches 180-190 ° C (we recommend the use of a kitchen thermometer for best results). Dip 3-4 croquettes in the oil at a time so as not to lower the temperature of the oil too much. Cook them by turning them over with a skimmer until they are well browned on all sides. Drain them and put them on a plate lined with absorbent paper to drain excess oil. Serve the potato croquettes while they're still hot!

Octopus salad with parsley
Ingredients:
- Octopus 1 kg cleaned
- Carrots 1
- Celery 1
- Garlic 1 clove
- Bay leaves 2 leaves
- Ground black pepper to taste
- Fine salt to taste

FOR THE DRESSING
- Parsley 10 g
- Lemon juice 2 tbsp - freshly squeezed
- Extra virgin olive oil 2 ½ tbsp
- Black pepper 1 pinch
- Fine salt 1 pinch

To make octopus salad with parsley, first peel the carrot with a vegetable peeler, then chop it roughly. Do the same with the celery. Put a large pot of water on to boil, and add the chopped carrot, celery, an unpeeled garlic clove, the bay leaves, and season with salt and pepper. Rinse the octopus under running water and, once the pot of water is boiling, immerse the octopus fully and let it cook over medium heat for 40-45 minutes, with the lid on the pot. While the octopus is cooking, use a skimmer to remove any residue and foam that forms on the surface of the cooking water. Once the octopus has finished cooking, let it cool in the cooking water so that it softens. Next, transfer it to a cutting board: Use a knife to remove the eyes, then remove the beak as well. Cut across the part where the head is to remove it, then empty it.

Cut the tentacles into pieces around inch (1 cm) long. Chop the head into small pieces as well and place everything in a bowl. Move on to the dressing: Squeeze the lemon to get 2 tbsp (10 g) of juice, then wash, pat dry, and finely chop the parsley, getting rid of the stems. Make the dressing by placing the parsley , lemon juice, and olive oil in a small jar (to emulsify it more easily). Season with salt and pepper. Close the jar and shake it to form an emulsion. Pour the dressing over the octopus, mix well, and serve your octopus salad with parsley right away!

Tuscan beans
Ingredients:
- **Dried cannellini beans 300 g**
- **Tomato puree 200 g**
- **Garlic 2 cloves**
- **Sage to taste**
- **Extra virgin olive oil q.s.**
- **Salt up to taste**
- **Black pepper to taste**

First, put the dried cannellini beans in a large bowl, cover them with plenty of cold water and leave them to soak for at least one whole night. The next day, transfer the beans with all their liquid to a saucepan: the beans should be completely covered, so add more water if necessary. Cook the cannellini beans over low heat for at least 50 minutes, skimming them occasionally with a slotted spoon.

After this time, drain the beans and keep the cooking liquid. Pour a drizzle of oil into a large frying pan, add the peeled garlic cloves and the sage leaves and leave to brown briefly, then add the tomato purée and let it reduce for a few minutes, still over low heat.
At this point add the cannellini beans, salt and pepper and also add the cooking liquid from the beans that you had kept aside.

Cover with a lid and cook for about 20 minutes on medium heat. Your beans are ready to be served piping hot!

Battered zucchini flowers
Ingredients:
- Zucchini flowers 15
- Fine salt to taste
- Peanut seed oil to taste - (for frying)

FOR THE CLASSIC BATTER
- Water 1 cup (220 g) - (mineral, lukewarm)
- Flour 00 (150 g)
- Fresh brewer's yeast 1 ½ tbsp (15 g)
- Fine salt ¾ tsp (6 g)
- Sugar ½ tbsp (6 g)

FOR THE TEMPURA
- Water 1 cup (200 g)
- Flour 00 1 cup (100 g)
- Egg yolks 1

To make the battered zucchini flowers, start by preparing the batter. First, dissolve 1½ tbsp (15 g) of fresh brewer's yeast, crumbled by hand, in a little room-temperature water taken from the 1 cup (220 g) of water you need for the batter, emulsifying with a whisk. Next, pour the flour into another bowl, add the rest of the room-temperature water, and mix with a whisk until you get a smooth mixture without any lumps.

Then add the brewer's yeast dissolved in the water, continuing to whisk. Now add ¾ tsp (6 g) of salt and ½ tbsp (6 g) of sugar, mixing again to combine the ingredients, and then cover with plastic wrap. Leave to rest for around 30 minutes at room temperature.
In the meantime, clean the zucchini flowers, starting by gently pulling off the stems. Then, still using your hands, pull off both the external pistils and the internal bud. Repeat these steps with all the zucchini flowers.

After 30 minutes, the classic batter will be well leavened, so now it's time for the frying. Pour the oil into a pot and heat to a maximum temperature of 170 ° -180 ° C (use a food thermometer to check). When the oil is almost at the right temperature, put the flowers into the batter, using kitchen tweezers to turn them so they are completely coated.

Next, take each flower out of the batter, allowing the excess to drain off, and then immerse the flowers in the hot oil, only doing a few at a time so the temperature doesn't go down too much. When the flowers are nice and golden, turn them and cook on the other side, too.

Then, take them out of the oil using a skimmer and place on a paper towel. Season with a pinch of salt and serve your battered zucchini flowers.
For a crispier version, once all of the flowers have been cleaned, as described above, you can make the tempura. Place the egg yolk in a bowl and, beating it with a whisk, add ¾ cup (100g) of flour little by little, and then slowly pour in 1 cup (200 g) of ice-cold water.

Continue to beat until you get a smooth mixture. Immerse the flowers in the batter, turning them so they are completely coated. Heat the oil to a temperature of 170 ° -180 ° C, as indicated above, and fry your battered zucchini flowers, turning them over halfway through.
Once they're cooked, remove them from the oil using a skimmer and transfer to a paper towel. Season with salt and serve them still hot!

Caponata
Ingredients:
- Eggplant 1 kg
- Celery 400 g
- White onions 250 g
- Cluster tomatoes 200 g
- Green olives in brine 200 g - pitted
- Salted capers 1 (50 g) - rinsed
- Pine nuts 50 g
- Sugar 60 g
- White wine vinegar 60 g
- Basil to taste
- Tomato paste 2 ½ tbsp (40 g)
- Extra virgin olive oil to taste
- Fine salt to taste

FOR FRYING THE EGGPLANT
- Extra virgin olive oil to taste

To make caponata (eggplant salad), first clean the onion and slice it thin. Trim the celery and cut it into thin slices. Cut the green olives in half and remove the pits. Wash and dry the eggplants, trim and cut them into approx. 1-inch (2.5 cm) thick pieces. Do the same with the tomatoes. Heat a frying pan and toast the pine nuts for a few minutes until they are golden in color. Now take your eggplants: put the olive oil in a high-sided pan and heat it, pour a few eggplant pieces in at a time and fry them for a few minutes. Once they are golden, drain them with the skimmer and place them on a tray lined with absorbent paper to remove excess oil, then set aside.

In a large pan pour a generous round of olive oil, heat it and then pour in the onion. Fry well until the onion has a light golden color, then add the celery; let it brown well, then add the capers, olives, roasted pine nuts and tomatoes. Brown for a few moments, then cover with the lid and cook over low heat for 15-20 minutes. In the meantime, prepare the sweet-and-sour sauce: pour the vinegar, tomato paste and sugar into a small pot.

Mix well with a teaspoon and, after 15-20 minutes of cooking, add salt and pour the sauce into the pan. Turn up the heat and stir until the smell of vinegar has evaporated. Turn off the flame, add the fried eggplant and sprinkle with plenty of basil. Mix everything well, transfer the caponata (eggplant salad) in an ovenproof dish and put it in the fridge. This dish should be served cold or at room temperature and will taste even better the next day.

Fennel au gratin
Ingredients:
- **Fennel 1 kg**
- **Butter 1 stick (35 g)**
- **Parmigiano Reggiano DOP cheese 35 g- (for sprinkling)**

FOR THE BECHAMEL
- **Whole milk 300 g**
- **Butter 1 stick (30 g)**
- **Flour 00 5 tbsp**
- **Fine salt to taste**
- **Nutmeg to taste**

To make fennel au gratin, clean and tip the fennel, remove the base and outermost, tougher leaves; cut each one in half and wash under running water, then cut into large slices. Plunge the fennel in abundant hot salted water and blanch them for 5-6 minutes.

In a capacious pan melt 1 stick of butter on a low flame, drain the fennel thoroughly and once the butter has melted, add the vegetables to the pan to brown for another 5 minutes, turning them over occasionally so that a crust forms on both sides. Remove from the heat when done, and start preparing the bechamel. Heat the milk in a saucepan, in another saucepan melt the butter and gradually sprinkle in the sieved flour, stirring all the while with a whisk to prevent lumps from forming.

Now add the previously heated milk and continue to stir until the sauce thickens; add the salt and the nutmeg. Now take the previously browned fennel slices and place them on the bottom of a round baking tray that is big enough for the vegetables to be arranged in a single layer; we used a 10 inch tray. Arrange them in a circle along the edge and work your way towards the center.

Pour the bechamel over them, sprinkle with the grated Parmigiano Reggiano cheese and bake in a static oven preheated to 180°C for 15-20 minutes, until a golden crust forms on the surface. Remove the fennel au gratin from the oven, leave to cool and then serve.

Mussels au gratin
Ingredients:
- **Mussels 500 g**
- **Breadcrumbs 100 g**
- **Grana Padano DOP cheese 1 tbsp - (grated)**
- **Garlic 1 clove**
- **Lemon peel 1**
- **Parsley 10 g**
- **Extra virgin olive oil 2 ½ tbsp (30 g)**
- **Black pepper to taste**

To make the mussels au gratin, first of all clean them, discarding any open mussels and keeping only the closed ones. After rinsing them under running water, remove the beard that sticks out of the shells, by pulling outwards. Open the mussel gently, making sure that when you open it, the mussel remains intact and attached to the shell. Repeat the process with all of the mussels and keep their water, filtering it through a strainer, as this will be used later on to wet the breadcrumbs.

As you open the mussels, place them on a baking tray lined with parchment paper. Next, prepare the breadcrumbs. Pour them into a bowl, together with the grated Grana Padano cheese, the chopped fresh parsley, the zest of the lemon, a crushed garlic clove and a sprinkling of black pepper.

Now pour in 2½ tbsp (30 g) of olive oil and cup (150 g) of filtered mussel water. Stir to achieve a smooth, moist mixture.

Using a spoon, stuff the mussels, drizzle them with olive oil, and bake them on the top shelf of a conventional oven preheated to 390°F (200°C) for 12 minutes and then on maximum power in broil mode for another 3 minutes. Once cooked, take your mussels au gratin out of the oven and serve immediately.

Sautéed mushrooms
Ingredients:
- Mushrooms 800 g
- Garlic 1 clove
- Parsley to taste
- Butter 2 tbsp
- Extra virgin olive oil 3 tbsp

Slice the mushrooms. Heat the butter with the oil and a halved garlic clove in a non-stick frying pan. Season the mushrooms. Add the mushrooms to the pan, sauté over high heat for a 5minutes. Season with salt and pepper. Add the finely chopped parsley. Remove from the heat and serve the sautéed mushrooms hot or cold, depending on your menu.

Vitello tonnato
Ingredients:
- Veal 800 g - (steak)
- Celery 1
- Carrots 1
- Yellow onions 1
- Garlic 1 clove
- White wine 250 g
- Water 1l
- Bay leaves 1 leaf
- Cloves 3
- Extra virgin olive oil 3 tbsp
- Ground black pepper ½ tsp
- Fine salt 2 pinches

FOR THE SAUCE
- Eggs 2
- Tuna in oil 3 oz (100 g) - drained
- Anchovies in oil 3 fillets
- Salted capers 2 tsp (5 g)
- Caper berries to taste - for decoration

Start by cleaning the vegetables you'll need to cook the meat. Wash them, peel and tip the carrot, then cut it into pieces. Tip the celery and cut it into pieces too. Peel the onion and cut it in half. Place the ingredients in a bowl and add the whole peeled garlic.

Now clean the meat: remove any cartilage and fat filaments. Place the eye of round, chopped vegetables, the laurel leaf, 2-3 cloves and the black peppercorns in a large pan. Add the white wine and the water, which should cover all the ingredients. Add two pinches of salt and then the oil. Switch on the stove and bring to the boil, then remove the foam as soon as it forms on the surface. Put the lid on and lower the flame slightly before leaving to cook for around 40-45 minutes; remember that every lb of meat requires a cooking time of around 30 minutes. The important thing is that the temperature in the middle of the meat cut never exceeds 65°C: use a cooking thermometer to check this. Once you have cooked the meat cut, drain it and leave it to cool thoroughly. Then remove the laurel, pepper and cloves. Take 1/3 of the resulting broth, simmer and reduce it on a high flame for around ten minutes. The leftover meat broth will be useful for other preparations, like risottos; once cooked, drain the vegetables in a container. Now prepare the boiled eggs. Place the eggs in a saucepan with abundant cold water. Switch on the stove and as soon as the water comes to the boil, set the timer to 9 minutes.When boiled, drain the eggs and rinse them in cold water. Peel them once cooled and cut them into 4 pieces. Add the egg slices to the bowl with the vegetables. Add the drained tuna too, along with the anchovies in oil and the desalted capers (to desalt them, place them under fresh running water); lastly, add a little broth. Use an immersion blender and add a little more broth if needed . Blend into a smooth cream with whatever consistency you prefer. By now the meat should have cooled down. Slice it thinly with a smooth bladed knife. Arrange the slices on a serving dish and pour the cream over them. Lastly, decorate with the caper fruits, some whole and some sliced: your vitello tonnato is ready.

Neapolitan eggplants
Ingredients:
- **Eggplant 1 kg**
- **Copper tomatoes 500 g**
- **Basil 10 leaves**
- **2 cloves garlic**
- **Salt up to taste**
- **Extra virgin olive oil to taste**

TO FRY THE EGGPLANTS
- **Peanut oil 1 l**

To prepare the mushroom eggplants, first wash the coppery tomatoes and cut them into cubes. Now pour a generous drizzle of oil and two cloves of garlic into a pan, cook, add the tomatoes and cook over low heat for about 20/25 minutes.
Wash and trim the eggplants. Cut the eggplants into cubes of about 2cm. Heat the seed oil in a pan. When it reaches 170 °, fry the eggplants a little at a time.
Once they are golden brown, gradually drain on paper for fried or kitchen paper. Once the sauce is ready, you can remove the garlic cloves. Season with salt and pepper and let the sauce cool. Finally, add the eggplants to the sauce. Flavor with the chopped basil and mix gently. The mushroom eggplants are ready to be enjoyed.

Polenta chips
Ingredients:
- Corn flour foil 250 g
- Water 1 l
- Extra virgin olive oil 1 tbsp
- Rosemary to taste
- Coarse salt to taste

FOR FRYING IN THE PAN
- Vegetable oil to taste

To prepare the polenta chips, start with the polenta. Place a saucepan with water and oil on the fire. As soon as it reaches a boil, pour the corn flour while stirring rapidly. As soon as it starts getting the right consistency, lower the heat and continue to cook, stirring with a wooden spoon, for about 30-40 minutes until the polenta has reached a fairly solid consistency. Turn off the flame and grease a 38x25 cm rectangular pan. Pour the polenta still hot, and level the surface with a spatula trying to obtain a thickness of 1 cm. Finally cover with parchment paper and level the surface with a rolling pin to make it smooth. Let it cool for at least 2 hours in the refrigerator.

Take the pan with the polenta and turn it over on a cutting board. With a smooth blade cut sticks about 2 cm wide. Then cut in the other direction to create rows of sticks of about 8 cm long: your chips are ready to be fried. Place a pan with plenty of oil on the stove, and heat it until it reaches a temperature of 180 ° C (use a kitchen thermometer to measure it). As soon as the oil reacheds the right temperature, dip a few pieces of polenta at a time for about 8 minutes until they are golden brown. Drain with skimmer and place on a tray lined with absorbent paper to eliminate excess oil. Finely chop the rosemary and mix it with coarse salt. Transfer the polenta chips in a basket lined with paper towels, and serve them with a sprinkle of the rosemary and salt mix. Enjoy the still hot and steaming polenta chips!

Mediterranean-style eggplant rolls
Ingredients:
- Long eggplant (4 slices) 120 g
- Mozzarella 100 g
- Tomato puree 200 g
- Pitted olives 15 g
- Basil 4 leaves
- 1 clove garlic
- Extra virgin olive oil 2 tbsp
- Salt up to taste
- Black pepper to taste

Start preparing the sauce: heat the oil in a saucepan, add a clove of garlic and brown it for 5 minutes over low heat. When the oil is flavored, pour the tomato pulp, add salt and pepper and cook for another 15 minutes. While the tomato sauce is cooking, wash the eggplant and cut it into slices about 1 cm thick with the help of a mandolin: you will need to make 4 long slices of uniform thickness. Heat a plate well and grill the eggplant slices on both sides, then transfer them to a plate or cutting board.
When the tomato sauce is ready, remove the garlic clove. Chop the mozzarella with your hands and preheat the oven to 180 ° in static mode. Now you are ready to assemble the rolls: spread a layer of tomato on the surface of the eggplants, add a little frayed mozzarella, a teaspoon of olives and a basil leaf.
Roll up the stuffed eggplants and place them in a small baking dish with the closure facing down. Finally cover the rolls with a little tomato sauce and a few pieces of mozzarella. The rolls are now ready to be baked: bake them in the preheated static oven at 180 ° for about 10 minutes, just enough time for the cheese to melt. Once out of the oven, your Mediterranean-style eggplant rolls are ready to be tasted still racy!

Stuffed Baked Potatoes
Ingredients:
- Potatoes (4 of the same size) 860 g
- Ground beef 120 g
- Sweet provola 40 g
- Parmigiano Reggiano DOP to grate 40 g
- Garlic 1 clove
- Extra virgin olive oil 30 g
- White wine 15 g
- Salt up to taste
- Black pepper to taste

To prepare the stuffed baked potatoes, start by washing and drying the tubers well. We advise you to choose potatoes of the same size in order to obtain uniform cooking afterwards. Arrange the potatoes on a baking tray covered with parchment paper. Bake them in a preheated static oven at 190°C for about 1 hour (cooking times depend on the size of the potatoes, to get the best results, test cooking by inserting a toothpick into the potatoes). In the meantime, heat the olive oil in a pan with the peeled garlic clove, once the garlic has flavored the oil, remove them and add the minced meat, crush it to crumble it and brown it for about 10 minutes, then blend with the white wine and, once the alcohol has evaporated, turn off the heat and keep aside.

When the potatoes have finished cooking (make sure they are soft by inserting them with a toothpick) take them out of the oven, let them cool slightly, then cut them in half lengthwise. With a teaspoon, remove the potato pulp leaving a border of about half a centimeter and collect it in a bowl.

Once you have hollowed out all the potatoes, mash the pulp with a fork to obtain a puree. Add the browned minced meat, salt and pepper.

Cut the provola into cubes and add it to the filling, stir to mix the ingredients. Now stuff your potatoes with the filling, helping you with a spoon. Season the potatoes with the grated cheese, then place them on a dripping pan covered with parchment paper and put them under the grill for 5 minutes to brown the surface. Serve your stuffed baked potatoes piping hot!

Main Course

Porcini mushroom risotto
Ingredients:
- Rice 320 g
- Porcini mushrooms 400 g
- Vegetable broth 1 l
- Yellow onions 1 - small
- Garlic 1 clove
- Butter 30 g
- Extra virgin olive oil 2 tbsp
- Fine salt to taste
- Black pepper to taste
- **FOR GARNISHING**
- **Parmigiano Reggiano DOP cheese 50 g- to be grated**
- **Butter 30 g**
- **Parsley 2 spoonfuls - to be minced**

To make porcini mushroom risotto, first prepare the vegetable broth. Cut the mushrooms into slices approximately 7-8 mm thick, keeping the whole section intact where possible.

Heat the oil in a non-stick pan and briefly fry a clove of crushed garlic, then turn up the heat and add the mushrooms. Sauté the mushrooms over high heat for approximately 10 minutes until they become brown, then add salt and pepper and remove from the heat. The browned mushrooms will give the risotto a pleasant toasted note.

In the meantime, peel and finely chop the onion. Melt the butter in a saucepan, add the onion, and let it cook over low heat for 10-15 minutes, adding a ladle of broth if necessary. When the onion has softened, add the rice and toast for a couple of minutes.

When the rice has become almost transparent, cook it by adding one ladle of broth at a time and stirring frequently; make sure that the bubbles from boiling remain constant and that the heat is not too high. When the rice is very al dente,, add the porcini mushrooms a few minutes before it is ready and finish cooking, adjusting the salt and pepper if necessary.

Once cooked, stir the risotto over low heat, adding the butter and grated Parmesan cheese, and mix well. If you prefer a less dry risotto, add another ladle of broth. Garnish with fresh chopped parsley, and your porcini mushroom risotto is ready to be served!

Meatballs with tomato sauce
Ingredients:
- Beef 220 g - ground
- Sausage 165 g
- Breadcrumbs 30 g
- Parmigiano Reggiano DOP cheese 25 g - grated
- Eggs 1
- Parsley 1 tbsp - chopped
- Oregano 1 pinch - dried
- Nutmeg 1 pinch - ground
- Fine salt to taste
- Black pepper to taste
- Extra virgin olive oil to taste

FOR THE SAUCE
- Tomato puree 350 g
- Water 50 g
- Fine salt 1 tsp
- Oregano to taste - dry
- Black pepper to taste

To prepare meatballs with tomato sauce, start with the meat mixture: cut stale bread into pieces and place it in a mixer with blades and pulse until crumbly. Set the crumbs aside and remove the twine from the sausages, cut them gently lengthways and finally remove the casing. Squeeze the meat out with a knife blade or a fork, then place it in a bowl together with the ground meat. Add oregano, a pinch of grated nutmeg, and chopped parsley. Finally, add grated Parmesan cheese and the breadcrumbs you made as well as an egg and knead everything with your hands, adding salt and pepper and mix until you have obtained a homogeneous mixture. Use this mixture to form little balls, taking a piece of the mixture and shaping it with both hands. As soon as all the meatballs are ready, heat some oil in a non-stick pan and when the oil is hot, place the meatballs in the pan, cooking them on both sides for a couple of minutes. Pour in tomato puree add water, season with salt and pepper, lower the heat and continue cooking for 15-20 minutes. Once ready, season with dried oregano and enjoy your meatballs with tomato sauce still hot!

Saffron risotto
Ingredients:
- **Saffron threads 1 tsp**
- **Rice 320 g**
- **Butter 125 g**
- **Onions 1**
- **Grana Padano DOP cheese 80 g - to be grated**
- **White wine 40 g**
- **Water to taste**
- **Vegetable broth 1 l**
- **Fine salt to taste**

FOR GARNISHING
- **Saffron threads to taste**

To make the saffron risotto, first put the threads in a small glass, pour just enough water to cover them completely, stir and leave to infuse overnight, this way they will release all their color. Next, prepare the vegetable stock. For this recipe you will need one quart. Peel and finely chop the onion so it will dissolve while being cooked and not be detected when tasting the risotto.

In a large saucepan pour 50 g of butter from the total amount for this recipe, melt it over low heat, then add the chopped onion and let it stew for 10-15 minutes, adding some broth to avoid drying the sauté: the onion must be transparent and soft. Once the onion is stewed, pour in the rice and toast it for 3-4 minutes, so that the grains will seal and keep cooking well. Sweat with the white wine and let it evaporate completely. Now proceed with cooking for about 18-20 minutes, adding the stock one ladle at a time, as needed, as it is absorbed by the rice: the grains must always be covered by stock.

Five minutes before the cooking time is up, pour the water with the previously infused saffron threads, stir to flavor and dye the risotto to a nice golden color. Once cooked, turn off the heat, add salt, stir in the grated cheese and the remaining 75 g of butter.

Stir and cover with a lid. Let it rest for a couple of minutes. At this point, the saffron risotto is ready, garnish the dish with a few more saffron threads, and serve the risotto hot.

Knödel
Ingredients:
- Stale bread 250 g
- Speck 150 g
- White onions 50 g
- Eggs 2
- Whole milk 250 g
- Butter ¾ tbsp (10 g)
- Black pepper to taste
- Parsley to taste
- Chives to taste

To make your Knödel, first prepare the meat broth and keep it warm. Next, peel and finely chop the onion. Cut the speck into very small pieces of around 110 inch (2-3 mm).

Melt the butter in a pan over low heat, then add the onion and speck. Brown for 5 minutes, stirring frequently.
Then turn off the heat and set aside. Chop the chives and parsley, then cut the stale bread into cubes of around ¼ inch (0.5 cm).
Pour the bread into a bowl and add the milk (200 g and add more if the mixture is too dry and not very malleable). Add the eggs and the chopped chives and parsley.
Continue adding the warm speck and onion , and start mixing everything together. If the mixture is too dry, add more milk. If it's gone too sticky or soft, try adding a little flour to the mixture. Once the mixture is ready, moisten your hands a little with cold water and shape the dumplings by rolling the dough between your hands. The dumplings should be around 2 inches (5 cm) in diameter.
Place them on a tray as you shape them. You should end up with around 10 of them. Once they're ready, you'll need to cook your dumplings in the boiling meat stock, which should take around 15 minutes at a moderate simmer. Serve your Knödel (Tyrolean-style dumplings) piping hot.

Gnocchi alla Romana

Ingredients:
- **Semolina 250 g**
- **Whole milk 1 l**
- **Butter 100 g**
- **Egg yolks 2**
- **Parmigiano Reggiano DOP cheese 100 g - grated**
- **Pecorino cheese 40 g**
- **Fine salt 1 tsp 7 g**
- **Nutmeg to taste**

To prepare gnocchi alla romana, place the milk in a pan over the heat, and add butter (30 g), salt, and a pinch of nutmeg; as soon as the milk starts to boil, whisk in the semolina, stirring vigorously to prevent the formation of lumps.

Cook the mixture over low heat for a few minutes, until it has thickened; remove the pan from the heat and add the two yolks to the mixture, stirring this time with a wooden spoon.

Add the Parmesan cheese and stir again. Now pour half of the dough, still hot, on a sheet of baking paper and using your hands, give it a cylindrical shape. To avoid scalding your hands, first put them under cold running water. Once you have obtained a uniform cylinder, wrap it in baking paper. Do the same with the other half of the dough you had put aside. Place the two rolls in the refrigerator for about twenty minutes.
Once cooled, you will have a compact dough that you can easily slice with a knife. To make cutting easier, we recommend wetting the blade with water. Once you have obtained about 40 pieces, place them on a previously buttered baking tray and sprinkle them with melted, not hot, butter 70 g.
Sprinkle the surface with Pecorino Romano and bake in a static preheated oven at 200° C for 20-25 minutes (if you use a convection oven, 350° F, 180° C, for 15 minutes). Now turn on the grill and gratin the top for 4-5 minutes. Once ready serve your gnocchi alla romana hot!

Frittata
Ingredients:
- **Eggs 8**
- **Pecorino cheese 50 g - to be grated**
- **Parmigiano Reggiano DOP cheese 50 g - to be grated**
- **Fine salt to taste**
- **Black pepper to taste**
- **Extra virgin olive oil 1 tsp (5 g) - to grease the pan**

To prepare the frittata, crack the eggs and place them in a large bowl, then beat them lightly with a fork (or whisk). Pour in the grated Parmesan and Pecorino cheese, then add salt and pepper to taste.

Place a 30 cm non-stick pan over the heat and heat the oil for a few moments. Add the beaten eggs and let them cook over low heat for 8 minutes, covering the pan with a flat lid; move the pan occasionally to keep the frittata from sticking to the bottom.

Once the required time has elapsed, flip the frittata: place the serving plate on the pan and turn it upside down, keeping the plate and pan tightly together so that the frittata does not slip out: now you will find yourself with the cooked part of the frittata facing upwards, so slide the frittata inside the pan, so that the other side can cook for another 8 minutes, this time without the lid. Once ready, serve the frittata hot.

Pumpkin risotto
Ingredients:
- **Carnaroli rice 320 g**
- **Pumpkin 600 g**
- **Yellow onions 3**
- **Vegetable broth 1.5 l**
- **Parmigiano Reggiano DOP cheese 80 g**
- **White wine 60 g**
- **Butter 50 g**
- **Black pepper to taste**
- **Fine salt to taste**
- **Extra virgin olive oil 20 g**

To cook pumpkin risotto, start by preparing a light vegetable broth, which you will use to cookthe rice. Cut the vegetables, put them in a large saucepan, cover them with water and add salt. Cover with a lid, bring to a boil and cook for about 1 hour. Filter the broth and keep it warm. Then start preparing the pumpkin: clean it, cut it into slices and then into small cubes. Finely chop the onion and put it in a large pan with the heated oil. Let the onion sauté over very low heat for about 10 minutes, until it is very soft. Then add the pumpkin and brown it for a few minutes, stirring to keep it from sticking. Start adding one ladle of broth, and then add more, little by little until the pumpkin is cooked (about 20 minutes): it must be very tender and creamy. Heat another large frying pan, add in the rice and toast it. We use the dry method because toasting the rice, an essential step to ensure the grains will develop their resistance to overcooking, cannot be done in a humid environment such as the one created in the other pan.

Keep toasting the rice over high heat until it becomes opalescent, turning it often to avoid burning it. This will take 2-3 minutes. Then add the white wine and stir immediately to avoid sticking. As soon as the wine has completely evaporated, pour the rice into the pan with the pumpkin. Mix well to combine the flavors and prevent the rice from sticking.

After the wine has evaporated, add a ladle of hot broth, and gradually add the next one only after the previous one has been absorbed, until it is properly cooked. This will take 15-20 minutes, depending on the type of rice used. Towards the end of cooking, season with pepper and salt. Finally, remove from the burner, add the butter and grated Parmesan cheese. Mix with care, then add a final ladle of broth if you prefer a creamier risotto. Let it rest for a minute before serving.

Baked pasta

Ingredients:

- Rigatoni 600 g
- Eggs 4
- Parmigiano Reggiano DOP cheese 3 tbsp - to be grated
- Scamorza (provola) cheese 300 g

FOR THE MEATBALLS

- Pork 250 g - ground
- Sausage 150 g
- Parmigiano Reggiano DOP cheese 100 g - to be grated
- Bread 100 g
- Parsley 2 tbsp - shredded
- Eggs 2
- Fine salt to taste
- Black pepper to taste
- Nutmeg 1 pinch

FOR THE SAUCE

- Tomato puree 1 l
- White onions 1
- Garlic 1 clove
- Extra virgin olive oil 4 tbsp
- Fine salt to taste
- Basil 5 leaves
- Black pepper to taste

BÉCHAMEL SAUCE

- Whole milk 1 l
- Flour 00 80 g
- Butter 80 g
- Fine salt to taste
- Nutmeg 1 pinch

To prepare the baked pasta, start with the mix for the meatballs. First take the sausage, cut it in half and remove the casing. Then coarsely chop the meat with a knife.

In a larger bowl pour the ground meat and add the sausage, the grated Parmesan cheese, chopped parsley and bread crumbs previously crumbled in the mixer.

Then add the eggs and season with salt and pepper. Work the dough with your hands until a homogeneous mixture is obtained. Cover it with transparent wrap and let it rest until the meatballs are prepared. Then, start preparing the sauce: in a large non-stick pan add the oil, a whole clove of garlic and a finely chopped onion.

When the oil is hot, pour in the tomato puree . Season with salt and pepper and cook for 30 minutes covered over low heat, stirring occasionally. In the meantime, roll the meatballs about 1tbsp (10 g) each and place them on a plate.
This mixture will yield about 70 meatballs. After the cooking time of the sauce, remove the garlic clove and pour the meatballs into the sauce. Add salt and pepper and stir with a spatula. Let it simmer over low heat for 15 minutes. Then add the chopped basil leaves and continue cooking for another 5 minutes. Finally, prepare the eggs. Boil them for at least 8-10 minutes, then cool them under cold running water. Once they are cold, peel the boiled eggs and cut them into slices with a special tool or a sharp knife and set them aside in a bowl.
Cut the scamorza cheese into slices, then into strips, then into cubes. Put it in a bowl and set it aside. Now prepare the béchamel sauce: heat the milk in a small saucepan. Heat the butter chunks in a separate pan and let them melt over low heat. Turn off the heat and add the flour to the melted butter, stirring vigorously with a hand whisk to prevent lumps from forming. Put the saucepan back over low heat and cook the cream until it is a golden brown.

Then add the milk, which is now hot, and season with nutmeg and salt. Cook the béchamel for 5-6 minutes over low heat until it thickens, continuing to stir with the hand whisk. Transfer the béchamel into a bowl and cover it with transparent wrap until it is used to prevent forming a crust on the surface. Boil the pasta in plenty of salted water and drain halfway through cooking. Take the meatball sauce, now ready, and add it to the pasta. Mix the ingredients well with a spoon.

Then spread a veil of béchamel on the bottom of an ovenproof dish and create a first layer of rigatoni pasta and meatballs. Spread half the boiled egg slices on top of the pasta and half of the diced scamorza cheese then sprinkle with half of the grated Parmesan cheese. Season the first layer with a few tablespoons of béchamel sauce and proceed with the second layer of pasta and meatballs ,distributing it evenly over the first. Complete the layer with evenly spread egg slices.

Sprinkle with diced scamorza cheese and béchamel. Sprinkle with the remaining grated Parmesan cheese and bake at 180° in a static oven for about 15 minutes (or ventilated at 160°C for 7 minutes). After cooking, set the oven function to broil and leave for about 5 minutes. The baked pasta is ready: let it rest at room temperature 5-10 minutes before eating.

Tomato risotto
Ingredients:
- **Rice 400 g**
- **Canned tomatoes 400 g**
- **Tomato puree 2 tbsp**
- **Vegetable broth 1 l**
- **Golden onions 1**
- **Grana Padano PDO 40 g**
- **Extra virgin olive oil 3 tbsp**
- **Butter 20 g**
- **Basil to taste**
- **Salt up to taste**

To prepare the risotto with tomato, start frying a finely chopped onion in 3 tablespoons of oil over low heat for about 10 minutes; the onion must not burn but become transparent. After this time, pour in the rice and toast it for a couple of minutes. Then add a ladle of vegetable broth and let it evaporate.

Add the peeled tomatoes to which you have added a teaspoon of sugar to remove the acidity, mix well and add a ladle of broth. Add two tablespoons of tomato sauce to taste. Continue to incorporate a ladle of broth every time the risotto dries, until cooked. When the cooking is almost completed, add some chopped basil, according to your tastes and season with salt if necessary.

Then remove the saucepan from the heat and stir in the butter, finally add the grated Grana Padano and mix. Serve the tomato risotto hot and garnished with a few basil leaves.

Lentil soup
Ingredients:
- **Dried lentils 250 g**
- **Leeks 100 g**
- **Potatoes 250 g**
- **Cherry tomatoes 180 g**
- **Bay leaf 2 leaves**
- **Extra virgin olive oil to taste**
- **Turmeric powder 1 tsp**
- **Water 1 l**
- **Black pepper to taste**
- **Salt up to taste**
- **Oregano to taste**

FOR THE CROUTONS
- **Black bread with cereals 1**
- **Extra virgin olive oil to taste**
- **Salt up to taste**
- **Black pepper to taste**
- **Oregano to taste**

To prepare the lentil soup, finely cut the white part of the leek. Peel the potatoes and cut them into 1 cm cubes. Heat a little oil in the pan, pour in the leek and brown it.

Add the potatoes to the casserole. Also add the rinsed lentils and water. Season with turmeric and bay leaves, stir and from the boiling point, cook over medium-low heat for 25-30 minutes, during which you will stir from time to time. Do not add the salt now, otherwise the lentils will remain tough. Meanwhile, prepare the croutons: cut the bread into cubes.

Pour the croutons on a baking tray, season with salt, pepper, oil and fresh oregano. Toast the bread in a preheated oven at 200 ° in the ventilated mode for 8 minutes. Wash and cut the cherry tomatoes in half.

Then add the cherry tomatoes and continue cooking for about ten minutes. Check that you have reached the degree of cooking suitable for your tastes, season with salt and pepper and remove from the heat, let it rest for a few minutes. Serve the lentil soup hot, adding a drizzle of raw oil, a sprinkling of pepper and the croutons.

Spinach and ricotta cannelloni

Ingredients:

Cannelloni 500g

FOR THE FILLING
- Spinach 250 g
- Cow's milk ricotta cheese 150 g
- Eggs 1
- Garlic 1 clove
- Extra virgin olive oil to taste
- Grana Padano DOP cheese 50 g - grated
- Nutmeg 1 pinch
- Black pepper to taste
- Fine salt to taste

FOR THE BÉCHAMEL SAUCE
- Whole milk 500 g
- Flour 00 40 g
- Butter 3 tbsp
- Fine salt 1 pinch
- Nutmeg to taste
- Black pepper 1 pinch

FOR BAKING AU GRATIN
- Grana Padano DOP cheese to taste

Pour the oil into a pot, add the garlic, let it brown and then remove it. Wash and drain the spinach well, then add it to the pot.

Season with salt and let it cook, covered, for around 5 minutes, until the spinach has wilted. Once cooked, let the spinach cool. Meanwhile, prepare the béchamel sauce. First, warm the milk. Then add the butter to another pot and let it melt completely. Now sift the flour and, once the butter has melted, add it to the butter and stir vigorously. After a couple of minutes, you'll get a hazelnut-colored roux. Remove the pot from the heat for a moment and slowly pour in the hot milk.

Keep stirring and season the béchamel with a pinch of salt and pepper and some grated nutmeg. Continue to cook the béchamel over medium heat for 5-6 minutes until you get the desired consistency, then transfer to a glass bowl and cover with plastic wrap. The spinach will be cool by now; transfer to a cutting board and chop roughly with a knife.

Place the chopped spinach in a large bowl, add the ricotta, stir with a fork, and then add the eggs. Season with salt, pepper, and nutmeg and stir to combine. Finally, add the grated cheese.

Stir the ingredients together well. Now transfer this mixture to a pastry bag and put it in the fridge until you're ready to use it.
Next, blanch your cannelloni one at a time in boiling, slightly salted water, for about 1 minute each.
Place around 100 g of filling in the middle of the cannelloni, using the pastry bag. Now spread 2 heaping spoonfuls of béchamel in a baking dish. Arrange your cannelloni in the dish and cover with the remaining béchamel, distributing it well. Sprinkle with the grated cheese and bake in a conventional oven preheated to 200°C for around 15 minutes. Then switch to broiler mode at 230°C and cook for another 5 minutes until a golden crust has formed on top. Your spinach and ricotta cannelloni are now ready to be served piping hot!

Eggplant parmigiana
Ingredients:
- **Eggplants 1.5 kg**
- **Tomato puree 1.4 l**
- **Mozzarella 500 g**
- **Parmigiano Reggiano DOP cheese 150**
- **Yellow onions 1**
- **Extra virgin olive oil to taste**
- **Black pepper to taste**
- **Basil - several leaves**
- **Fine salt to taste**
- **Peanut seed oil to taste - for frying the eggplant**
- **Coarse salt 35 g - for purging the eggplant**

To prepare the eggplant parmigiana, start by washing and drying the eggplant. Then with a knife remove the stem and slice the eggplant lengthwise with a vegetable slicer, or alternatively with a knife, to obtain slices 4-5 mm thick.

As you place the slices inside a colander, sprinkle them with a very small amount of coarse salt between the layers, well distributed (you can also use a little fine salt); continue this way until you finish it all. On top of the eggplants, place a plate with a weight on it to let the eggplants purge the excess water and slightly bitter taste, the enemy of fried food. Leave it like this for at least 1 hour. Remember to rinse the slices well under running water, one by one if necessary, to remove the salt and pat them dry before use. In the meantime, slice and cut the mozzarella into strips, after which you will have very small cubes. If you don't have another colander, you can place them on a very clean cloth. In the meantime, make the sauce. In a large saucepan pour a drizzle of extra virgin olive oil and add the chopped onion, stir often so as not to burn it and let it brown for a couple of minutes.

Then add the tomato puree and a little water, the salt and let it simmer for 45 minutes. When finished cooking do not forget to add the basil leaves by hand.

Heat plenty of vegetable oil and in the meantime rinse the portion of eggplant that you are going to fry and dry it with oil blotting paper: always proceed a little at a time so they do not darken. Fry a few slices at a time in boiling oil at 170° C.

After cooking 2-3 minutes, drain on absorbent paper; do the same with all the others. At this point you should have everything you need, so move on to putting it together. Cover the bottom of an 20x30cm baking dish with a little sauce, then make the first layer by arranging the eggplant slices horizontally.
Grate some black pepper, sprinkle with parmesan cheese and pour some cubes of mozzarella, distributing them evenly. And finally pour on a little more sauce, just enough to color the inside.

Repeat the same procedure this time by arranging the eggplant slices on top ; continue this way to make the layers by inverting the direction of the slices each time. Between layers, remember to press gently with the palms of your hands in order to compact them. On the last layer pour the remaining tomato puree , the cubes of mozzarella and parmesan cheese. Now it's time to bake your eggplant parmigiana in a hot oven at 200° C for 40 minutes. Once ready, let it cool a few minutes before serving.

Pumpkin lasagna
Ingredients:
- Lasagna 500 g
- Pumpkin 1.2 kg - flesh, already cleaned
- Vegetable broth 100 g
- Extra virgin olive oil 50 g
- Rosemary 3 sprigs
- Fine salt to taste
- Black pepper to taste
- Parmigiano Reggiano DOP cheese 40 g - grated
- Garlic 2 cloves
- Provola cheese 250 g

FOR THE BÉCHAMEL SAUCE
- Whole milk 500 g
- Butter 3 tbsp 50 g
- Flour 00 50 g
- Nutmeg to taste

To make the pumpkin lasagna, start by preparing the vegetable broth. Then turn to cleaning the pumpkin: Cut it in half, remove the seeds and stringy parts, and then remove the skin. Cut the flesh into strips and then dice.

Rinse the rosemary, dry, and chop the needles finely; in this step you can chop up the garlic cloves, too, or else you can fry the cleaned whole cloves in a nonstick pan with lightly heated oil. Add the chopped rosemary, and once the garlic has turned golden you can remove it. Then, over very low heat, add a ladleful of broth to keep the chopped rosemary from burning and get it to release its aroma. Let it infuse for a few moments and then add the diced pumpkin. Turn up the heat and sauté the pumpkin well, stirring often. Season with salt and pepper; once the pumpkin is nicely browned, add a ladleful of vegetable broth. Lower the heat, cover with a lid, and leave to cook for around 15 minutes, stirring and adding a ladleful of broth as needed, until it has softened.

While the pumpkin is cooking, turn your attention to the béchamel sauce: Warm the milk in a saucepan, making sure it doesn't reach a boil, and season with some nutmeg. While the milk is heating up, melt the butter in another saucepan over low heat, and once fully melted, remove from the heat and sprinkle in the flour, continuing to whisk vigorously to keep lumps from forming. Place it back on the stove once you've got a roux, always keeping the heat moderate to make it golden, and then add the milk.

Stir well to combine the ingredients and allow to thicken for a few minutes. At this point, you'll have all the ingredients ready to assemble the pumpkin lasagna. Take a 7x11-inch (20x30-cm) baking dish and add a layer of béchamel, then a layer of egg pasta sheets , until the surface of the dish is covered.

Add another layer of béchamel, then the diced pumpkin and provola cheese. Next add another layer of lasagna sheets and béchamel. Continue by adding pumpkin and provola and then again with alternating layers until finishing with béchamel, pumpkin, and grated Parmigiano Reggiano cheese. Bake the pumpkin lasagna at 180°C in a preheated conventional oven for 30 minutes. If you'd like, complete the cooking by putting the lasagna under the broiler for a few minutes until you see a light crust form on the surface. Now, take the baking dish out of the oven, let it rest for a few minutes at room temperature, and then serve your pumpkin lasagna still steaming.

Gnocchi alla sorrentina
Ingredients:
- Red potatoes 1 kg
- Flour 00 300 g
- Eggs 1
- Fine salt to taste
- Semolina to taste

FOR THE TOMATO SAUCE
- Tomato puree 600 g
- Basil 6 leaves
- Garlic 1 clove
- Extra virgin olive oil to taste
- Fine salt to taste

TO GARNISH
- Mozzarella cheese 250 g
- Parmigiano Reggiano DOP cheese 70 g

To make the gnocchi alla sorrentina, start with the potatoes to make the gnocchi: Wash them under running water to remove any dirt, then place in a large pot, add water, and cook for around 30-40 minutes . Next, turn to the sauce: Add a drizzle of oil to a pot along with a whole clove of garlic, crushed, and the tomato puree; season with salt and pepper.

Allow the flavors to develop with the basil leaves, then cover with a lid and leave to cook for around 30 minutes over medium/low heat. Drain the potatoes well once they're ready. Sift flour onto a pastry board and create a well. Using a potato ricer, press the still-warm potatoes out into the well in the flour, or peel and mash the potatoes and place in the well.

Add the egg and salt to the potatoes, then start to knead: Do this fairly quickly, for just as long as it takes to compact the ingredients and give the dough a uniform and soft consistency. Cover with a clean, dry dishcloth. Bring water to cook the gnocchi to a boil in a large pot, salting the water once boiling. Meanwhile, take one portion of the dough at a time, keeping the rest covered, and roll into a cylinder around 2-3 cm thick. Sprinkle with some flour and cut the gnocchi from the cylinders using a dough cutter. To give them the classic ridges, you can use a gnocchi board or the prongs of a fork.

As you make them, you can put the gnocchi on a tray covered with a clean dishcloth. Once the gnocchi are ready, remove the garlic from the sauce and pour nearly all of the sauce into a very large bowl; the remaining sauce will be used at the bottom of the baking dish later on.
Boil the gnocchi in the pot in at least 2/3 batches; be sure that the water in the pot is simmering gently and not boiling vigorously to avoid damaging the gnocchi. They'll only need to cook for a few minutes, and as soon as they've risen to the surface, drain using a skimmer and, little by little, add them to the bowl where you put the sauce. Stir gently with a spoon. Pour the remaining sauce into a baking dish, drizzle over some oil, and then pour in the gnocchi.
Cover with a layer of diced mozzarella and a sprinkling of Parmigiano. Then add another layer of gnocchi, the remaining mozzarella and Parmigiano. Cook your gnocchi alla sorrentina in broil mode in a conventional oven preheated to 250°C, for 5 minutes. Serve the dish piping hot!

Spaghetti frittata
Ingredients:
- **Spaghetti 350 g**
- **Eggs 5**
- **Whole milk 100 g**
- **Parmigiano Reggiano DOP cheese 50 g - for grating**
- **Smoked scamorza cheese 100 g**
- **Smoked bacon 50 g**
- **Thyme 1 sprig**
- **Black pepper 1 pinch**
- **Extra virgin olive oil to taste**
- **Garlic 1 clove**

To make spaghetti frittata, first place a pan full of salted, it will be used to cook the pasta. Meanwhile, make the filling: dice the smoked bacon and scamorza cheese. As soon as the water boils, pour in the spaghetti and cook them until very firm to the bite.

Pour the eggs into a large bowl, add the thyme leaves and milk, then salt and pepper. Season with grated cheese and mix well to obtain a homogeneous mixture. Incorporate the filling and stir again.

As soon as the pasta is cooked, drain it in a bowl and season it with a drizzle of olive oil. Add the pasta to the filling and stir again to blend. Take a flared round pan (we used one measuring 12 inches (30 cm) at the top and 10 inches (26 cm) at the bottom). Brown a clove of garlic in oil. Remove the garlic clove and pour in the spaghetti. Distribute them evenly with a spatula, then cook over a high heat for 1 minute so that the base hardens, then lower the heat, cover with the lid and cook for 15 minutes. It's time to turn the frittata: shake the pan to make sure it is detached from the bottom, place a plate of the diameter of your pan on top of the frittata, turn the pan upside down and cook uncovered for another 5 minutes. The frittata is ready, enjoy it sliced warm or cold!

Pasta

Rigatoni carbonara
Ingredients:
- **Rigatoni 320 g**
- **Bacon 150 g**
- **Egg yolks 6 - average size**
- **Pecorino Romano cheese 50 g**
- **Black pepper to taste**

To prepare rigatoni carbonara start by putting a pot of salted water on the burner to cook the pasta. In the meantime, remove the pork rind from the bacon and cut it first into slices and then into strips about 1cm thick. The removed rind can be reused to flavor other things. Put the pieces into a non-stick pan and brown for about 15 minutes over medium heat, being careful not to burn it or it will smell too strong.

Meanwhile, put rigatoni in boiling water and cook for the time indicated on the package. In the meantime, pour the yolks into a bowl, add most of the Pecorino cheese needed for the recipe and the remaining part will be used just before serving.

Season with black pepper and whip by hand. Add a tablespoon of cooking water to dilute the mixture and stir. In the meantime the bacon will be cooked, turn off the burner and set it aside. Drain the pasta directly into the pan with the bacon and stir it briefly to season it. Remove from heat and pour the mixture of eggs and pecorino cheese into the pan. Mix quickly to combine.

To make it very creamy, if necessary, you can add a little cooking water to your pasta. It serves rigatoni carbonara immediately with the remaining pecorino cheese and ground black pepper on top.

Spaghetti with clams
Ingredients:
- **Spaghetti 320 g**
- **Clams 1 kg**
- **Garlic 1 clove**
- **Parsley 1 small bunch**
- **Extra virgin olive oil to taste**
- **Black pepper to taste**
- **Fine salt to taste**
- **Coarse salt to taste - for the clams**

To make spaghetti with clams, start by cleaning the clams. Make sure there are no broken or empty shells which have to be discarded. Then beat them against the sink or on a cutting board. This step is important to check that there is no sand inside: healthy clams will remain closed, while those full of sand will open. Then place them in a colander over a bowl and rinse them. Place the colander in a bowl and add plenty of coarse salt. Let the clams soak for 2-3 hours.

Once the time has passed, the clams will have purged any residual sand. Heat some oil in a pan. Then add a clove of garlic and, as the oil takes on flavor, drain the clams well, rinse them, and plunge them in the hot pan. Cover with a lid and let them cook for a few minutes over high heat.

The clams will open with heat, so shake the pan from time to time until they are completely open. As soon as they are all open, turn off the heat immediately, otherwise the clams will cook too much. Collect the juice by draining the clams, and do not forget to discard the garlic. In the meantime, cook the spaghetti in plenty of boiling salted water and drain halfway through the total cooking time of the spaghetti.

Then pour the sauce into a pan, add the spaghetti, and continue cooking using some cooking water. Your pasta will finish cooking in the pan. When cooked, add the clams and chopped parsley. Heat everything on high for a few seconds and the spaghetti with clams is ready: serve immediately!

Genovese
Ingredients:
- **Pasta 320 g**
- **Beef 600 g**
- **Yellow onions 1 kg**
- **Celery 75 g**
- **Carrot 75 g**
- **Parsley 1 sprig**
- **Bay leaves 1 leaf**
- **White wine 150 g**
- **Extra virgin olive oil to taste**
- **Fine salt to taste**

To make pasta alla genovese, start by peeling and thinly slicing the onion. Peel and finely chop the carrots. Finely chop the celery too, leave the tuft to one side.

Tie the celery tuft, parsley and laurel leave together with cooking twine for a bouquet garni. Lastly, prepare the meat by removing any excess fat and cutting it into pieces.
Add a generous amount of oil to a large saucepan, followed by the onions, the celery and the carrot. Leave to flavor on a low flame for a few minutes, then add the meat. Add the bouquet garni and a pinch of salt, stir and leave to flavor for a few minutes. Lower the flame, cover with the lid and cook for around 3 hours. There is no need to add water or squash because the onions will release enough liquid into the cooking sauce so that it does not dry out. However, it is important to check and occasionally stir it. Remove the bouquet garni once the 3 hours are up. Now add part of the wine and simmer on a high flame. Stir and continue to cook for another hour without the lid, gradually add the remaining wine as the sauce thickens. Once the cooking time is up, cook the ziti in boiling salted water.
Drain the pasta when firm to the bite and place it back in the saucepan. Stir well to amalgamate the sauce, then serve your pasta alla genovese, sprinkled with some pepper and grated Parmigiano if you wish!

Pasta and beans
Ingredients:
- **Ditaloni rigati pasta 320 g**
- **Dried Borlotti beans 200 g**
- **Tomato puree 250 g**
- **Lard 80 g**
- **Prosciutto crudo 80 g**
- **Onions 1**
- **Celery 1**
- **Carrots 1**
- **Garlic 1 clove**
- **Rosemary 3 sprigs**
- **Bay leaves 2**
- **Extra virgin olive oil 10 g**
- **Black pepper to taste**
- **Fine salt to taste**

To prepare the pasta and beans, first leave the dried beans to soak overnight. The next day, rinse them, transfer them to a saucepan, cover with plenty of cold water, add bay leaves, and boil them for around 80 minutes.

Meanwhile, prepare the other ingredients for the recipe. Start by peeling and finely chopping the onion, celery, and carrot, and then cut the prosciutto and lard into strips.

Heat the oil in a pot, add a peeled clove of garlic and the chopped vegetables and fry for around 5 minutes. Then add in the strips of prosciutto and lard and cook for a couple more minutes. Remove the beans from the water using a slotted spoon and add them to the vegetable mixture.

Next, add a ladleful of the bean cooking water to the mixture, setting the rest of the cooking water aside to use later. Now add the tomato purée to the pot, season with salt moderately, add pepper, and cook for 20 minutes over medium heat, after which time you can add the pasta. Before adding the pasta, take two ladlefuls from the mixture and pour them into a container. Blend using an immersion blender and set the resulting cream aside.

Add the ditaloni rigati pasta directly to the pot , cover with the cooking water from the beans, and allow the pasta to cook, stirring from time to time, still over medium heat. Once the pasta is cooked al dente, add the previously blended mixture and the chopped rosemary, then turn off the heat, put the lid on, and leave to rest for 3 minutes. A final sprinkling of black pepper and your pasta and beans dish is ready to be served!

Neapolitan-style pasta and potatoes
Ingredients:
- **Mixed Pasta 320 g**
- **Potatoes 750 g**
- **Celery 150 g**
- **Carrots 150 g**
- **White onions 1**
- **Lard 130 g**
- **Tomato paste 20 g**
- **Rosemary 1 sprig**
- **Parmigiano Reggiano DOP cheese 1 - rind**
- **Extra virgin olive oil to taste**
- **Fine salt to taste**
- **Black pepper to taste**

To prepare the Neapolitan-style pasta and potatoes, start by peeling the celery, carrot and onion, before chopping them finely.

Next, peel the potatoes and roughly chop them into small pieces of around an inch (2 cm). Finally, slice and then chop the lard. At this point you'll have everything you need. Now turn your attention to the stove. Pour a glug of oil into a pan, add the lard and warm over low heat for a few minutes.

Then add the chopped onion, carrots, and celery. After a few minutes, add the potatoes and allow the flavor to develop for a few minutes, stirring occasionally to keep everything from burning. Add the rosemary and the cheese rind (you can wash it first and scrape off the outer part), then add the tomato paste and stir. Pour in 2 cups (600 g) of hot water and season with pepper, and salt. Finally, cover with the lid and cook over low heat for 30 minutes, adding a little more water if needed. Once the potatoes have softened, mash some of them with the back of a wooden spoon, then pour in the mixed pasta.

Immediately add another cup (250 g) of hot water and bring everything to a boil. Leave the pasta to cook, stirring occasionally and adding more water if necessary. Make sure it has the right amount of salt. Remember that the mixture should be creamy and almost dry once it is cooked, though. Finally, remove the sprigs of rosemary and serve your Neapolitan-style pasta and potatoes topped with a drizzle of oil.

Pasta alla Gricia

Ingredients:

- **Rigatoni 320 g**
- **Bacon 250 g**
- **Pecorino Romano cheese 60 g - to grate**
- **Fine salt to taste**

To prepare pasta alla gricia, first place a pot full of water on the burner that will be used to cook the pasta. At this point take the bacon and cut slices 1 cm thick. Pour the bacon into a pan already hot, without adding more fat;

Let it sizzle on medium heat for about ten minutes until it is golden and crisp, taking care not to burn it. In the meantime the water will have come to a boil, salt and cook the pasta; while the pasta cooks, finely grate Pecorino cheese. When 2 minutes are left before the pasta is done, slow down the cooking of the bacon by adding a ladle of cooking water. The cooking of the bacon will stop and the starch released from the pasta will create a pleasant cream. Jiggle the pan a little bit to move the pieces of bacon.

At this point your pasta is done, add it directly to the sauce, preserving the cooking water. Stir for about 1 minute, shake the pan and stir. Then remove the pan from the heat, sprinkle with a third of grated Pecorino cheese and add a little more cooking water if necessary.

Stir and toss the pasta again; you will notice that a tasty cream will have been created. You can then serve pasta alla gricia and garnish each plate with the remaining Pecorino cheese.

Tagliatelle with porcini mushrooms
Ingredients:
- **Tagliatelle 320g**
- **Porcini mushrooms 500 g (clean)**
- **Butter 50 g**
- **Extra virgin olive oil 3 tbsp**
- **Fine salt to taste**
- **Garlic 1 clove**
- **Parsley 1 sprig**
- **Black pepper to taste**

Cut into slices mushrooms . In a large frying pan, put in the butter and melt it over very low heat; when it has almost completely melted, pour in the oil, leave to heat slightly over low heat and then pour in the porcini mushrooms and a whole clove of garlic, cleaned or chopped if you prefer (optional).

Season with salt and pepper to taste, then let the mushrooms cook for about 10 minutes. When finished cooking you can remove the garlic clove if you have added it. Once prepared, keep them warm. Then mince the parsley very finely and set it aside. Bring the water to a boil and salt to taste; cook the tagliatelle for 3-4 minutes.

Then drain them directly into the seasoning while preserving the cooking water. Set the heat to low under the pan with the seasoning and mix the ingredients to combine them. Add the finely chopped parsley and, if needed, add a ladle of pasta cooking water to prevent the tagliatelle from being too dry. Then serve the tagliatelle with porcini mushrooms as soon as they are ready!

Calamarata
Ingredients:
- Calamarata (pasta shape) 400 g
- Squid (cleaned) 600 g
- 1 clove garlic
- Fresh chilli 1
- 1 sprig parsley
- Cherry tomatoes 400 g
- White wine 60 g
- Triple tomato concentrate 25 g
- Salt to taste.
- Black pepper to taste
- Extra virgin olive oil to taste

To prepare the calamarata, start with the garlic: you can peel it easily by pressing it with the palm of your hand before removing the coat. For the fresh chilli, you can use it with the seeds or alternatively ruminate them if you prefer less spiciness, before chopping it finely.

Wash the tomatoes, dry them and divide them into 4 parts.

Cut the squid into large rings of about 2 cm. Move to the stove; boil plenty of salted water in a pan, boil and then cook the pasta. Meanwhile, heat the oil in a saucepan with the garlic clove and the chopped chilli. As soon as the bottom is hot, raise the temperature and sear the squid rings. When they are sealed, it only takes a few seconds, blend with the white wine and wait for the alcohol to have completely evaporated. Then remove the garlic, add the cherry tomatoes and tomato paste.

Stir, season with salt and then lower the heat, let it cook for about ten minutes. When cooked, sprinkle with chopped parsley. In the meantime, you can cook the pasta until half cooked.

As soon as the pasta is cooked, take a ladle of cooking water and pour it into the pan then drain the calamarata and dip it into the pan. Mix a few instants.

On an aluminum foil put another sheet of parchment paper, place a couple of ladles of pasta in the middle and close the parchment paper first and then the aluminum one. Arrange the packets on a dripping pan and bake in a static oven, already hot at 200 °, for about 10 minutes. Your calamarata is ready, you just have to serve it!

Bucatini all'amatriciana
Ingredients:
- **Bucatini 320 g**
- **Peeled tomatoes 400g**
- **Bacon 150g**
- **Pecorino Romano cheese 75g - for grating**
- **Fine salt to taste**
- **Extra virgin olive oil to taste**
- **Fresh chili pepper 1**
- **White wine 50 g**

To prepare bugatini Amatriciana, first boil the water to cook the pasta in, then add salt. Prepare the sauce: take the bacon, remove the pork rind and cut it into slices about 1 cm thick then into strips about 1/2 cm wide.

Heat a drizzle of oil in a pan, preferably a stainless steel skillet, add the whole chili pepper and the bacon cut into strips; brown over low heat for 7-8 minutes until the fat has melted and the meat is crunchy; stir often to prevent it from burning. Once the fat has melted, pour in the white wine, turn up the heat and let it evaporate.

Transfer the bacon to a plate and set aside, pour the peeled tomatoes into the same pan, breaking them up with your hands directly into the cooking liquid, continue cooking the sauce for about 10 minutes. As soon as the water boils, pour in the bucatini. Add salt to taste, remove the chili pepper from the sauce, add the bacon strips to the pan and stir to mix. Once the bucatini are cooked, drain them and add them directly to the sauce in the pan. Sauté the pasta very quickly to mix it well with the sauce. To finish, sprinkle with grated pecorino cheese : your bucatini all'Amatriciana is ready to be served!

Lasagne Bolognese
Ingredients:
- Remilled durum wheat semolina 350 g
- Flour 00 150 g
- Spinach 250 g
- Eggs 2
- Egg yolks 3

FOR THE BOLOGNESE SAUCE
- Beef 300 g - (minced, coarsely ground and mixed)
- Bacon 150 g
- Carrots 50 g
- Celery 50 g
- Yellow onions 50 g
- Red wine 100 g
- Tomato puree 300 g
- Vegetable broth to taste
- Extra virgin olive oil 1 tbsp
- Fine salt to taste
- Black pepper to taste

FOR THE BÉCHAMEL SAUCE
- Butter 70 g
- Flour 00 70 g
- Whole milk 1 l
- Fine salt 1 pinch
- Nutmeg to taste

TO SEASON
- Butter to taste
- Parmigiano Reggiano DOP cheese 270 g

To prepare lasagne alla Bolognese, start with the meat sauce. Prepare the vegetable broth and ensure to keep it warm. Then take the bacon, cut it into strips first and then chop it well. Separately, finely chop the carrots, onions, celery and set aside.

In a saucepan, pour a drizzle of oil and the pancetta bacon. Use a ladle to spread it well and let it brown for a few minutes. Then add the chopped vegetables and cook for 5-6 minutes. Then add the minced meat. Stir and raise the heat. Let the meat brown slowly, it must be well browned to seal the juices and be soft.

Deglaze with red wine and let it evaporate completely before adding the tomato puree. The Bolognese sauce must cook for two hours. When it starts boiling again, you can add some hot broth, one or two ladles, and let the sauce cook for another couple of hours at least.

Let it cook with the lid on, without covering the pan completely. Check and stir from time to time, add more broth when needed and let it cook. Now move on to the pasta. First, pour the spinach into a pan, add a little water, cover with a lid and cook until they are wilted, it will take 5-6 minutes in total. At this point, drain them, let them cool and squeeze them well. Transfer the spinach to a mixer and blend them until you get a puree. You will need to get approx 100 of it. Now on a pastry board pour the semolina and 00 flour, add the spinach and create a fountain shape. Add the lightly beaten eggs
and egg yolks. Begin to knead everything starting from the center, this way the eggs will not slip out of the fountain. Knead well until you get a homogeneous dough.

Wrap it in plastic wrap and let it rest for 30 minutes at room temperature. In the meantime, prepare the béchamel sauce. Heat the milk in a saucepan, without boiling it. In another pan, place the butter and let it melt.

Add the flour in one go and cook for a few minutes until you get a golden roux. Then, pour the hot milk in three times, mixing well.

Add salt and flavor with nutmeg. Continue to mix until you get a creamy béchamel. Transfer to a small bowl, cover with plastic wrap and set aside. As soon as 30 minutes have elapsed, take the dough back and take a piece. Cover the rest of the dough with plastic wrap to keep it from drying out.

With the help of a little semolina flatten it slightly on the pastry board to form a rectangle and roll out the dough in the machine. Start from a wider thickness, then fold the dough and pass it over. When you feel it is too wet, sprinkle with a little semolina. Gradually reduce the thickness until you get a sheet just over 0.5 mm thick. Transfer it to a pastry board and cut into large rectangles 30x20 cm. Continue this way until the dough is finished and in the meantime put a pot of water on the stove and add salt. When it starts to boil, immerse one sheet at a time, wait 30-40 seconds and using a skimmer drain it. Transfer it to a tray with a cloth and dab to remove excess water. Continue this way, placing the cooked sheets side by side, without overlapping them. As soon as the Bolognese sauce is ready, season with salt and pepper and proceed to the composition of the lasagna.
Take a large 30x20 cm lasagna pan and grease the bottom. Add a thin layer of béchamel and one of Bolognese sauce. Then place the first sheet, add a layer of béchamel and a layer of meat sauce. Add grated Parmesan cheese and place another sheet of pasta on top.
Add another layer of béchamel and one of meat sauce, add grated cheese and continue like this until you have 5 layers. After placing the last sheet, add the Bolognese sauce in order to completely cover the pasta sheet. Sprinkle with grated cheese, add some tufts of butter and bake in a preheated static oven at 170 ° C for 40 minutes.

Spaghetti cacio e pepe
Ingredients:
- **Spaghetti 320 g**
- **Black pepper to taste - corns**
- **Pecorino Romano cheese 200 g- medium seasoning, to be grated**
- **Fine salt to taste**

To prepare spaghetti cacio e pepe, first of all grate the Pecorino cheese. Boiling some water in a pan and when it boils you can add salt to taste. Once salted, you can cook the spaghetti. In the meantime, pour the whole peppercorns on a cutting board, then crush them with a meat pestle or a grinder. This will release more of the pungent scent of the pepper.
Pour half of the crushed pepper into a large non-stick pan, toast over low heat stirring with a wooden spoon, then add a couple of ladles of cooking water. The bubbles you see appearing are from the starch contained in the water. Drain the spaghetti when it is very al dente (keeping the cooking water aside to use later) and pour the pasta directly into the pan with toasted pepper; it will continue cooking with the seasoning. Stir the pasta continuously with the kitchen tongs to make it and add a ladle of water or two if necessary, to continue cooking. Keep pouring a ladle of water only when needed (when you see that the pan is almost completely dry) and stir with kitchen tongs. In the meantime, when the pasta is ready, prepare the Pecorino cream (don't start this operation before because the cream would get too thick): pour about half of the grated Pecorino cheese into a bowl. Add a ladle of cooking water to the grated Pecorino cheese. Stir vigorously with a whisk and add more water when needed. Then add the remaining half of the Pecorino cheese, keeping a little bit aside to garnish later. Add a little more water if needed: at this stage you will have to carefully adjust the amount of Pecorino cheese to the water to obtain a cream of the right consistency and without lumps.

Finish cooking your pasta, adding a little more hot water if necessary; before adding the Pecorino cream, briefly stir the cream by placing the bowl over the steam of the pan with hot water, always stir with the whisk, so as to bring the cream back to a temperature similar to the one of your pasta if necessary. Turn the heat off under the pan with spaghetti and pour in the Pecorino cream.

While pouring the Pecorino cream onto your spaghetti, stir it continuously with the kitchen tongs, pour the Pecorino you kept aside in too, stir and sauté the pasta again, then transfer your spaghetti cacio e pepe to a plate and season with the remaining pepper, enjoy immediately in all its creaminess!

Seafood spaghetti
Ingredients:
- Spaghetti 320 g
- Mussels 1 kg (clean)
- Clams 1 kg (clean)
- Squid 300 g (clean)
- Scampi 8 (clean)
- Cherry tomatoes 300 g
- Extra virgin olive oil 4 tbsp
- Garlic 1 clove
- Parsley 1 sprig - to be chopped
- White wine 3 tbsp (40 g)
- Fine salt to taste
- Black pepper to taste

Heat 2 tablespoons of olive oil in a large saucepan and when it is hot, pour in the clams and mussels, cover immediately with a lid and wait until they are all completely open, about 3-4 minutes.

Once the mussels and clams are open, remove the lid and pour them into a container. Do not discard the cooking liquid but strain it through a tight mesh strainer and keep it warm.

Then shell both clams and mussels and set aside the flesh and some shells still full, while you can discard the empty shells.

Cut the squid into strips. Now wash the tomatoes and cut them into wedges. In the meantime, place a pot full of salted water on the stove and bring it to a boil, it will be used to cook the spaghetti. Next, drizzle a pan with 2 tablespoons of extra virgin olive oil and add a clove of garlic. Once it is golden brown, pour in the squid and add a pinch of salt. Cook for 5 minutes then sweat with the white wine, let the wine evaporate, remove the garlic , add the cherry tomatoes and cook for another 5 minutes. Meanwhile, cook the spaghetti in boiling water.

Add the scampi to the sauce, season with salt and pepper. Drain the spaghetti directly into the pan 4 minutes before their cooking time is up. Continue cooking and pour the mussels and clams cooking water you had set aside. Lastly, add the shelled mussels and clams. At the end of cooking, turn off the heat, season with a chopped sprig of parsley and toss one last time. Serve seafood spaghetti very hot.

Pasta alla sorrentina

Ingredients:
- **Pennette pasta 320 g**
- **Tomato puree 500 g**
- **Mozzarella cheese 125 g**
- **Extra virgin olive oil 2 ½ tbsp (30 g)**
- **Garlic 1 clove**
- **Basil to taste**
- **Fine salt to taste**
- **Parmigiano Reggiano DOP cheese 65 g**

To prepare pasta alla sorrentina, you'll need to start by preparing the sauce. Pour the oil into a large pan and add the peeled garlic clove, fry for 1 minute, and then add the tomato puree. Season with salt as needed, add a few basil leaves, and stir.

At this point, cover with a lid, and leave to cook for 30 minutes over low heat before removing the garlic clove. Heat a pot full of water to cook the pasta, and in the meantime, cut the mozzarella into cubes. Once the water has reached a boil, cook the pasta before draining it and adding it to the sauce, stirring well to combine. Pour around half of the pasta into a 10-inch (25-cm) round baking dish to form the first layer, before placing half of the mozzarella cubes on top and sprinkling with a little Parmigiano Reggiano cheese. Cover with the remaining pasta, then add the mozzarella, and finally cover with the Parmigiano Reggiano. Broil in the oven for around 5 minutes, until the pasta is nicely baked and the mozzarella has melted (if you don't have a broil function, you can put the dish on the top rack and turn the oven on full power, but be careful not to burn it!). Garnish your pasta alla sorrentina with some fresh basil and serve immediately!

Spaghetti puttanesca
Ingredients:
- **Spaghetti 320 g**
- **Peeled tomatoes 800 g**
- **Salted capers 2 tsp (10 g)**
- **Parsley 1 small bunch - to be chopped**
- **Anchovies in oil 25 g**
- **Olives 100 g**
- **Garlic 3 cloves**
- **Dried chili pepper 2**
- **Extra virgin olive oil 2 ½ tbsp (30 g)**
- **Fine salt to taste**

To make puttanesca pasta, first rinse the capers under running water to remove excess salt, then dry them and chop them coarsely. Take the pitted gaeta olives and crush them with the blad of a knife.

Wash and dry the parsley, then chop it. Place a pot full of water over heat and bring to the boil (salt when it boils); it will be used to cook the pasta. In the meantime, pour the oil, the peeled whole garlic cloves and chopped dried chilli pepper into a large pan. Add the anchovy filets and desalinated capers. Brown over medium heat for 5 minutes stirring frequently, so the anchovies melt and release their aroma. After this time, pour in the lightly crushed peeled tomatoes, stir with a spoon, and cook for another 10 minutes over medium heat. Meanwhile, boil the spaghetti.
When the sauce is ready, remove the garlic cloves and add the crushed olives. Flavour the sauce with fresh chopped parsley.
In the meantime the pasta will also finish cooking. Drain it directly into the pan and sauté for half a minute, just enough time to mix all the flavors together. Serve the spaghetti alla puttanesca very hot.

Pennette with mushrooms
Ingredients:
- **Pennette rigate pasta 320 g**
- **Porcini mushrooms 400 g**
- **Smoked bacon 200 g**
- **Tomato puree 400 g**
- **White onions 60 g**
- **Cream 30 g**
- **Extra virgin olive oil 3 tbsp**
- **Parsley to taste**
- **Fine salt to taste**
- **Black pepper to taste**

To prepare pennette pasta with mushrooms, start by cleaning the mushrooms. Remove any excess soil first using a small knife, then a slightly dampened cloth . Then cut them into slices, about 1/5 inch (.5 cm) thick.

Bring a pot with plenty of salted water to a boil. Move to the bacon: slice it and cut some cubes about a 1/5-inch thick (0.5 cm). Heat 120 g of oil in a pan and fry the smoked bacon over high heat, stirring frequently. It will just take a few minutes, then set aside.

Peel and chop an onion, take the pan where you sautéed the bacon and heat another 20 g of oil with the cooking liquid. Add the chopped onion and let it brown briefly before adding the porcini mushrooms. Brown for about 5 minutes, stirring occasionally.

Add the tomato puree and cook over low heat for about 5-10 minutes. When it has cooked, add the bacon and cook for another 5 minutes. In the meantime, cook the pasta.

Over low heat, add the cream to the sauce and stir to mix . Chop the fresh parsley and complete your dish by staining the penne pasta directly into the pan. Stir, season with the chopped parsley and a little pepper to taste (and salt if needed). Just a few moments and the pennette pasta with mushrooms is ready to be served.

Fish and Seafood

Octopus salad with parsley
Ingredients:
- **Octopus to be cleaned 1 kg**
- **Carrots 1**
- **Celery 1 stalk**
- **1 clove garlic**
- **Bay leaf 2 leaves**
- **Black pepper in grains to taste**
- **Salt up to taste**

TO SEASON
- **Parsley 10 g**
- **Lemon juice 10 g**
- **Extra virgin olive oil 30 g**
- **Black pepper 1 pinch**
- **Salt up to 1 pinch**

To make octopus salad with parsley, first peel the carrot with a vegetable peeler, then chop it roughly. Do the same with the celery. Put a large pot of water on to boil, and add the chopped carrot, celery, an unpeeled garlic clove, the bay leaves, and season with salt and pepper.
Rinse the octopus under running water and, once the pot of water is boiling, dip it in the boiling water several times (4-5 will be enough) to get the tentacles to curl.
Then immerse the octopus fully and let it cook over medium heat for 40-45 minutes, with the lid on the pot. While the octopus is cooking, use a skimmer to remove any residue and foam that forms on the surface of the cooking water. Once the octopus has finished cooking, let it cool in the cooking water so that it softens. Next, transfer it to a cutting board: Use a knife to remove the eyes, then remove the beak as well. Cut across the part where the head is to remove it, then empty it.
Cut the tentacles into pieces around 1 cm long. Chop the head into small pieces as well and place everything in a bowl. Move on to the dressing: Squeeze the lemon to get 2 tbsp (10 g) of juice, then wash, pat dry, and finely chop the parsley, getting rid of the stems.

Make the dressing by placing the parsley, lemon juice, and olive oil in a small jar (to emulsify it more easily). Season with salt and pepper. Close the jar and shake it to form an emulsion.

Pour the dressing over the octopus, mix well, and serve your octopus salad with parsley right away!

Risotto alla pescatora
Ingredients:
- Carnaroli rice 2350 g
- Shallot 1
- White wine to taste
- Goatfish 7 oz (200 g) - (pre-gutted)
- Clams 2 ¼ lbs (1 kg)
- Squid 500 g) - (already cleaned, just the tail)
- Shrimps 250 g
- Extra virgin olive oil to taste
- Garlic 1 clove

FOR THE BROTH
- Water 2 l - ice cold
- Shallot 60 g
- Fennel 200 g
- Black peppercorn 3 - whole
- Basil 2 leaves
- Garlic 2 cloves

FOR CREAMING
- Extra virgin olive oil 100 g
- Fresh chili pepper 1 tsp (5 g)
- Basil 5 leaves
- White pepper 1 pinch

FOR THE CHERRY TOMATO COULIS
- Datterino tomatoes 250 g
- Sugar 1 pinch
- Fine salt 1 pinch
- Water 3 ½ tbsp (50 g)
- Garlic 1 clove

FOR PARSLEY OIL (OPTIONAL)
- Parsley 50 g- (leaves only)
- Extra virgin olive oil 100 g

To prepare risotto alla pescatora, you must first clean the clams. First of all, make sure that all are well closed and discard any open ones. Place them in a bowl with water and salt for a couple of hours. Then drain them and cook them. Pour a drizzle of oil into a pan and let it warm, then add a crushed garlic clove and as soon as the oil is hot pour in the clams.

Raise the heat, wait a few seconds then sweat with the white wine. Cover with a lid and cook for a few minutes until they all open. Now, using a strainer, filter the cooking water in a bowl.

Discard the closed clams, shell the others and set them aside. Now move on to the squid. Cut the tail in half, flatten it, lay it on a cutting board and cut it into very thin strips.
Set aside and proceed with the mullets. Cut the head and the final part of the tail, then fillet the fish to obtain 2 standard fillets. Save the scraps because they will be used to make the broth. Now clean the shrimp. Detach the head, shell and tail with your hands and set them aside, as they will also be used to flavor the broth.
Then with a small knife cut the back of each shrimp and remove the black vein. Next, make the broth. Finely chop the shallot and cut the fennel into thin strips.
Pour a little oil into a large pot. Add 2 cloves of garlic, shallot, shrimp shells and mullet bones. Let it brown, then add water with ice, fennel, peppercorns and basil leaves.
Also add the previously filtered clam water. Bring to a boil, then lower the temperature and cook for 15-18 minutes over low heat.Meanwhile, make the tomato coulis. Pour the tomatoes, sugar, salt, unpeeled garlic clove and the water in a pan. Wait until it starts boiling, then cook for 5-6 minutes. Now remove the garlic, turn off the heat and transfer everything to a mixer. Blend all ingredients and transfer to a bowl. Now the broth will be ready too, so filter it and keep it warm. Proceed to cook the rice.
Pour a drizzle of oil into a pan, add the chopped shallot and let it toast slightly. When it starts to sweat, add the Carnaroli rice and let it toast while stirring occasionally.
To know when the rice is well toasted, touch it with the back of your hand, without scalding yourself, and if it is hot add the white wine, about 1/4 cup (40 g). As soon as it has evaporated, wet the rice with a couple of ladles of broth.

As soon as it starts to boil, it will take about 13 minutes to cook, you will have to add more broth only when needed.After about ten minutes, the rice will be almost cooked, add the clams and stir. Then add the squid, stir again, add the shrimps and stir again.

Wait 13 minutes, then remove from the heat and stir. Add the oil, the thinly sliced chili pepper, a little white pepper and some basil leaves, breaking them up with your hands. Add the tomato coulis, shake the pan at the same time to mix.

Cover with a lid, let it rest for a minute and in the meantime quickly sear the mullets. Pour a drizzle of oil into a pan, let it warm, then add the mullet fillets. After a few seconds turn them over and finish cooking on the other side.

Then transfer them to a tray with absorbent paper to dry them. Back to the rice now, taste it. Adjust the salt, white pepper and, if necessary, add a little more oil. Stir it one last time before serving. Pour a ladleful of rice in the middle of a plate.

Tap with the palm of your hand under the bottom of the plate to distribute the rice evenly. Place three mullet fillets on top of each portion and finish off with a sprinkle of parsley oil. Serve risotto alla pescatora still hot!

Stewed cod
Ingredients:
- Cod 1500 g
- Yellow onions 200 g
- Flour 00 100 g
- Tomato puree 600 g
- Extra virgin olive oil 3 tbsp (40 g)
- Salted capers 3 tbsp (30 g) - (to be disalinated)
- Taggiasca olives 6 tbsp (60 g)
- Oregano 1 tbsp - dried
- White wine 3 tbsp (40 g)
- Black pepper to taste
- Fine salt to taste
- Parsley to taste

To prepare stewed cod, start by desalinating the capers: rinse them thoroughly under running water. Now check there are no bones in the fish. Run your fingers along the surface of the cut of fish and if you find any, remove them with pincers. Now cut the cod into 4 pieces, each around 1.2 inches in size, without removing the skin, as it will keep the fish intact during cooking. Lastly, peel and thinly slice the onion.
Heat a saucepan on the stove. Add the oil and then the onion; brown on a low flame, stirring occasionally, for around 4-5 minutes. Once softened, leave the onion to one side, without gathering up the oil too and quickly dredge the cod pieces with flour. Be sure to remove any excess flour. Turn the flame up and add the cod pieces and cook for 1-2 minute per side: turn the pieces over when golden. Add the white wine, simmer and reduce, then turn the flame down a little and add the tomato puree. Add the onions to the condiment, followed by the olives and desalinated capers, flavor with the oregano and lastly, add a pinch of salt and pepper. Stir delicately ,
put the lid on and cook for around 40 minutes on a low flame. Your stewed cod is now ready, all you need to do is add some fresh parsley to taste and enjoy it with a few slices of bread.

Baked sea bream
Ingredients:
- Sea bream 900 g (clean)
- 2 cloves garlic
- 1 sprig rosemary
- Thyme 1 sprig
- 2 slices lemons
- Black pepper to taste
- Salt up to taste

FOR POTATOES
- New potatoes 400 g
- Salt flakes to taste
- Dried oregano to taste
- Extra virgin olive oil 40 g

Fill the cavity of the sea bream with the sprigs of rosemary.
Also add the sprigs of thyme, the two cloves of garlic, then add salt and pepper. Finally, insert two slices of lemon.
Now move on to the potatoes. Wash them well and without peeling cut each into 4 wedges. Transfer to a bowl seasoned with oil and salt flakes. Add the dried oregano and mix well. Now transfer the sea bream to a large pan and add the potatoes.
Arrange them well around the fish, without overlapping them. Add some more rosemary and lemon slices if you prefer. Bake in a static oven at 180 ° for 40 minutes. Halfway through cooking, stir the potatoes for even cooking. Remove from the oven and serve your sea bream in the oven.

Venetian style cod
Ingredients:
- Stockfish 500 g - (already soaked)
- Extra virgin olive oil 280 g
- Lemons 0
- Garlic 1 clove
- Bay leaves 2 leaves
- Fine salt to taste
- Black pepper to taste

FOR GARNISHING
- Parsley to taste
- Extra virgin olive oil to taste

To prepare Venetian style cod, start by buying previously soaked dried cod, otherwise leave it to soak for 3 days in a bowl and change the water every day. Now remove the skin from the dried cod and cut into slices. Fill a saucepan with cold water and add the unpeeled garlic clove, 1-2 laurel leaves and half a lemon.

Place the dried cod in the water, bring to the boil and leave to cook for around 30 minutes on a low flame; skim the froth that will form on the using a skewer. The cooking time may vary according to the piece of dried cod you are using, so check that is well-done. Once the time is up, drain the dried cod and save the cooking water.

Place the dried cod in a bowl and check for any bones; leave it to cool, then place it in a planetary mixer bowl fitted with a whisk, or a leaf spatula. Switch on the planetary mixer at a low speed and gradually add the oil.

Once you have incorporated the oil, gradually add tbsp of cooking water and continue stirring to obtain a homogeneous cream with a spreadable consistency. Add salt and pepper to taste, garnish with parsley and a drizzle of oil, then serve your puree of dried cod on slices of grilled polenta!

Cod Vicentina
Ingredients:
- Stockfish (soaked for about 3 days) 1 kg
- White onions 300 g
- Desalted salted sardines 40 g
- Flour 00 to taste
- Coarse salt to taste
- Whole milk 180 g
- Grana Padano PDO 20 g
- Black pepper to taste
- Extra virgin olive oil 180 g
- Parsley to taste

To prepare the Vicenza-style cod, the stockfish you will use must already have been soaked for about 3 days and dried overnight. Then first of all chop the onion and desalt the sardines, rinsing them carefully under water. Then pour them into a pan together with the chopped onion, add a generous drizzle of oil, mix everything together and cook for about 50-60 minutes over low heat until the sardines have melted and the onions are well dried and you have obtained a sort of cream with an amber color.
Now move on to the cod. Take the tenderloin soaked, boned and opened with the skin intact. Then stuff with part of the onion mixture, spreading it only on one half, season with coarse salt and a pinch of freshly ground pepper.
Finally sprinkle with flour, you'll need just a veil. Close the cod as if it were a sandwich and cut into pieces about 6 cm wide.
Equip yourself with a saucepan (choose one of a size that allows you to have the pieces of cod close together) and spread about half of the remaining onion mixture on the bottom. Arrange the pieces of stockfish vertically inside the pan. The pieces will have to be arranged next to each other.
Cover with the remaining onion, sprinkle again with a little flour, add a pinch of coarse salt,
pepper, Grana Padano and pour over all the milk.

Then add the oil slowly until the cod is completely covered. At this point let everything cook for about 4-5 hours on low heat, trying to touch it as little as possible during cooking. If you prefer, you can cover with a lid, but leave a part uncovered to let the steam escape. After 5 hours the cod will be soft, white and not too flaky (in large chunks), the aroma will be intense.
Finally, add the chopped parsley, mix everything together and serve with slices of polenta, as tradition dictates.

Seafood Salad
Ingredients:
- Mussels 1 kg - to be cleaned
- Clams 750 g - to be cleaned
- Octopus 700 g - to be cleaned
- Shrimps 500 g - to be cleaned
- Squid 400 g to be cleaned
- Carrots 2
- Celery 2 ribs
- Garlic 1 clove
- Bay leaves 4 leaves
- Parsley to taste
- Ground black pepper to taste
- Coarse salt to taste

FOR THE DRESSING
- Lemon juice 3 tbsp (40 g)
- Extra virgin olive oil 3 tbsp (40 g)
- Parsley to taste
- Fine salt to taste
- Black pepper to taste

To make this seafood salad, start by cleaning the clams: Discard any whose shell is broken or open, placing the rest in a bowl and covering them with water. Add a handful of coarse salt, stir gently, and leave to soak for a couple of hours, changing the water every so often.

In the meantime, cook the octopus: Chop the celery and carrots roughly and add them to a pot filled with plenty of water, together with the parsley and bay leaves. Add the peppercorns as well and bring to a boil. Dip the octopus 'tentacles in the boiling water 4-5 times to get them to curl.

Then immerse the entire octopus in the water, cover the pot with a lid, and leave it to cook for 30-35 minutes over medium heat, skimming off any residue that forms on the surface of the water from time to time. Meanwhile, clean the mussels: Remove the beard by pulling firmly with your hand, and any incrustations and barnacles using the blade of a knife. Then rinse under running water, scrubbing the shells well with steel wool. Put the mussels aside and turn to cleaning the shrimp: Remove the head, legs, and tail, then remove the shell and pull out the intestine gently. Now clean the squid: Separate the head from the body and remove the cuttlebone, then remove the fins and skin. Then cut into rings.

At this point, check on the octopus: Prick it in the middle with a fork and when it's ready, it will be tender but still firm. Transfer the cooked octopus to a colander and let it cool, then remove the vegetables from the cooking water and add the squid. Boil for around 4-5 minutes, depending on the size.

Pour in the shrimp, too, and blanch for 30 seconds, then drain the squid and shrimp and set aside. Once the clam soaking has passed, drain them and tap them one by one on a cutting board to make sure there's not any leftover sand. If there is, you will need to discard the clams that still have sand in them. Add a drizzle of oil to a pot and brown a clove of garlic in it. Then add the mussels and clams and cover the pot with a lid.

Cook over high heat for 5 minutes, just enough time for them to open. Drain the cooking liquid into a bowl - you can use it in other recipes. Discard any mussels and clams that are still closed and remove the open ones from their shells and place in a bowl; be sure to keep a few in the shells to use as garnish. Take the octopus, which should have cooled by now, and clean it, first cutting across the head at eye level to remove them.

Remove the insides from the head and the beak on the underside, in the middle of the tentacles. Cut the tentacles into 2-cm pieces and place in a large bowl.

Lastly, prepare the citronette dressing: Place the oil and lemon juice in a small bowl, then chop the parsley and add it to the bowl as well. Season with salt and pepper and emulsify with a fork.

Take the bowl with the octopus and add the shelled mussels and clams, squid, and shrimp. Dress with the citronette emulsion and stir well. Garnish with the whole mussels and clams you set aside, and then serve up your delicious seafood salad!

Drowned octopus
Ingredients:
- Octopus (already cleaned) 1 kg
- Peeled tomatoes 800 g
- Dried chilli pepper to taste
- 1 clove garlic
- 1 sprig parsley
- White wine 50 g
- Extra virgin olive oil 40 g
- Salt up to taste
- Black pepper to taste

Put the peeled garlic in a large pan, along with the oil and dried chilli. Heat well for 1-2 minutes, also tilting the pan so that the oil can flavor well with the garlic and chilli, but being careful not to let them burn. At this point, add the baby octopus and let them cook for 2-3 minutes over high heat, turning them from time to time.

Deglaze with the white wine and, again with tongs, turn the baby octopus, letting it cook for a couple of minutes. Add the peeled tomatoes and parsley sprigs, then add salt and pepper. Cover the pot with a lid, and cook over low heat for 30-40 minutes, depending on the size of the baby octopus. To check if they are cooked, do the test by piercing them with a fork: if they are tender it means that they are cooked to perfection. Remove the garlic, always using kitchen tongs; the poached octopus are ready to serve!

Octopus and potato salad
Ingredients:
- **Octopus 1 kg (clean)**
- **Potatoes 1 kg**
- **Bay leaves 2 leaves**

FOR THE CITRONETTE DRESSING
- **Parsley 1 bunch**
- **Black pepper to taste**
- **Extra virgin olive oil 60 g**
- **Fine salt to taste**
- **Lemon juice ¼ cup 60 g**

To prepare a warm octopus and potato salad, start with the potatoes: place a large saucepan filled with cold water on the heat and submerge the potatoes in their skins, after washing them thoroughly: leave them to cook for about 30-40 minutes from the moment they come to a boil (a fork test will tell you if they are cooked: if you can insert the fork without resistance, they are ready). Pour plenty of water into another pan, add the bay leaves and bring to a boil. Once the water reaches boiling point, submerge the whole octopus in the water, cover with the lid and cook for 50 minutes over moderate heat. For optimum cooking, allow about 20-25 minutes per 500 g of octopus. Meanwhile, when the potatoes are cooked, drain, and peel them, taking care not to burn your fingers
and cut them into 1-inch (2-3 cm) chunks. Set aside and keep warm. Prepare the citronette dressing: pour the squeezed lemon juice into a dressing shaker and add the olive oil, season with salt and pepper, close the spout, then shake the bottle to mix.
Wash and finely chop the parsley. As soon as the octopus is ready, drain it and leave to cool for 10 minutes. Place on a cutting board, separate into two halves, cut off the head and detach the tentacles from the central body, then cut everything into chunks measuring approximately 1 inch (2-3 cm). Tip the octopus into a large bowl, add the warm potato cubes, and dress the salad with citronette flavored
with the chopped parsley. Mix everything gently to coat with the aromatic dressing. Your warm octopus salad is ready to serve!

Venetian style cod

Ingredients:
- Stockfish(500 g) - (already soaked)
- Extra virgin olive oil 1 cup (280 g)
- Lemons 1
- Garlic 1 clove
- Bay leaves 2 leaves
- Fine salt to taste
- Black pepper to taste

FOR GARNISHING
- Parsley to taste
- Extra virgin olive oil to taste

To prepare Venetian style cod, start by buying previously soaked dried cod, otherwise leave it to soak for 3 days in a bowl and change the water every day. Now remove the skin from the dried cod and cut into slices. Fill a saucepan with cold water and add the unpeeled garlic clove, 1-2 laurel leaves and half a lemon.

Place the dried cod in the water, bring to the boil and leave to cook for around 30 minutes on a low flame; skim the froth that will form on the using a skewer. The cooking time may vary according to the piece of dried cod you are using, so check that is well-done. Once the time is up, drain the dried cod and save the cooking water.

Place the dried cod in a bowl and check for any bones; leave it to cool, then place it in a planetary mixer bowl fitted with a whisk, or a leaf spatula. Switch on the planetary mixer at a low speed and gradually add the oil.

Once you have incorporated the oil, gradually add 7 tbsp of cooking water and continue stirring to obtain a homogeneous cream with a spreadable consistency. Add salt and pepper to taste, garnish with parsley and a drizzle of oil, then serve your puree of dried cod!

Neapolitan-style octopus
Ingredients:
- Octopus (already cleaned) 1 kg
- Peeled tomatoes 800 g
- Dried chilli to taste
- Garlic 1 clove
- Parsley 1 sprig
- White wine 50 g
- Extra virgin olive oil 40 g
- Salt up to taste
- Black pepper to taste

To prepare the poached baby octopus, start with the baby octopus: if you have already cleaned baby octopus, rinse them well under running water. Once the octopuses are ready to be cooked, put the peeled garlic in a large pan, together with the oil and dried chilli pepper.

Heat well for 1-2 minutes, also tilting the pan so that the oil can be flavored well with the garlic and chilli pepper, but being careful not to let them burn. At this point, pour the octopus and let them burn for 2-3 minutes over high heat, turning them from time to time with the help of tongs.

Deglaze with the white wine and, again with tongs, turn the octopuses and let them cook for a couple more minutes. Add the peeled tomatoes and the sprigs of parsley, then salt and pepper.

Cover the pot with a lid 10, and let it cook over low heat for 30-40 minutes, depending on the size of the octopuses. To check if they are cooked, test them by piercing them with a fork: if they are tender it means that they are perfectly cooked. Remove the garlic, again using kitchen tongs; the poached octopus are ready to serve!

Seafood risotto
Ingredients:
- Rice 320 g
- Mussels 1 kg (clean)
- Clams 500 g (clean)
- Squid 350 g - already cleaned
- Shrimps 300 g - (the tails)
- Parsley 1 sprig
- Garlic 2 cloves
- White wine 6 tbsp (90 g)
- Vegetable broth to taste
- Extra virgin olive oil to taste
- Butter 70 g
- Fresh scallion 50 g
- Celery 25 g
- Carrots 25 g
- Chili 1
- Fine salt to taste
- Black pepper to taste

Empty the inside of the calamari and remove the skin. Cut into strips, then into large pieces, each roughly 0.8 inches in size.
Start by cooking the mussels: heat them in a large pan on a high flame. Put the lid on and leave them to open; shake the pan occasionally. It takes around 2-3 minutes for them to open. Filter the liquid through a colander into a container.
Set aside 2-3 whole mussels for each plate, you'll need them for the final decorative touch . Now cook the clams. Put the pan back on the stove and add the clams. Cover with the lid and leave them to open, shaking the pan occasionally. Will open in 1-2 minutes; as soon as this happens, filter and add the liquid to the same container used for the mussel liquid.

Leave to cool for a few moments before shelling and once more set aside 2-3 whole pieces per plate. Heat the vegetable broth, clean the celery, carrot and fresh spring onion. Finely chop the vegetables with a knife, peel the garlic cloves and leave them whole. Lastly, clean and then finely chop the chili and the parsley. Leave to one side and return to the stove. Heat a saucepan on the stove, add a generous drizzle of oil, followed by the finely chopped garlic and parsley.

Leave to flavor for ten minutes or so on a low flame, stirring occasionally. Once the vegetables have softened, remove the garlic, turn up the flame to the maximum setting and add the calamari. Saut for 1 minute before adding the shrimp tails.

Cook for another minute and as soon as the liquid evaporates, add 1.3 oz of white wine, simmer and reduce. Remove from the heat when the alcohol has fully evaporated and place the calamari and shrimps in a bowl; cover with the lid to keep them hot. Add the rice and toast for around 1 minute on the highest setting, stirring all the while to prevent any grains from burning.
Once toasted, add the remaining part of the white wine (so 2 oz) and wait for the alcohol to evaporate before cooking the rice with the vegetable squash. You can add the squash gradually by the ladle, until fully cooked. Add the mussel and clam liquid and stir occasionally, but not too much.

1-2 minutes before the end of the cooking time, add the shrimps and calamari, the mussels and clams and leave to flavor. Remove from the heat, add the very cold and diced butter and stir to obtain a creamy consistency.

Add the finely chopped parsley and the freshly ground pepper. Stir and leave to rest for a few minutes before placing on dishes. Your seafood risotto is ready: garnish the dishes with the mussels and clams to set aside for later.

Cuttlefish with peas
Ingredients:
- Peas 500 g
- Clean cuttlefish 1 kg
- White onions 1
- Extra virgin olive oil 4 tbsp
- Salt up to taste
- Parsley to taste
- Vegetable broth to taste
- Peeled tomatoes 500 g
- White wine 50 g
- Black pepper to taste

To make the cuttlefish with peas, first make the vegetable broth. Cut the cloak into rather wide strips. Heat the olive oil in a large pan, pour the chopped onion and simmer over medium heat for about 10 minutes, adding hot vegetable broth as needed to avoid drying the onion too much.

When the onion is very soft and transparent, add the cuttlefish, salt and pepper. The cuttlefish may release water so you can raise the heat to dry them. When they have lost their water, add the white wine and let it evaporate. Finally, add the peas, the peeled tomatoes previously crushed and deprived of the stalk; add a ladle of broth and continue cooking over low heat for 15/20 minutes. Meanwhile, wash, dry and chop the parsley too. When the cuttlefish with peas are soft, turn off the heat, flavor with fresh parsley and serve immediately.

Octopus in the Neapolitan style
Ingredients:
- Octopus 600 g
- 4 cloves garlic
- Parsley 1 bunch
- Cherry tomatoes 500 g
- Extra virgin olive oil 4 tbsp
- Black pepper to taste
- Salt up to taste
- Chilli pepper to taste
- Pantelleria capers 1 tbsp
- Gaeta olives 2 tbsp
- 4 slices bread

Taranto-style mussels
Ingredients:
- Mussels 1 kg
- Tomato pulp 400 g
- 2 cloves garlic
- Fresh chilli 1
- White wine 50 g
- Extra virgin olive oil 40 g
- Black pepper to taste
- Salt up to taste
- Parsley to taste
- TO ACCOMPANY:
- 8 slices bread

Pour half the indicated amount of oil into a pan and add a peeled and whole clove of garlic; let it brown and add the mussels. Add a sprig of whole parsley and the white wine to deglaze, then cover with a lid and let the mussels hatch: it will take about 4 minutes, as soon as they open you can turn off the heat. Meanwhile, remove the seeds from the chilli pepper and chop finely.

Pour the remaining part of the oil into another pan, add the chilli pepper and the other crushed garlic clove, let the sauce brown over a very low heat and stirring occasionally. Then add the tomato pulp, season with ground pepper and a pinch of salt (just a pinch because the mussels are already very tasty), being careful not to overdo it because the mussels will already be very tasty. Let the sauce cook for 5-6 minutes, mixing it from time to time. Filter the mussels by collecting the broth in a small bowl, so as to pour it more easily into the sauce. Cook for another 10 minutes; intato remove the garlic and parsley from the mussels and set aside.

Only the crunchy accompaniment is missing: slice the bread, arrange it on a dripping pan lined with parchment paper and sprinkle it with a drizzle of oil, then toast it for a few minutes in the oven under the grill at 250 ° for 3 minutes, until it is well gilded.
Once the sauce is ready, add the mussels and mix. Then finely chop the parsley and add it to your Taranto-style mussels. Wait another 3 minutes, sprinkle with a generous sprinkling of black pepper again if you prefer, mix one last time and serve the Taranto-style mussels with the toasted bread!

Meat

Roman-style veal
Ingredients:
- Sliced veal 4 slices of veal
- Raw ham 4 thin slices
- Sage 4 leaves
- Butter 50 g
- White wine ½ cup
- Black pepper to taste
- Flour 00 50 g
- Extra virgin olive oil 1 ½ tbsp
- Water 1 ½ tbsp

Start by slicing the veal nut, then place each slice on a cutting board, remove any nerves and fat and then beat it with a meat tenderizer to make it thin. Place a thin slice of raw ham in the middle,
and a sage leaf. Use a toothpick to keep the ingredients together. Pour 40 g of butter into a pan and melt over medium-high heat.
Flour the slices of meat on one side only and gradually place them in the pan with the sauce, increase the temperature so that the veal are golden brown. Pepper to taste, but do not salt because the raw ham will make the dish tasty.
When the meat is golden underneath, blend with the white wine and let it evaporate. As soon as the alcohol has evaporated completely, cover with the lid and cook for another minute. Transfer the veal to a plate and keep them warm.
Now take care of the accompanying sauce: add 20g of butter and water in the same pan with the cooking liquid of the meat. Reduce until you have created a slightly dense cream. Now spread the cream on the bottom of a serving plate and place the slices of meat on top. The veal are ready to serve.

Pork stew
Ingredients:
- **Pork loin 800 g**
- **Potatoes 450 g**
- **Celery 1 rib**
- **Carrots 1**
- **White onions 1**
- **Rosemary 2 sprigs**
- **Butter 20 g**
- **Dark beer 800 g**
- **Salt up to taste**
- **Black pepper to taste**
- **Flour 00 (for flouring) 50 g**
- **Garlic 1 clove**

To make the pork stew, start by cutting the loin into cubes of a couple of centimeters, then flour them on all sides and set aside. Meanwhile, wash and peel the vegetables for the sauté: the carrot, celery and onion, then chop them finely with a knife.

Now chop the rosemary needles with a knife, melt the butter in a large saucepan, then pour the mixture for the sauté and also squeeze in a clove of garlic.

To finish, flavor with the chopped rosemary and let the sautéed mixture simmer over a moderate heat for about 5 minutes and then add the pork. Brown the meat for at least 5 minutes and then sprinkle it with the beer, let it evaporate and then cover with the lid, add salt and pepper and continue cooking for 40 minutes. Meanwhile, peel the potatoes. Cut them into cubes as large as those of meat.

After 40 minutes of cooking the meat, add the potato cubes and continue cooking for another 30 minutes with the lid on, enough time to cook the potatoes too and create a delicious creamy sauce. Once ready, serve the pork stew piping hot.

Cotechino (Pork sausage) with lentils

Ingredients:
- **Precooked cotechino 300 g**

FOR THE LENTILS
- **Dried lentils 300 g**
- **Celery 1**
- **Carrots 1**
- **White onions 1**
- **Extra virgin olive oil 2 ½ tbsp (35 g)**
- **Bay leaves 3 leaves**
- **Rosemary 2 sprigs**
- **Vegetable broth 500 g**
- **Fine salt to taste**
- **Black pepper to taste**

To make cotechino with lentils, first soak the lentils in cold water for 2 hours. Drain and rinse them under running water. In the meantime, cook the cotechino following the instructions on the package, in our case it should be immersed in cold water and cooked for about 20 minutes from the time water starts boiling.

Now proceed with the vegetables: peel the carrots and mince them by cutting them first into strips and then into cubes. Do the same with the celery, then peel and chop the onion.

Pour the olive oil into a pan and heat it. Add the chopped vegetables and sauté them for a couple of minutes. Then add the lentils, previously soaked in cold water.

Season with pepper, salt and add the rosemary sprigs and bay leaves with kitchen twine, facilitating the removal of the herbs after cooking. Cover the lentils with hot vegetable broth and cook for 20 minutes or more depending on the desider consistency, adding more broth if necessary. Once the lentils are cooked, remove the herbs and keep the lentils warm. In the meantime cook the cotechino, drain it and unwrap it.

Transfer it to a cutting board taking care not to burn your fingers. Peel it and slice it. Serve the plate of cotechino with the lentils hot.

Chicken strips Sorrento style

Ingredients:
- **Chicken breast 500g**
- **Tomato puree 300 g**
- **Mozzarella cheese 100 g**
- **Shallot 1**
- **Basil 4 leaves**
- **Flour 00 to taste - to dust**
- **Parmigiano Reggiano DOP cheese 3 tbsp (20 g) - grated**
- **Extra virgin olive oil to taste**
- **Fine salt to taste**
- **Black pepper to taste**

To prepare the chicken strips alla sorrentina, begin with the sauce. Peel a shallot and chop it finely. Add to a pan with a drizzle of extra virgin olive oil and cook for a few minutes over low heat, stirring often to stop the shallot from burning. Add the tomato puree, salt to taste, and add a ladle of water.

Cover and cook over medium heat for 20 minutes 4. Meanwhile, prepare the chicken. Cut the breast into strips about ½ inch (1 cm) thick and then into irregular pieces about 2 inches (5 cm) long.

Coat the chicken strips in flour and place them on a baking sheet lined with parchment paper. Heat some oil in a frying pan and then sear the chicken by cooking over high heat for 2-3 minutes, turning occasionally. When the strips are golden brown, season with salt, and then add the tomato sauce. Cook for another 2 minutes and then turn off the heat. Add the diced mozzarella and the basil leaves, torn up by hand. Season with ground black pepper and mix everything together. Pour into a casserole dish, sprinkle the surface with grated Parmigiano cheese . Broil in a preheated oven at (460°F) 240°C under the broiler for 8-10 minutes or however long it takes for the mozzarella to melt and form a lightly browned crust on the surface. Your chicken strips alla sorrentina are ready to serve. All you have to do now is get them to the table piping hot.

Venetian liver
Ingredients:
- **Veal liver 600 g**
- **White onions 800 g**
- **Bay leaf 1**
- **Dry white wine 60 g**
- **Butter 30 g**
- **Extra virgin olive oil q.s.**
- **Salt up to taste**
- **Black pepper to taste**

To make the Venetian-style liver, first peel the onions and cut them into rings about half a cm thick. Heat the oil in a pan with a bay leaf, then add the onions and cook over low heat for 15 minutes; they will have to wither without taking on colour. In the meantime, take care of the liver: remove the skin and any cartilage, then cut it into strips about 2 cm wide. When the onions are wilted, add the liver and raise the heat.
Stir for a couple of minutes, then pour in the white wine, add salt and pepper and cook for a few more minutes.
Once ready, turn off the heat and add the butter, then mix well to mix it: in this way the dish will be creamier. Your Venetian liver is ready!

Lemon scaloppini
Ingredients:
- **Sliced veal 8**
- **Lemon juice 3 tbsp (50 g)**
- **Fine salt to taste**
- **Black pepper to taste**
- **Flour 00 to taste - for breading**
- **Butter 3 tbsp (40 g)**

To prepare lemon scalloppini, start by squeezing the fruit to obtain the juice. Then cover the meat with parchment paper, so as not to tear the fibers, and beat using a tenderizer. Strike firmly but not too hard, to tenderize the tissues without tearing the pulp.

Coat the sliced veal in flour, remove any excess flour, then melt the butter on a low flame in a capacious pan and add the sliced veal. Turn up the flame and brown for a couple of minutes on one side and then on the other.

Add salt and black pepper to taste, then add the lemon juice to the pan and cook on a low flame for 2-3 minute. As soon as the sauce thickens and becomes creamy, remove from the flame and serve the lemon scalloppini immediately!

Veal stew with potatoes
Ingredients:
- **Veal 1 kg- chunks**
- **Potatoes1 kg**
- **Carrots 1**
- **Celery 1 rib**
- **White onions 1**
- **Extra virgin olive oil 1 ½ tbsp**
- **Meat broth 1 l**
- **Fine salt to taste**
- **Black pepper to taste**
- **Flour 00 3 tbsp**
- **White wine 50 g**
- **Sage 1 sprig**
- **Rosemary 1 sprig**
- **Thyme 1 sprig**

To prepare veal stew with potatoes start by washing and peeling the carrot, onion and celery, then chop. Take the veal meat and cut it first into slices and then into pieces.

Take a large saucepan with high sides, heat the olive oil, add the chopped mixture for soffritto, season for 5 minutes over moderate heat, then add the veal chunks, season with salt and pepper to taste and brown the meat for 4-5 minutes. Now sprinkle with the previously sifted flour, mixing it well in the cooking liquid to avoid lumps.

Once the flour has been absorbed, add the white wine to the stew, let it evaporate completely, then add the meat stock to cover. Season with the sprigs of aromatic herbs previously tied together , so they can be easily removed from the pan.

Cover the stew with a lid and continue cooking for 1 hour, stirring occasionally. After this time, remove the aromatic herbs with kitchen tongs. In the meantime, wash and peel the potatoes and cut them into cubes the size of the veal pieces.

Add the diced potatoes to the stew. Continue cooking for another hour with the lid on, stirring occasionally until the potatoes and veal are tender. Serve the veal stew with potatoes hot.

Roast veal with potatoes
Ingredients:
- **Veal sirloin 600 g**
- **Potatoes 1 kg**
- **White wine 3 tbsp**
- **Rosemary 2 sprigs**
- **Garlic 2 cloves**
- **Extra virgin olive oil 3 tbsp**
- **Fine salt to taste**
- **Black pepper to taste**

To prepare the roast veal in with potatoes start with the latter. After washing and drying them well, peel them and then cut them into cubes of about an inch or so; the most important thing is that they are all the same thickness. Pour them into a bowl and add the oil, salt and pepper and peeled garlic.

Add a sprig of chopped rosemary and mix everything, with your hands or with a wooden spoon, then transfer to a dripping pan greased with oil and bake, in a preheated oven in static mode, at 200° C for 20 minutes.
In the meantime, tie up the roast. First of all, remove the whitish tissues that could turn hard during cooking, making the meat tough. So with one hand you hold a raised flap of meat while with the other hand you use a sharp knife, the one for filleting fish will do, then keep trimming these parts until the piece of meat is completely clean. Now you can tie it together. Unroll a large amount of kitchen string and place it underneath the meat lying horizontally on the cutting board.

Tie the two ends together with a double knot on the outer side: for convenience we start from the left to the end. Now pass the string around your hand twice, until it forms a loop.
Then put the meat inside and tighten the string by pulling the upper or lower end until it reaches the center. This is the first knot, repeat until the piece of veal is completely wrapped: in the meantime, remember to leave about a half an inch of space between one knot and the other.

At the end, turn the meat over on the other side, keeping the ends still, and tie it all together with a double knot on the side opposite to the first one.

Splint the meat by passing the other sprig of rosemary under the knots and then salt and pepper the cutting board. Place the piece of meat on it and start massaging it, making the seasoning stick to all the parts.

Heat the oil in a frying pan and add the meat, leaving it sealed on all sides over a medium-high flame. Every minute or so, to turn it with tongs or wooden spoons making sure that the meat browns well.

When all sides of the piece of meat are well sealed, steam with the white wine and let it evaporate for a few moments, then turn off the stove. Put the meat on the center of the drip pan by making space among the potatoes.

Sprinkle the piece of veal with the sauce and insert a roast thermometer until it reaches the center of the meat. Continue cooking at 200° C, until the meat thermometer reaches 65°C, approximately 35 minutes. After your roast veal with potatoes is done: wait a few minutes before removing the string and slicing this treat!

Meatloaf
Ingredients:
- Beef 1.3 lbs - ground
- Sausage 400 g
- Bread 200 g - fresh
- Pecorino cheese 150 g - for grating
- Whole milk 200 g
- Eggs 2
- Thyme 3 sprigs
- Nutmeg ½ tsp - ground
- Fine salt to taste
- Black pepper to taste
- Extra virgin olive oil to taste

FOR THE POTATOES
- Red potatoes 500 g
- Shallot 2
- Sage - several leaves
- Thyme 3 sprigs
- Fine salt to taste
- Black pepper to taste
- Extra virgin olive oil to taste

To prepare the meatloaf in the oven, first remove the crust of the fresh bread with a knife, cut it into cubes and transfer it to a bowl: in all, you will need about 150 gof crumb. Pour the milk into the bowl so that the bread absorbs and softens. In the meantime, break the sausage into small pieces after removing the casing.

Pour the ground beef into another bowl, then add the sausage, the grated Pecorino cheese, the bread soaked in milk and squeezed slightly, whole eggs, nutmeg, a few fresh thyme leaves, salt and pepper.
Knead the mixture with your hands to mix all the ingredients uniformly, then make it the shape of a cylinder making sure to push it together well. Place the meatloaf on a sheet of baking paper, brush it with olive oil and set it aside for a moment.

Now preheat the oven to 180° C in static mode and prepare the side dish: rinse the potatoes under running water and divide them in half, then clean the shallots and cut them into 8 parts.

Transfer the potatoes into a bowl and add the thyme leaves, coarsely chopped sage leaves, salt and pepper . Add the shallots , season with olive oil and mix well.

At this point take a large baking tray, grease the bottom with olive oil and pour the mixture of potatoes and shallots inside. Place the meatloaf in the center of the pan and bake in a preheated static oven at 180° C for 80-90 minutes. After the cooking time has elapsed, take the meatloaf out of the oven and serve it hot together with the potato side dish!

Veal Milanese

Ingredients:
- Veal loin slices 1 kg
- Eggs 4 - large
- Breadcrumbs 300 g
- Clarified butter 300 g
- Salt to taste

FOR THE POTATOES
- Grated potatoes 500 g
- Clarified butter 100 g
- Rosemary 1 sprig
- Fine salt to taste
- Black pepper to taste
- Garlic 1 clove

Using a meat pounder, beat the the slices of meat slightly, so that the thickness is evened out but without reducing it. Use a knife again to remove the extra connective tissue, which would make the cutlet shrink during cooking.

Set aside the meat and prepare the eggs. Break them into a bowl and mix them slightly with a whip, without breaking them up too much. If they're small, add another one. Put the breadcrumbs into a large bowl. Take the cutlets by the bone and first dip them in the breadcrumbs, then dip them in the eggs and again in the breadcrumbs, pressing well with your hands so that the breadcrumbs stick better. Make a double breading by dipping the cutlets again in the eggs and again in breadcrumbs, pressing well but without flattening the meat too much. Repeat this operation for all the cutlets, then using the flat side of the blade of a knife, tap the slices to even out and set the breadcrumbs. Finally, with the dull edge of the blade, make a sort of grid on the ribs by first pressing horizontal lines and then vertical. Repeat the same for all the others and start preparing the potatoes. Wash the potatoes with a little water and baking soda, then dry them.

Then get your vegetable slicer and a bowl full of water. Make slices about 1/10" (2-3 mm) thick and gradually transfer them into the bowl filled with water; this way they will release some starch but will not oxidize. Put some water in a pan, salt it and bring it to a boil. Then drain the potatoes and pour them into the water.

Blanch them for about 90 seconds a half minutes then drain them again and cool them slightly under cold water jet. This precooking will reduce the cooking time in butter. Dry the potatoes with a dish towel and in the meantime heat a large saucepan. Add the clarified butter and let it melt. Then add a lightly crushed poached clove of garlic to the potatoes, a sprig of rosemary and let it all brown over a high flame, stirring occasionally. In the meantime, take another larger pan, which will be used to cook your cutlet and melt the butter.

As soon as it is hot but not too hot, place the cutlets, making sure that the part with the lines is in contact with the pan. After about 4 minutes, the cutlets will be well browned, then turn them and with a spoon collect some cooking fat and sprinkle it on the rib bone; this way there will be no bloody streaks and you will get a clear bone. Cutlets will have to cook for about another 4 minutes, this time depends on the thickness of the cut and you will want a pinkish meat inside.

Potatoes will have the same cooking time; when they are cooked, you can salt them and season them with a little pepper. Drain the potatoes on a sheet of absorbent paper, remove the garlic and blot them with another sheet to remove the excess fat, even if it is very little due to the type of potatoes chosen.

When cutlets are ready, using a pair of tongs, transfer them to a plate with absorbent paper and again with a sheet of paper gently dab, to eliminate the excess fat. At this point everything is ready, all you have left to do is put them on a plate. Place the potatoes on the side of the plate, near the cutlet and season with maldon salt. Serve your Milanese cutlet hot.

Steak
Ingredients:
- Sliced veal 400 g
- Tomato puree 400 g
- Garlic 2 cloves
- Oregano to taste
- Extra virgin olive oil to taste
- Fine salt to taste
- Black pepper to taste

TO DECORATE
- Basil to taste

To prepare the steak pizzaiola, start with the sauce: heat the oil in a pan and add the crushed garlic cloves. After a couple of minutes, pour the tomato puree and a drop of water used to rinse the jar. Simmer for about 15 minutes over low heat.

In the meantime, prepare the meat: make small cuts on the edges of the slices where there is some fat to prevent them from curling during cooking, then transfer the slices on a sheet of parchment paper. Cover with another sheet and beat them lightly, being careful not to tear the meat; you will need to obtain a uniform thickness of about 3-4 mm. When the sauce has reduced, flavor with oregano, salt and pepper, then remove the garlic.

Dip the slices of meat in the sauce (if they are too big you can cut them in half) and let them cook 2 minutes per side. Garnish with a few basil leaves, if you wish, and immediately serve your steak pizzaiola!

Ligures rabbit
Ingredients:
- **Rabbit 1.5 kg**
- **Taggiasca olives 100 g**
- **Onions 1**
- **Rosemary 1 sprig**
- **Red wine 1 glass**
- **Garlic 2 cloves**
- **Thyme 1 tbsp**
- **Extra virgin olive oil about 5 tablespoons**
- **Meat broth to taste**
- **3 bay leaves**
- **Salt up to taste**
- **Pine nuts 2 tbsp**

First, cut the rabbit into at least a dozen pieces.

Once this operation is finished, put the olive oil in a large saucepan, heat it, and let the chopped onion and garlic wither over a low heat; add the rabbit and brown it, then add the bay leaves, thyme (or marjoram) and the chopped rosemary needles. Cook until the rabbit has taken on a nice golden colour.

Let it cook for a few minutes and then add the glass of red wine, let the wine evaporate, then add the Taggiasca olives.

Then add the pine nuts, mix everything well and then cover the rabbit with a lid and cook for about an hour until the rabbit becomes tender (the meat should detach easily from the bone). From time to time add a ladleful of stock to the pot and cook over low heat. Serve the rabbit by sprinkling it with plenty of cooking sauce and enjoy your meal!!

Roman-style tripe

Ingredients:
- Tripe 1 kg
- Guanciale 100 g
- Pecorino Romano cheese 100 g
- Celery 2 ¾ tbsp (40 g)
- Carrots 5 ½ tbsp (80 g)
- White onions 6 tbsp (90 g)
- Extra virgin olive oil 2 tbsp (30 g)
- Canned tomatoes 400 g
- White wine 3 ⅓ tbsp (50 g)
- Mint 3 leaves
- Garlic 1 clove
- Fine salt to taste
- Black pepper to taste

To prepare the Roman-style tripe, start by cleaning it, then put it in a colander and rinse it well under running water, then drain. In the meantime, prepare the chopped aromatic mixture by peeling the carrot and cutting it into cubes, do the same with the celery, removing its top leaves, and then the onion, removing the peel. If you do not wish for an intense flavor, remove its core. Then cut the slice of guanciale into cubes. In a saucepan, pour the extra virgin olive oil together with the chopped celery, carrot, and onion, then add the peeled garlic clove, let it season for a few moments over high heat, then add the cubes of guanciale and lastly, the tripe.

Pour the white wine and let it evaporate completely, add salt and pepper, then the crushed tomatoes, stir everything and let it cook for 2 hours, there will be no need to cover or add water, as the tripe will release juices during cooking. After the first hour of cooking, add the mint leaves and continue cooking. After two hours of cooking, remove the garlic clove, Turn off the heat, add the grated pecorino romano cheese, stir a few moments and serve the Roman-style tripe hot.

Beef stew with peas
Ingredients:
- Beef 800 g - (neck, brisket)
- Peas 400 g - shelled
- Celery 1
- Carrots 1
- Yellow onions 1
- Flour 00 to taste
- Dry white wine 80 g
- Vegetable broth 500 g
- Fine salt to taste
- Black pepper to taste
- Extra virgin olive oil to taste
- Triple concentrated tomato paste 2 tsp (10 g)

To prepare beef stew with peas, start by peeling and finely chopping the celery, carrot and onion. Now take the meat and cut it into 1-1/2-inch (2-3 cm) chunks, and place them in a bowl with flour. Make sure they are well coated in flour, and eliminate the excess flour by putting the pieces in a sieve. Now place a thick-bottomed pot on the stove. Heat some of the oil and add the pieces of meat. Let them brown for a few minutes over a high flame, stirring frequently, to seal in the juices. As soon as the meat is well browned, sweat with the white wine and let the alcohol evaporate. Lower the temperature a little and add the chopped aromatic herbs, letting them cook briefly.

Pour in the hot vegetable broth, then season with salt and pepper, and add the tomato paste. Stir one last time and let everything simmer gently for about 85 minutes with the lid on. Occasionally stir to prevent the meat from sticking to the bottom and make sure the broth has not dried out too much. If it has, just add a little more broth.
At the end of cooking, remove the lid, add the peas and cook for another 5 minutes. Your beef stew with peas is now ready to be served!

Palermitan cutlet
Ingredients:
- Chicken breast slices 400 g
- Breadcrumbs 130 g
- Pecorino to grate 30 g
- Extra virgin olive oil 50 g
- Parsley 2 g
- Salt up to taste
- Black pepper to taste
- Lemons (optional) to taste
- Mint (optional) to taste

To prepare the Palermitan cutlet, start with the meat. Beat the slices of meat with the special hammer or a meat mallet to soften the meat and reduce its thickness. Then transfer the slices of meat onto a plate, brush them with oil on both sides and set them aside while you continue with the preparation.

Then prepare the breading: wash the tuft of fresh parsley. Dry it and finely chop the leaves with the help of a mezzaluna or a knife. In a large bowl, put the breadcrumbs and add the chopped parsley. If you like, you can also add a few leaves of chopped fresh mint. Then add the grated pecorino to the mixture.

To flavor the breading, add the salt and pepper and mix everything together. Now you can pick up the meat set aside and pass it in the breading slice by slice, pressing well with your hands to make the mixture adhere.

Heat the grill well over medium heat and cook the meat for 10-15 minutes 10, turning it a couple of times halfway through cooking until the slices of meat are well grilled on both sides. If you prefer, you can cook the cutlet in a preheated static oven at 190° for about 15 minutes (if a convection oven at 170° for about 10 minutes). The Palermitan cutlet will then be ready to be served piping hot.

Chicken stew with peppers

Ingredients:
- Chicken - whole about 1.3 kg
- Peeled tomatoes 400 g
- Yellow onions 1
- Carrots 1
- Celery 1 rib
- Garlic 1 clove
- Red wine ½ cup
- Extra virgin olive oil to taste
- Rosemary 1 sprig
- Parsley 1 sprig - chopped
- Fine salt to taste
- Black pepper to taste

Start by cutting the vegetables. After peeling the onion, peel the carrot and trim it, finally remove the top from the celery and chop it all until it is diced about 2-3 mm). Then start cleaning the chicken. Cut it into pieces separating the thighs, chest and wings. At this point you have everything you need so go to the stove. Heat a drop of oil in a saucepan, do not overdo it because the skin of the chicken will release a lot of fat. Light the flame and let it warm up for a few moments, then put in the chicken pieces, starting with the skin side down.

Let it brown for about ten minutes, turning it after a bit. When the chicken is well colored add the chopped celery, carrot and onion and then the peeled clove of garlic. Then add salt, pepper and rosemary, stir and let it flavor together for another minutes.

Blend with red wine and let the alcoholic part evaporate completely. Now remove the rosemary and garlic clove and add the chopped peeled tomato pieces.

Mix everything together and cover with a lid, let cook over moderate heat for 30-35 minutes. Remember that if the chicken is bigger then you will need to increase the cooking a little bit more, and vice versa if it is smaller. In any case, the chicken is considered ready as soon as the meat detaches from the bones.

When finished cooking, make sure it is salted right and then sprinkle with parsley. One last stir and your chicken cacciatora is ready. Enjoy your meal!

Dessert

Tiramisù
Ingredients:
- Ladyfingers 300 g
- Eggs 4 very fresh
- Mascarpone cheese 500 g
- Sugar 100 g
- Coffee 300 g
- Unsweetened cocoa powder to taste - for the surface

To prepare tiramisu, start with very fresh eggs: carefully separate the egg whites from the yolks, remembering that to whip the egg whites well they must not contain any trace of yolk. Then whip the egg yolks with a hand mixer, pouring in only half of the sugar. As soon as the mixture has become clear and frothy, and with the mixer still running, you can add mascarpone cheese, little by little. When all the cheese is incorporated, you will have obtained a thick and compact cream; set it aside. Clean the mixer attachments very well and beat the egg whites, pouring in the remaining sugar a little at a time.

Whisk them into stiff peaks; you will know they're ready if the mixture does not move when you overturn the bowl. Take a spoonful of egg whites and pour it into the bowl with egg yolks and sugar and stir vigorously with a spatula, to thin the mixture. Then proceed to add the remaining egg whites, little by little, stirring very gently from bottom to top. Once ready, place a generous spoonful of cream on the bottom of a 12x8in baking pan and spread it evenly. Then soak the ladyfingers for a few moments in the cooled coffee, which you will have sweetened to your liking (we added only 1 teaspoon of sugar), first on one side and then the other. Arrange the soaked ladyfingers on top of the cream, side by side, to create the first layer, over which you will spread part of the mascarpone cheese cream. Make sure to level it carefully so that you have a smooth surface. Continue to arrange the coffee-soaked ladyfingers, then add another layer of cream.

Level the surface, sprinkle it with unsweetened cocoa powder, and allow it to set in the fridge for a couple of hours. Your Tiramisù is ready to be enjoyed!

Mimosa cake
Ingredients:
- Sugar 250 g
- Flour 00 140 g
- Potato starch 120 g
- Eggs 8 - at room temperature
- Vanilla bean 2
- Fine salt 1 pinch

FOR 850 G PASTRY CREAM
- Egg yolks 5
- Sugar 175 g
- Whole milk 500 ml
- Heavy cream 125 ml
- Cornstarch 7 tbsp
- Vanilla bean 1
- **FOR THE CHANTILLY CREAM**
- Heavy cream 100 ml
- Powdered sugar 2 ½ tbsp

FOR THE LIQUEUR SYRUP
- Water 130 g
- Sugar 75 g
- Grand Marnier liqueur 70 g
- **TO DECORATE**
- **Powdered sugar to taste**

To prepare the classic mimosa cake you first need to make the two sponge cakes. Make sure you have two 8" (20 cm) diameter pans and that both fit into the oven on the same shelf next to each other. If this is not the case, you will have to make one sponge cake at a time (just halve the indicated amounts). Preheat the oven to 325° F (160°) in static mode. Crack open the eggs, put them in a stand mixer and start whipping them at moderate speed. Cut both the vanilla pods, take out the seeds and add them to the mixing bowl with a pinch of salt. At this point slowly add the sugar.

Continue to whip for about 15 minutes until the eggs have tripled in volume and you have obtained a fluid and creamy mixture, slightly thickened. Stop the mixer and place a strainer directly over the bowl. Sift together the flour and starch and gently fold the powder in with upward movements from the bottom using a spatula, so as not to risk separating the mixture. When it is homogeneous, butter and flour the two 8" (20 cm) diameter cake pans. Divide the dough equally between the 2 cake pans. Bake your sponge cake in a static oven preheated to 160° C, on the lower shelf, for about 50 minutes. Make sure they are baked by testing with a toothpick; if it emerges completely dry, you can take them out of the oven. Let them cool completely before you take them out of the pan. Then place them on a cooling rack to finish cooling.

TO PREPARE THE DIPLOMATIC CREAM

Now make the cream to fill the mimosa cake. Start with the pastry cream: cut the vanilla pod, take out the seeds and set them aside. Pour the milk, cream and the empty pod into a pan and heat it all on low until it is almost boiling. In the meantime, beat the yolks together with the sugar and vanilla seeds in a bowl; it won't be necessary to whip them, just mix everything together. Sift the corn starch directly into the mixture and stir again. As soon as the milk is hot, remove the pod using kitchen tongs. and pour one ladle of it into the egg yolk mixture, stirring with a whisk to dissolve it. Pour everything into the pan with the hot milk and, stirring constantly, let it thicken over low heat. Once ready, place it in a low and wide ovenproof dish and let it cool completely, covering it with transparent wrap when the cream is still hot. After it has cooled, pour the fresh cream into a bowl, add the powdered sugar and start whipping with the beaters. As soon as the cream is whipped well, take the cream and transfer it into another bowl. Whip lightly to soften it and start adding the cream. Add one spoonful and stir vigorously to dilute the cream, then incorporate the remaining cream by moving the spatula very gently from the bottom to the top. Cover again with plastic wrap and put in the refrigerator to set for about 30 minutes.

FOR THE SYRUP

In the meantime, prepare the syrup for the cake too. Pour the water, liqueur and sugar into a saucepan. Turn on the burner and, while stirring, heat the syrup until the sugar has melted, then pour it into another bowl and let it cool.

TO ASSEMBLE THE DESSERT

As soon as everything is cool, you can assemble the dessert. First remove the outer crust from both sponge cakes, starting with the edges, then from the top and finally from the bottom. At this stage try to remove only the darker part, so as to reduce waste. You can use the scraps as indicated at the bottom of the recipe. Take one of the two sponge cakes and use a bread knife to cut 3 uniform layers. To cut the sponge cake as regularly as possible, you can cut laterally: make two notches with the bread knife to set the measure, then slowly sink the blade crosswise to obtain the first layer, helping the movement by turning the sponge cake as you cut to make it homogeneous and precise. Place the first layer of sponge cake on a plate (we used a turntable, but a normal serving plate will do fine), then a pastry ring (you can also fill the cake without one): using a spoon, spread the previously prepared syrup over the whole surface of the disc and let it cool down. Now add about 1/4 of the cream and level it with a spatula. Insert the second disc into the ring, bathe again and cover with another layer of cream as previously described.

Now insert the last disc and soak it again with the remaining syrup. Add one more layer of cream, saving some for the edges, and level evenly. Take the second sponge cake and cut it into vertical slices, then make some rather small cubes from each of them and put them in a small bowl. Gently remove the ring from the mimosa cake and use a spatula to add the remaining cream to the edges of the cake. Using a spoon, place the sponge cake cubes over the entire surface, including the edges: the cubes will easily stick to the diplomatic cream. Once the whole surface has been carefully covered, place the cake in the fridge for a couple of hours. When serving, dust your classic mimosa cake with powdered sugar!

Caprese with lemon

Ingredients:
- Almond flour 170 g
- White chocolate 100 g
- Lemon zest 3
- Butter at room temperature 100 g
- Egg yolks at room temperature 80 g
- Egg whites at room temperature 175 g
- Powdered sugar 150 g
- Potato starch 40 g
- Baking powder for cakes 5 g
- Lemon flavor 2 ml
- Salt up to 1 pinch

TO DECORATE
- Powdered sugar to taste

To make the lemon caprese, first grate the white chocolate and the lemon zest, then set aside. Pour the soft butter into a bowl, add half the sugar dose and whisk the mixture with an electric whisk. Once the ingredients have been collected, flavor with lemon zest. and a pinch of salt. Keeping the whips in action, also pour the egg yolks and when the mixture is amalgamated
add the lemon flavor. Set the dough aside and, in another large bowl, pour the almond flour and grated white chocolate. Sift the remaining powders here: starch and yeast.

Stir and set aside. Now pour the egg whites and the remaining half of sugar into a bowl, whip with an electric whisk until you get a shiny and fluffy mixture. Now take the egg mixture and stir in, alternating them, 1/3 of the egg whites and 1/3 of the mixed powders and continue until all the ingredients are used up. Once ready, the dough will be quite compact, grease and flour a mold with a diameter of 22 cm with the starch, then pour the mixture and level it with the spatula to distribute it evenly.

Bake the cake in a preheated convection oven at 170 ° for 45 minutes; once ready, take it out of the oven, let it cool and then turn out your lemon caprese and serve, sprinkling the surface with icing sugar.

Pastiera napoletana (Neapolitan ricotta cheese Easter pie)
Ingredients:
- Flour 00 250 g
- Lard 50 g
- Butter 50 g
- Sugar 80 g
- Wildflower honey 20 g
- Eggs 1
- Whole milk 2 ¾ tbsp
- Lemon peel 1
- Orange peel 1
- Fine salt 1 pinch

FOR THE WHEAT CREAM
- Cooked wheat 200 g
- Whole milk 80 g
- Butter 1 ¾ tbsp
- Lemon peel to taste
- Orange peel to taste
- Fine salt 1 pinch

FOR THE FILLING
- Sheep's milk ricotta cheese 200 g
- Sugar 180 g
- Candied citron 50 g
- Wildflower honey 1 tbsp
- Eggs 2
- Egg yolks 1
- Orange blossom water to taste
- Whole milk 1.5 tbsp
- Orange peel to taste
- Lemon peel to taste

TO GARNISH
- Powdered sugar to taste

To prepare the pastiera, start by preparing the shortcrust pastry dough. On a work surface, sift the flour and add a pinch of salt to form a volcano, making sure you can see the work surface underneath in the center. In the center add butter, lard, and sugar. Mix these 3 ingredients well by hand. Continue to mix and add the honey, egg, milk, and citrus peels. Continue to mix the ingredients in the center of the flour until you obtain a kind of soft batter. Then begin to add the flour slowly and mix with the help of a dough scraper if needed.

Shape the dough into a ball. To make it more homogeneous, you can lightly dust the work surface with a little flour. Then continue to knead the dough to make it completely smooth and homogeneous. Cover it with plastic wrap and let it rest in the refrigerator for 1 hour.

While the dough is resting, prepare the wheat cream. Pour the precooked wheat in a pan and add a pinch of salt. Mash the wheat a little to make it uniform and pour in the milk and add the butter. You can also add a piece of orange and lemon peel. Bring it to the verge of boiling which will take just a few minutes. Use a fork to mash the wheat as it cooks and continue to stir. Once it is about to boil, turn off the heat and transfer the wheat mixture to a low and wide pan to cool. In a separate bowl, add the drained ricotta cheese and the sugar. Stir until you obtain a soft cream and then let it rest in the refrigerator for about an hour. After the time has elapsed, take out the cold wheat mixture from the refrigerator, remove the citrus peels and place the wheat mixture in a large bowl. Add the diced candied citron and stir briefly. At this point, if you want, you can use a hand blender for a few seconds to obtain a mixture with a less rustic consistency.

Take the bowl with the ricotta cheese and sugar, add the honey, stir, and add the wheat mixture, stirring constantly to combine the ingredients. In another bowl, add the eggs, yolk, and orange blossom water.

Then add the milk, zest a little bit of lemon and orange, and mix everything well. Add this mixture to the ricotta cheese and wheat cream in two or three parts and continue to mix. The filling is now ready. Take the dough out of the refrigerator and divide it into two parts, one larger than the other. Roll out the larger part on a work surface with a rolling pin, making sure they are both lightly floured, until you obtain a thickness of 1/8 inch (3 mm). Then roll the dough around the rolling pin.

Unroll it over an 8-inch (20 cm) flared pastiera cake mold. Let it adhere well to the bottom and sides, then remove the excess dough by passing the rolling pin over the edges. Trim with a small knife and prick the base with a fork. Place the filling inside, gently beat the mold on the work surface to eliminate any air bubbles. Roll out the remaining dough and make seven ½-inch (1-2 cm) thick strips. Place the first 4 strips over the filling reaching over the edge of the pastiera mold in a diagonal direction. Then add on top of the 4 strips the other 3, again reaching over the edges, to create a grid pattern. Then eliminate the excess dough. The pastiera is now ready to be baked in a preheated static oven at 180° C for about 50-55 minutes on the lowest rack. Then take the Neapolitan pastiera out of the oven and when it has completely cooled you can either remove it from the mold or serve the cake directly in it. Sprinkle a little powdered sugar just before serving and enjoy!

Margherita cake
- **Flour 00 90 g**
- **Potato starch (50 g**
- **Sugar 150 g**
- **Baking powder ½ tsp**
- **Eggs 3**
- **Egg yolks 3**
- **Fine salt ¼ tsp**
- **Lemon peel 1**
- **Butter 90 g**

FOR THE DECORATION
- **Powdered sugar to taste**

To prepare your margherita cake, melt the butter over very low heat and then leave to cool. Pour the eggs and sugar into the bowl of a stand mixer. Turn the mixer on, using the whisk attachment on a medium speed. Add the salt and grated lemon zest before the eggs are fully whipped.

Whip on a high speed for 8 minutes. Add the egg yolks one at a time. Combine the flour, baking powder, and starch in another bowl, and sift the mixture onto a sheet of parchment paper, twice. Reduce the speed of the mixer and add all of the dry ingredients at the same time. Increase the speed to achieve an even consistency, then turn off the mixer. Take some of the dough, transfer it to a bowl, add the melted butter, and mix quickly using a spatula to create an emulsion . Add a little more of the mixture to the bowl and mix until you achieve an even consistency. Pour the mixture back into the bowl of the stand mixer and mix from the bottom up. As soon as you have achieved an even consistency, transfer it into a greased and floured 8-inch (20-cm) cake pan, possibly Teflon-coated. Bake in a conventional oven preheated to 190°C for 40 minutes. After this time, take the cake out of the oven and leave to cool. Turn your margherita cake out onto a wire rack, garnish with powdered sugar, and serve.

Italian trifle
Ingredients:
- Eggs 2
- Flour 00 30 g
- Potato starch 30 g
- Sugar 60 g
- Fine salt 1 pinch
- Vanilla bean 1

FOR THE PASTRY CREAM
- Whole milk 400 g
- Heavy cream 100 g
- Egg yolks 4
- Cornstarch 45 g
- Sugar 140 g
- Vanilla bean 1
- Dark chocolate 50 g

TO DECORATE
- **Unsweetened cocoa powder to taste**
- **Alchermes 100g**

Start by making the pan sponge cake. Pour the eggs into a bowl at room temperature and beat them with a whisk while adding the sugar a little at a time. Continue for about ten minutes or until the mixture becomes clear and frothy. Next, place a strainer in the bowl and pour in the flour and potato starch.

Fold in the dry ingredients with gentle upward movements, making sure that no residue is left on the bottom of the bowl. Pour the dough into a previously buttered and floured 7-inch (18 cm) round mold. Level the surface with a rubber spatula and bake in a preheated oven, in static mode at 160°C for about 40 minutes, placing the drip pan on the lower shelf (not in contact with the base); leave to cool and then remove from the pan.

PREPARATION OF THE PASTRY CREAM AND ASSEMBLY

Meanwhile, prepare the pastry cream. Pour the milk and cream into a saucepan, scrape the vanilla seeds, keeping them aside, from the pod and place the latter into the saucepan. Let it warm up to just under the boiling point. In the meantime, pour the vanilla seeds on the yolks, add the sugar, beat quickly and then sift the corn starch. By now the milk and cream should be hot, so discard the pod
and pour a couple of ladles into the egg mixture to dilute it. Then pour into the pan and stir with a whisk while cooking for a few minutes. As soon as the cream thickens, you can turn off the heat 15.

Divide the cream into two bowls and pour the chocolate into one. Take advantage of the fact that the cream is still very hot to help you dissolve it, then cover both creams with plastic wrap and let them cool down. Take the cooled pan sponge cake, use 70 g of it, cut it into vertical slices 1/4-inch (1 cm) thick, and trim to fit into 4 glasses of 2/3 cup 150 ml capacity. Soak the sponge cake with alchermes, without exaggerating and proceed by pouring a little chocolate cream first and then the vanilla cream. Tap the glass to distribute the cream evenly and continue layering with soaked sponge cake, and the two types of cream. Level the surface with a spatula and repeat for the other glasses. Finally put them in the refrigerator to settle for at least a couple of hours. Sprinkle unsweetened cocoa on your glasses of before serving and enjoy your dessert!

Struffoli (Sweet fritters)
Ingredients:
- Sugar 3 tbsp
- Flour 00 400 g
- Butter 60 g - to be melted
- Orange peel 1
- Eggs 3
- Egg yolks 1
- Fine salt 1 pinch
- Anise liqueur 1 tbsp

FOR THE TOPPING
- Colored sprinkles to taste
- Wildflower honey 175 g
- Candied orange 30 g
- Candied citron 30 g
- Food decorations to taste - silver-colored candy
- Candied cherries to taste

FOR FRYING
- Peanut seed oil to taste

To make honey balls, melt the butter and let it cool. In the meantime, put the flour, sugar, eggs, a pinch of salt, grated orange peel, and melted butter in a bowl with the anise liqueur. Start kneading by hand in the bowl, then transfer the dough to a pastry board and knead until a compact and homogeneous dough ball is created .

Cover with a clean cloth, then let rest for at least 30 minutes at room temperature. After the rest time has elapsed, take the brick, divide it into 6-7 equal parts with a knife. With each piece, create sticks approximately 1/3 inch (1 cm) thick. Cut the sticks into small 1/3 inch (1 cm) pieces and place them on a sheet, ensuring that they do not overlap.

To cook the balls: heat the peanut oil in a pot, and when it is hot, dip theballs with a skimmer. For optimal frying, make sure that the oil reaches a temperature of approximately 180° C with a food thermometer. To keep the temperature stable, only cook a few fritters at a time. Mix with a skimmer to obtain a uniform cooking; 2-3 minutes will be enough to obtain a golden color at the right point; drain them and transfer to a tray covered with absorbent paper to dry the excess oil.

Let the balls cool and melt the honey in a pot over low heat, when the honey has melted pour over the Struffoli and stir to amalgamate. Turn off the heat and let cool, then add the colored sugar.

Cut the candied oranges and citron into small cubes, pour them into the pot with the balls, and stir gently with a spoon.

Take a serving dish, place a glass jar in the center of the dish that will be used to create the crown shape, and distribute the balls around the jar. When the honey has solidified, gently remove the jar from the center of the dish. Decorate with candied cherries and silver-colored candied almonds, then serve your Struffoli.

Tuscan chestnut cake
Ingredients:
- **Chestnut flour 500 g**
- **Water 650 g**
- **Pine nuts 100 g**
- **Rosemary 1 sprig**
- **Raisins 80 g**
- **Walnut kernels 100 g**
- **Extra virgin olive oil 5 tbsp (40 g)**
- **Fine salt 1 tsp (5 g)**

To prepare the Tuscan chestnut cake, first wash the raisins in fresh water and soak them in a bowl of cold water for 10 minutes to rehydrate them. Coarsely chop the walnut kernels with a knife, then peel off the fresh rosemary needles.

Sift the chestnut flour into a large bowl and add the 650g of water a little at a time, stirring with a hand whisk; when the mixture is smooth and homogeneous, add the chopped walnuts and whole pine nuts, making sure to set a small amount aside that will later be used on top of the cake before baking.

After 10 minutes, squeeze and dry the raisins, then add them to the mixture, adding a small amount at a time; mix well and add salt.

Oil a 12 inch (32 cm) low round cake tin and pour the mixture, leveling it with a spatula. Sprinkle the surface of the cake with the pine nuts, walnuts and raisins set aside, distributing them evenly.

Lastly, add the rosemary needles, a drizzle of oil, and cook in a static oven preheated to 195° C for approximately 35 minutes. When a crust forms cracks on the surface and the nuts have a nice golden color, take the cake out. When cool, serve and enjoy the Tuscan chestnut cake.

Graffe (Donuts)
Ingredients:
- Whole milk 120 g - warm
- Flour 00 130 g
- Brewer's yeast 0.6 tsp (3 g)

FOR THE DOUGH
- Potatoes 300 g
- Manitoba flour 400 g
- Flour 00 70 g
- Eggs 3
- Sugar 50 g
- Butter 100 g - (softened)
- Acacia honey 1 tsp (8 g)
- Lemon peel 1
- Fine salt 1 ¼ tsp (8 g)

FOR BUTTERING
- Butter 2 tbsp (30 g)

FOR FRYING AND SUGARING
- Peanut seed oil 1 l
- Sugar 200 g

To prepare the graffe donuts, wash the potatoes, then boil them; it will take about 30 minutes depending on the size of the potatoes. Prepare the yeast in the meantime: in a bowl add the dehydrated brewer's yeast to the sifted flour and mix it with the lukewarm milk until a homogeneous mixture is obtained.

Cover the yeast with transparent wrap and let it rise in the oven with the light on for 1 hour (otherwise cover it with a wool cloth and let it rise in a place away from drafts). When the potatoes are cooked, peel them, mash them with a potato masher and let it all cool down. Place the two sifted flours and the honey in a stand mixer with flat beaters.

Add the sugar, the mashed potatoes, whichby now have cooled down and the grated rind of a whole lemon, well washed and dried.

Beat the eggs slightly and add them , then turn on the mixer with the flat beater: when the dough is firm and collected on the beater, replace it with the dough hook and add the yeast. Continue working the mixture until the yeast is well incorporated, then add the salt and the softened butter one piece at a time, waiting for it to be absorbed before proceeding with the next.

Then put the dough on the work surface lightly greased with a little melted butter and work it with your hands to make it smooth. Make it into a ball and place it in a bowl covered with transparent wrap, and let rise for 2 hours in the oven with the light on (or covered with a lid and left in a place away from drafts). The ideal temperature to make it rise is 79-82° F (26-30° C).

After this time, put the dough on the work surface, greased with the remaining melted butter, and make it cylindrical in shape, then divide it into portions of about 60 g: shape each part into a ball, flatten it slightly and pierce it in the center, then gently widen the hole: with our amounts you'll have 20 graffe. Place the donuts made this way on a drip pan lined with baking paper, cover with transparent wrap or a cloth and let rise in the oven off with the light on for 1 hour: they should double in volume. When leavening is complete, start heating the seed oil in a large saucepan, it should reach 325° F (160° C). Cut the baking paper under each graffe so as to make a support and not have to move them by hand and risk ruining their shape. When the oil has reached the indicated temperature, gently immerse them with the baking paperand then remove the paper . Fry them one at a time, a couple of minutes on each side to brown evenly.

When they are well browned on both sides, drain the graffe from the oil with a skimmer and let them dry on a tray lined with paper towels. Place the granulated sugar in a container that you must roll the doughnuts in still hot to cover them completely with sugar: your graffe are ready, serve them hot!

Chocolate salami
Ingredients:
- Dark chocolate 200 g- (55%)
- Butter 100 g
- Cookies 100 g
- Sugar 150 g
- Rum 2 tbsp
- Unsweetened cocoa powder 1 tbsp

TO DECORATE
- Powdered sugar to taste

To prepare the chocolate salami, first take the ingredients out of the refrigerator so that they are at room temperature. Chop the dark chocolate with a knife and melt it in the microwave or in a bain-marie, then let it cool. Meanwhile, pour the butter and sugar into a separate bowl and start working with a whip.

When you have reduced the butter to cream, pour the rum slowly while continuing to mix. Finally add the warm chocolate, give a quick stir and also add the unswetened cocoa powder, making sure to mix everything until you get a homogeneous mixture.

Crumble the dry biscuits with your hands and add them to the chocolate mixture, then mix with a spatula to incorporate them evenly.

Now take a sheet of baking paper and pour the mixture into the center, shaping it with your hands to give it a cylindrical shape. Lift the bottom flap and wrap the paper around the cylinder, then roll up the ends to seal it.

Transfer the roll to the refrigerator and let it harden for at least 2-3 hours. After this time, remove the baking paper and sprinkle with powdered sugar. Your chocolate salami is ready to be sliced and enjoyed!

Torta caprese
Ingredients:
- 50% dark chocolate for grating 170 g
- Peeled almonds (to be ground into powder) 85 g
- Whole hazelnuts (to be reduced to powder) 85 g
- Icing sugar 170 g
- Softened butter 170 g
- Potato starch 25 g
- Bitter cocoa powder 14 g
- Egg whites at room temperature 148 g
- Egg yolks at room temperature 85 g
- Powdered yeast for cakes 4 g
- Vanilla pod
- Salt up to 1 pinch

TO DECORATE
- **Powdered sugar to taste**

To prepare torta caprese, start by placing the butter at room temperature into a bowl (take it out of the fridge at least a couple of hours before using it), half of the sugar and the seeds scraped off half a vanilla bean. Using a handheld mixer on medium-high speed, whisk the butter and after 6-7 minutes add the pinch of salt and egg yolks. The eggs should also be left at room temperature for at least 12 hours.

After a few minutes the mixture will be frothy, so turn off the mixer, clean the bowl with a spatula collecting all the mixture and set it aside. In another bowl mix the dry ingredients: add the grated chocolate, the powdered almonds, and the powdered hazelnuts. Next, sift the potato starch, baking powder and bitter cocoa powder.

Mix everything well and set aside. In another bowl pour the egg whites and the remaining powdered sugar. Make sure that the whisks are clean, otherwise the egg whites will not whip.

After a few minutes the egg whites will be shiny and frothy: you don't have to whip them stiff, but they need to hold the classic bird beak. When all preparations are complete, preheat the oven to 170°C in convection mode and start combining them: fold a third of the whipped egg whites then a third of the dry ingredients into the egg yolks and butter mixture using a spatula, stirring gently from bottom to top. Add another third of the egg whites and one third of the dry ingredients and continue until you get a uniform mixture.

Pour the smooth and creamy mixture 22 cm round cake mold already buttered and floured with potato starch. Carefully level the surface and bake in a convection oven at 170°C for about 45 minutes.

Once baked, let the cake cool down in the mold, then turn it upside down to unmold it. Then turn it over again on a plate lined with baking paper and let it cool completely. Once cold, turn the cake upside down one last time, remove the baking paper and dust the surface with powdered sugar. Your torta caprese is ready to be enjoyed!

Panna Cotta
Ingredients:
- **Heavy cream 500 ml**
- **Vanilla bean 1**
- **Gelatin 8 g**
- **Sugar 80 g**

To make panna cotta, first soak the gelatin sheets in cold water for 10-15 minutes. Cut the vanilla pod lengthwise and extract the seeds by scraping with the tip of a knife. Put the liquid cream in a saucepan, then pour in the sugar.

Flavor with the vanilla seeds and also add the pod; heat everything over a low heat, but without boiling; when it comes to a boil, turn off the heat and extract the pod using kitchen tongs.

When the gelatin is softened, drain it without squeezing excessively, then dip it in the pot with hot cream. Stir with a wooden spoon or hand whisk until the gelatin has completely dissolved; there must be no lumps. At this point take 4 five-ounce molds and pour in the panna cotta using a ladle.

Once the molds are filled, put the panna cotta in the refrigerator to set for at least 5 hours. Once it has set, before serving it and for better demolding, dip each mold into boiling water for a few seconds. Then immediately demold the panna cotta on each serving plate: serve your panna cotta au natural, with caramel, melted chocolate, or fruit coulis.

Apple strudel
Ingredients:
- Flour 00 130 g
- Water 2 tbsp
- Vegetable oil 1 tbsp
- Eggs 1
- Salt 1 pinch

FOR THE FILLING
- Golden delicious apples 750 g
- Sugar 60 g
- Breadcrumbs 60 g
- Butter 3 tbsp
- Raisins 50 g
- Pine nuts 25 g
- Cinnamon powder 1 pinch
- Rum 2 tbsp
- Lemon peel 1

FOR DUSTING
- **Powdered sugar to taste**

To prepare the apple strudel, start by making the dough: Pour the sifted flour and salt into a bowl, then add the egg and water and begin to knead with your hands. Then add the oil and knead the mixture to form a smooth dough. If it's too sticky, you can add another 10-20 g of flour at most.

Transfer the dough to a flat surface and knead until elastic. When you've finished kneading, form a ball and transfer to a lightly greased bowl, cover with plastic wrap, and leave to rest for an hour in a cool place. In the meantime, soak the raisins in rum, or warm water if you prefer; melt 2 tbsp (30 g) of butter in a frying pan and toast the breadcrumbs when it begins to sizzle.

Stir with a wooden spoon to keep the breadcrumbs from burning and brown for a few minutes, then turn off the heat and leave to cool. Next, peel the apples, remove the cores, cut them into four wedges, and then into thin slices. Add the apples to a large bowl with the sugar, pine nuts, grated lemon peel, a pinch of cinnamon, and the raisins, which must be well drained and squeezed: The ingredients must release their aromas but they must not be allowed to steep for too long, or else the sugar will make them release too much water.

Melt the remaining butter in a small saucepan over a low heat. Then take the dough ball and roll it out on a lightly floured dish towel to form a rectangle measuring approximately 14x18 inches (35x45 cm). Brush the surface, except for the edges, with a little melted butter, and sprinkle with toasted breadcrumbs; this layer will absorb the juices that the apples release during cooking.

Place the apple mixture on top, then roll the strudel up from the longest side, taking care not to break the pastry (you can use the dish towel to help you). Seal the sides of the strudel as well so that the contents do not come out during cooking.
Then place the strudel on a baking sheet lined with parchment paper with the sealed end at the bottom. Brush with melted butter before placing in the oven. Cook the strudel in a conventional oven preheated to 200°C for approximately 40 minutes 180°C for 30 minutes if using a convection oven). Once cooked, sprinkle the strudel with powdered sugar and serve it warm, cut into slices.

Paradise cake
Ingredients:
- Butter 170 g
- Powdered sugar 170 g
- Sugar 3 tbsp
- Fine salt ¼ tsp
- Potato starch 70 g
- Powdered yeast for sweets 1 tsp
- Flour 00 (100 g
- Vanilla bean ½
- Egg yolks 4
- Eggs 2
- Lemon peel ½
- Orange peel ½

FOR SPRINKLING OVER THE CAKE
- **Powdered sugar to taste**

To prepare paradise cake, start by placing the sieved flour, potato starch and yeast in a bowl, then stir thoroughly with a spoon. Place the pieces of softened butter in another bowl, add the pulp of half a vanilla seed and grate the peel of half an untreated lemon; grate the peel of half an untreated orange too. Start beating the butter and vanilla with an electric whisk and add the powdered sugar. When the mixture becomes light and airy in consistency, add the egg yolks, then the salt, and continue to beat the mixture with the electric whisk, until soft and creamy. Leave to one side and place two whole eggs in another bowl, add the granulated sugar; beat with an electric whisk and as soon as the egg and sugar mixture becomes light-colored, smooth and frothy, add it to the butter, sugar and egg yolk mixture; alternate by adding the powders. Now add a little of the egg and sugar mixture and stir thoroughly with a spatula. Add some of the powders and continue to stir. Continue once more by adding some more of the powder to the liquid part, until there is none left. Alternating both parts creates a dough with a typically crumbly consistency, which characterizes the paradise cake.

Take a 9.5 inch (24 cm) mold, use a brush to butter it, then coat in flour and add the paradise cake mix. Smooth with a spatula for an even surface. Bake the paradise cake in a static oven preheated to 170°C for around 45-50 minutes (this will depend on your oven; cover the cake with a sheet of aluminum after 30 minutes if you notice it is becoming too dark, and continue to bake). When done (always use the toothpick test to check), remove it from the oven and wait around 20 minute before turning it over onto a serving dish.

Delicately remove the mold and leave to cool thoroughly for around 1 hour. Once cooled, sprinkle with the powdered sugar to create a homogeneous layer on the surface. Your paradise cake is ready to be enjoyed.

Baci di dama (Hazelnut cookies)
Ingredients:
- Butter 300 g
- Sugar 300 g
- Almond flour 300 g
- Flour 00 300 g
- Egg whites 3 tbsp (50 g) -
- Fine salt 1 pinch (3 g)

FOR THE FILLING
- Dark chocolate 375 g

To prepare baci di dama (Hazelnut cookies), start with the shortbread dough. Pour the soft but still firm cubed butter and sugar into the bowl of a stand mixer with a flat beater. Mix a few seconds at low speed until the dough is well combined. Add the almond flour and turn on the mixer again. Pour the egg whites into a bowl, add the salt and dissolve it. Pour everything into the batter . As soon as it's well mixed, turn off the machine and add the already sifted flour. Continue to mix at low speed, clearing the edges of the mixer bowl with a spatula every few seconds. As soon as the flour has been absorbed, transfer the dough onto a lightly floured surface. Add a light layer of flour on the top and pat it down without kneading. Cover the dough with plastic wrap and put it in the refrigerator for 2-3 hours. Then, transfer it to a slightly floured surface. Using two pastry rulers, roll out the dough with a rolling pin to an even thickness of about 1/2" (1 cm). Trim the first edge, then cut strips about 1" (2 cm) long using a pastry ruler and a knife.
Create the grid by making the other side 1" (2 cm) wide strips , obtaining cubes of about .4-5 g each. Make them into balls in the palm of one hand and place them on a drip pan lined with baking paper, spaced apart. With these amounts, you should get about 250 balls. Bake in a static oven preheated to 180°C for 12 minutes. As soon as the cookies are golden, take them out and let them cool down.

Now soften the chocolate and put it inside a baking paper cone. Turn one half of the half spheres upside down and squeeze some chocolate in the center and put on top of another half sphere, lightly pressing them together. Repeat this operation for all the cookies and let them solidify before enjoying them. If the air temperature is too hot, put the baci di dama in the refrigerator.

Italian Comfort Food

Part 2

Appetizers, side and snacks

Potatoes meatball
Ingredients:
- Potatoes 500 g
- Caciocavallo 100 g
- Breadcrumbs 80 g
- Grana Padano PDO to grate 60 g
- Eggs 2
- Parsley to taste
- Salt up to taste
- Black pepper to taste

TO COOK
- Extra virgin olive oil q.s.

To prepare the potato balls, first boil the potatoes starting from the cold water for about 30-40 minutes from the boil until they are soft, checking with the prongs of a fork. In the meantime, grate the caciocavallo with a grater with large holes. When the potatoes are cooked, peel them and mash them still hot in a bowl. Add the caciocavallo, salt, pepper and eggs. Also add the breadcrumbs, the grated Parmesan and the chopped parsley.

Mix with a fork until you get a homogeneous mixture. Now take small portions of dough of about 25 g each and form them into balls, then lightly crush them between the palms of your hands. As they are ready, place the meatballs on a tray.
Pour a finger of oil into a non-stick pan and put it on the heat. When the oil is hot, add the meatballs and brown them on both sides, it will take a few minutes. Drain the potato balls on absorbent paper and serve them still hot!

Zucchini rolls with prosciutto and robiola
Ingredients:
- Zucchini 2
- Robiola 100 g
- Raw ham 120 g
- Chives to taste
- Black pepper to taste
- Salt up to taste

To prepare the zucchini rolls with prosciutto and robiola, first wash the zucchini. Then trim them on both sides and cut 12 slices 2-3 mm thick. Grease a grill and heat it; then place the zucchini slices and cook for about 5 minutes.

Then turn them over and continue cooking on the other side as well. Then transfer the grilled zucchini to a tray and set aside for a moment. Transfer the robiola into a bowl and mash it lightly with a fork.

Season with salt, pepper and the chopped chives. Spread the zucchini on a cutting board and sprinkle the entire surface with the cheese.
Add a slice of ham, roll up and serve your zucchini rolls with prosciutto and robiola.

Stuffed Baked Potatoes
Ingredients:
- **Potatoes (4 of the same size) 860 g**
- **Ground beef 120 g**
- **Sweet provola 40 g**
- **Parmigiano Reggiano DOP to grate 40 g**
- **Garlic 1 clove**
- **Extra virgin olive oil 30 g**
- **White wine 15 g**
- **Salt up to taste**
- **Black pepper to taste**

To prepare the stuffed baked potatoes, start by washing and drying the tubers well. We advise you to choose potatoes of the same size in order to obtain uniform cooking afterwards. Arrange the potatoes on a baking tray covered with parchment paper. Bake them in a preheated static oven at 190°C for about 1 hour (cooking times depend on the size of the potatoes, to get the best results, test cooking by inserting a toothpick into the potatoes). In the meantime, heat the olive oil in a pan with the peeled garlic clove, once the garlic has flavored the oil, remove it and add the minced meat, crush it to crumble it and brown it for about 10 minutes, then pour in the white wine and, once the alcohol has evaporated, turn off the heat and set aside.

When the potatoes have finished cooking (make sure they are soft by inserting them with a toothpick) take them out of the oven, let them cool slightly, then cut them in half lengthwise. With a teaspoon, remove the potato pulp leaving a border of about half a centimeter and collect it in a bowl.

Once you have hollowed out all the potatoes, mash the pulp with a fork to obtain a puree. Add the browned minced meat, salt and pepper.

Cut the provola into cubes and add it to the filling, stir to mix the ingredients. Now stuff your potatoes with the filling, helping you with a spoon.

Season the potatoes with the grated cheese, then place them on a dripping pan covered with parchment paper and put them under the grill for 5 minutes to brown the surface. Serve your stuffed baked potatoes piping hot!

Mediterranean eggplants rolls
Ingredients:
- Long eggplants (4 slices) 120 g
- Mozzarella 100 g
- Tomato puree 200 g
- Pitted Taggiasca olives 15 g
- Basil 4 leaves
- Garlic 1 clove
- Extra virgin olive oil 2 tbsp
- Salt up to taste
- Black pepper to taste

To make the Mediterranean eggplant rolls, first start preparing the sauce: heat the oil in a saucepan, add a clove of garlic and brown it for 5 minutes over low heat. When the oil is flavored, pour the tomato pulp, salt and pepper and cook for another 15 minutes.

While the tomato sauce is cooking, wash the eggplants and cut it into slices about 1 cm thick: you will have to obtain 4 long slices of uniform thickness. Heat a plate well and grill the eggplants slices on both sides, then transfer them to a plate or cutting board.

When the tomato sauce is ready, remove the garlic clove. Break up the mozzarella with your hands and preheat the oven to 180° in static mode. You are now ready to assemble the rolls: spread a layer of tomato on the surface of the eggplants, add a little shredded mozzarella, a teaspoon of olives and a basil leaf.

Roll up the stuffed eggplants and place them in a small baking dish with the seam facing downwards. Finally cover the rolls with a little tomato sauce and a few pieces of mozzarella. The rolls are now ready to be baked: cook them in the preheated static oven at 180° for about 10 minutes, just long enough for the cheese to melt. Once out of the oven, your Mediterranean eggplant rolls are ready to be enjoyed still sparkling!

Fried mozzarella
Ingredients:
- **Mozzarella 500 g**
- **Medium eggs 3**
- **Whole milk 20 g**
- **Flour 00 to taste**
- **Breadcrumbs to taste**
- **Black pepper to taste**
- **Salt up to taste**

TO FRY
- **Peanut oil 1 l**

To prepare the fried mozzarella, first cut the mozzarella into 2 cm slices and then into cubes. Place it in a colander to drain.
Meanwhile, in a bowl, beat the eggs with salt and pepper, then add the milk.
Drain the mozzarella well, then dip each morsel first in the flour, then in the eggs and then in the breadcrumbs.
Do a double breading only in the egg and breadcrumbs. In a saucepan, heat the seed oil and when it has reached 170° -180°, dip the breaded mozzarella a few at a time.
Fry for a couple of minutes. When they are golden, drain them on absorbent paper. Fried mozzarella is ready to be tasted.

Tuscan beans
Ingredients:
- **Dried beans 300 g**
- **Tomato puree 200 g**
- **Garlic 2 cloves**
- **Sage to taste**
- **Extra virgin olive oil q.s.**
- **Salt up to taste**
- **Black pepper to taste**

To prepare the beans, first put the dried beans in a large bowl, cover them with plenty of cold water and leave them to soak for at least a whole night. The next day, transfer the beans with all their liquid to a saucepan: the beans should be completely covered, so add more water if necessary. Cook the beans over low heat for at least 50 minutes, occasionally skimming them with a slotted spoon.

After this time, drain the beans and keep the cooking liquid. Pour a drizzle of oil into a large frying pan, add the peeled garlic cloves and the sage leaves and leave to brown briefly, then add the tomato purée and let it reduce for a few minutes, still over low heat.

At this point add the beans, salt and pepper and also add the cooking liquid from the beans that you had kept aside. Cover with a lid and cook for about 20 minutes on medium heat. Your beans are ready to be served piping hot!

Supplì Alla Romana
Ingredients:
- Rice 500 g
- Minced beef 150 g
- Mozzarella 200 g
- Dried mushrooms 50 g
- Medium eggs 2
- Tomato puree 400 g
- Meat broth 1 l
- Grana Padano PDO 120 g
- Half onions
- Butter + 50 g for creaming 30 g
- White wine 100ml
- Extra virgin olive oil 2 tbsp
- Salt up to taste
- Black pepper to taste
- FOR BREADING AND FRYING
- Breadcrumbs to taste
- Eggs 2
- Peanut oil to taste

Melt the butter with the oil in a pan, add the chopped onion and the minced meat, then let it brown; add the previously soaked, squeezed and minced mushrooms.
Let it brown for another 5 minutes and then blend with the wine and add the tomato puree. Add salt and pepper and cook over medium heat until the sauce has reduced and thickened.
When the sauce is ready, add the rice and, stirring frequently, cook the rice adding, when needed, some meat broth until the risotto appears dry and compact.

Turn off the heat and add the butter and grated parmesan; mix well and then add the two beaten eggs. Stir until all the ingredients are incorporated and blended well, then pour the mixture onto a large flat plate and let it cool completely. In the meantime, cut the mozzarella into small pieces or strips and put it to drain in a colander, so that it loses the excess water. When the rice is cold, form the supplì by taking a little of the mixture with wet hands and giving it an oval shape: insert a couple of small pieces of mozzarella inside and in the center of the supplì, then close well. Do this until you run out of ingredients.

Once you have obtained all the supplì, dip them in the beaten egg and then in the breadcrumbs, making sure that the breadcrumbs adhere to all sides.

Then fry the supplì in plenty of hot oil (at least 180°). Put the rice balls to drain on a sheet of absorbent paper and serve piping hot.

Battered zucchini flowers
Ingredients:
- Zucchini flowers 15
- Fine salt to taste
- Peanut seed oil to taste - (for frying)

FOR THE CLASSIC BATTER
- Water 1 cup (220 g) - (mineral, lukewarm)
- Flour 00 1 150 g
- Fresh brewer's yeast 1 ½ tbsp
- Fine salt ¾ tsp
- Sugar ½ tbsp (6 g)

FOR THE TEMPURA
- Water 200 g
- Flour 00 100 g
- Egg yolks 1

To make the battered zucchini flowers, start by preparing the batter. First, dissolve 1½ tbsp of fresh brewer's yeast, crumbled by hand, in a little room-temperature water taken from the 220 g of water you need for the batter, emulsifying with a whisk. Next, pour the flour into another bowl, add the rest of the room-temperature water, and mix with a whisk until you get a smooth mixture without any lumps.

Then add the brewer's yeast dissolved in the water, continuing to whisk. Now add ¾ tsp (6 g) of salt and ½ tbsp (6 g) of sugar, mixing again to combine the ingredients, and then cover with plastic wrap. Leave to rest for around 30 minutes at room temperature.

In the meantime, clean the zucchini flowers, starting by gently pulling off the stems. Then, still using your hands, pull off both the external pistils and the internal bud. Repeat these steps with all the zucchini flowers.

After 30 minutes, the classic batter will be well leavened, so now it's time for the frying. Pour the oil into a pot and heat to a maximum temperature of 170°-180°C (use a food thermometer to check). When the oil is almost at the right temperature, put the flowers into the batter, using kitchen tweezers to turn them so they are completely coated.

Next, take each flower out of the batter, allowing the excess to drain off, and then immerse the flowers in the hot oil, only doing a few at a time so the temperature doesn't go down too much. When the flowers are nice and golden, turn them and cook on the other side, too.

Then, take them out of the oil using a skimmer and place on a paper towel. Season with a pinch of salt and serve your battered zucchini flowers.

For a crispier version, once all of the flowers have been cleaned, as described above, you can make the tempura. Place the egg yolk in a bowl and, beating it with a whisk, add ¾ cup (100g) of flour little by little, and then slowly pour in 1 cup (200 g) of ice-cold water.

Continue to beat until you get a smooth mixture. Immerse the flowers in the batter, turning them so they are completely coated. Heat the oil to a temperature of 170°-180°C, as indicated above, and fry your battered zucchini flowers, turning them over halfway through.

Once they're cooked, remove them from the oil using a skimmer and transfer to a paper towel. Season with salt and serve them still hot!

Shrimp cocktail
Ingredients:
- Shrimp 16 clean
- Iceberg lettuce 60 g
- Lemons 4 slices

FOR THE MAYONNAISE
- Very fresh egg yolks 1
- Sunflower oil 120 g
- Filtered lemon juice 15 g
- Salt up to taste
- Black pepper to taste

FOR THE COCKTAIL SAUCE
- Ketchup 45 g
- Worcestershire sauce 1 tsp
- Tabasco to taste
- Brandy 1 tsp

To prepare the shrimp cocktail, start with the mayonnaise. In the glass of a mixer, pour the egg yolk together with salt, pepper and the filtered lemon juice then pour the seed oil slowly, very slowly, while keeping the immersion blender running.

After a few moments you will have obtained the mayonnaise of the right creamy consistency, then proceed to the preparation of the cocktail sauce. Pour the mayonnaise into a bowl and add the ketchup, the worcestershire sauce, then the brandy and mix everything. Finally, add a few drops of Tabasco, mix again and keep aside in a cool place.

Arrange 4 tails at a time on a slotted spoon and immerse them for about 10 seconds in boiling water, the time necessary to blanch the prawns and make them curl a little, then drain them on a plate and continue with all the others. Finally cut the iceberg lettuce into strips and you have everything ready for the composition.

In a cocktail glass (a tall glass or other container is fine if you prefer), pour a dollop of cocktail sauce, then add a sprig of lettuce and pour a little more of the sauce. Arrange 4 prawns per glass and finally decorate with a slice of lemon. The shrimp cocktail is ready: serve immediately or put it in the fridge for half an hour!

Potato salad
Ingredients:
- **Potatoes 800 g**
- **Unsweetened natural white yogurt 125 g**
- **Delicate mustard 30 g**
- **Salt up to taste**
- **Parsley to chop 1 bunch**
- **Mayonnaise 100 g**
- **Chives 1 bunch**
- **Black pepper to taste**

To prepare the potato salad, start by boiling the whole potatoes in their skins for about 40 minutes starting with cold water. Check doneness with the prongs of a fork. Meanwhile, prepare the sauce: chop the parsley and chives. In a very large bowl, pour the yogurt.
Add the mayonnaise and mustard, then mix with a whisk.
Flavor with parsley and chives, then season with pepper and salt.
Stir again to mix. In the meantime the potatoes will be cooked, drain them, peel them and cut them into large cubes.
Pour them into the bowl with the sauce and mix gently to flavor them without breaking them. Keep the potato salad in the fridge until use.

Lentil stew
Ingredients:
- **Dried lentils (500 g)**
- **Tomato puree (1 l)**
- **Extra virgin olive oil to taste**
- **Carrots 1**
- **Celery 1 rib**
- **Yellow onions ½**
- **Garlic 1 clove**
- **Bay leaves 3**
- **Rosemary to taste**
- **Sage to taste**
- **Fine salt to taste**
- **Black pepper to taste**

To make the lentil stew, start with the vegetable mixture. Trim the carrot and chop into cubes of around 1/8" (4 mm). Do the same with the celery and onion. Next, chop the onion again to cut it into even smaller dice. Tie the aromatic herbs together with some string to form a small bunch. Add a good glug of oil to a large pot, followed by the chopped vegetables and an unpeeled clove of garlic. Let this brown over low heat for 5-7 minutes, until the vegetables are very soft. Rinse the lentils well under running water, then add them to the pot, along with the bunch of herbs. Now add the tomato purée. Fill the container the purée was in with water to rinse it, adding this water to the pot slowly until the lentils are covered. You'll need around (300 ml) of water. Stir and then leave to cook over low heat, covered, for 45-60 minutes. While the lentils are cooking, you'll need to stir them every once in a while and add more water when they start to get dry; in total, you should add around another (500 ml) of water. After 45 minutes have passed, taste the lentils to check the consistency and whether you need to cook them for longer.

Toward the end of the cooking time, adjust with water as needed. Season with salt and pepper , remove the bunch of aromatic herbs and clove of garlic. Serve the lentils hot or warm, finishing off the plates with a drizzle of olive oil and chopped rosemary and pepper to taste.

Broccoli au gratin
Ingredients:
- Clean broccoli 1 kg
- Parmigiano Reggiano DOP to grate 40 g
- Black pepper to taste

FOR THE BECHAMEL
- Whole milk 250 g
- Flour 00 25 g
- Butter 25 g
- Nutmeg to taste
- Salt up to taste

To prepare the broccoli au gratin, start with the homemade béchamel: melt the butter in a saucepan over low heat. Add the flour all at once and cook for a minute being careful not to let the bottom stick, stirring with a spoon. Pour the milk at room temperature in 3 times.

Thicken by stirring with a whisk, you must obtain a thick sauce without lumps. Season with salt, pepper and nutmeg. Clean the broccoli by obtaining the tops and wash them.
Blanch the broccoli in salted water for 6 minutes, then drain them in a bowl of water and ice. Pat the broccoli dry.
Pour some béchamel on the bottom of a baking dish, add a first layer of broccoli and more béchamel.
Make a second layer with the advanced broccoli and the béchamel, season with the grated cheese. Bake in a preheated static oven at 200° for 17 minutes, then switch to the grill at 230° for 4-5 minutes. Serve the broccoli au gratin hot.

Jewish-style artichokes
Ingredients:
- **Purple artichokes 4**
- **Vegetable oil to taste - for frying**
- **Fine salt to taste**

To prepare Jewish-style artichokes, start by cleaning the purple artichokes: remove the tough end part of the stalk left over from when the artichoke was harvested. Remove the outermost leaves until you can see the ones at the bottom that are lighter in color. To open the leaves out, beat the artichoke against a cutting board, holding it by the stalk, without pressing down too hard so as not to break the leaves.

As you beat them you can spread them out by hand and when the artichoke opens out like a flower, continue to clean the other ones. Heat the seed oil in a pan, just enough to immerse the artichoke heads in. Heat to (170°C): we recommend you monitor the temperature using a thermometer, to ensure the artichokes cook evenly. Now immerse the first artichoke. Take care during this step, be sure to protect yourself from any splashes of hot oil.

Hold the stalk with cooking tongs to press the artichoke down on the bottom; cook for 6-7 minutes. In this way the flower won't lose its shape. Towards the end of the cooking time, turn the artichoke over onto its side so that the stalk cooks too and then drain it. The first one is ready: drain it on some oil-absorbing cooking paper and repeat with all the others; once your Jewish-style artichokes are ready, don't forget to add salt!

Peppers with breadcrumbs
Ingredients:
- Red peppers 2
- Yellow peppers 2
- Extra virgin olive oil q.s.
- Stale breadcrumbs q.b.
- Pecorino to grate 40 g
- Capers 1 tbsp
- Oregano to taste
- Garlic 1 clove

To prepare the peppers with breadcrumbs, wash and dry the peppers well, cut them in half, remove the stalk and the internal seeds, then cut them into strips 2-3 cm wide. Cook the peppers in a pot with plenty of extra virgin olive oil for 15-20 minutes. In the meantime, prepare the crumb-based sauce: with the help of a mixer, chop the stale bread, then transfer it to a bowl and add the grated pecorino, the capers, a clove of minced garlic and
the oregano. Mix well to mix all the ingredients, then add the mixture to the peppers and cook for 20 minutes over medium heat, covering with a lid. When the peppers are almost ready, remove the lid and let everything cook, raising the heat to toast the bread. The peppers with breadcrumbs are ready: let them cool down and serve them as a side dish, or as a tasty appetizer; they are also excellent eaten cold.

Caramelized Tropea onions
Ingredients:
- **Tropea red onions 1 kg**
- **Sugar 70 g**
- **Cane sugar 80 g**
- **Water 250 g**

To prepare the caramelized Tropea onions, start by peeling the latter, eliminating both the skin and the two ends. Then move on to the cut, you can slice them not too finely with a smooth blade, collect the slices obtained in a container.

Pour the chopped onions into a large saucepan together with the granulated sugar and the cane sugar, mix well so that the ingredients blend well together and add the water.

Cook for about an hour over moderate heat, stirring gently from time to time so as not to flake the onions. When cooked, check the temperature with a kitchen thermometer, it should reach 108°; the compound will be darkened and the liquid almost completely dried. Your caramelized Tropea onions are ready, place them in a bowl and enjoy them to accompany meat or on crunchy toasted bread!

Pasta

Pasta alla sorrentina
Ingredients:
- **Fusilli pasta (320 g)**
- **Tomato puree (500 g)**
- **Mozzarella cheese (125 g)**
- **Extra virgin olive oil 2 ½ tbsp (30 g)**
- **Garlic 1 clove**
- **Basil to taste**
- **Fine salt to taste**
- **Parmigiano Reggiano DOP cheese ½ cup (65 g)**

To prepare pasta alla sorrentina, you'll need to start by preparing the sauce. Pour the oil into a large pan and add the peeled garlic clove , fry for 1 minute, and then add the tomato puree. Season with salt as needed, add a few basil leaves, and stir.
At this point, cover with a lid, and leave to cook for 30 minutes over low heat before removing the garlic clove. Heat a pot full of water to cook the pasta, and in the meantime, cut the mozzarella into cubes. Once the water has reached a boil, cook the pasta before draining it and adding it to the sauce, stirring well to combine. Pour around half of the pasta into a 10-inch (25-cm) round baking dish to form the first layer, before placing half of the mozzarella cubes on top and sprinkling with a little Parmigiano Reggiano cheese. Cover with the remaining pasta, then add the mozzarella, and finally cover with the Parmigiano Reggiano. Broil in the oven for around 5 minutes, until the pasta is nicely baked and the mozzarella has melted (if you don't have a broil function, you can put the dish on the top rack and turn the oven on full power, but be careful not to burn it!). Garnish your pasta alla sorrentina with some fresh basil and serve immediately.

Orecchiette with broccoli and sausage

Ingredients:
- Orecchiette pasta (320 g)
- Broccoli (300 g)
- Sausage (300 g)
- White wine 3 tbsp (40 g)
- Garlic 1 clove
- Thyme 2 sprigs
- Rosemary 1 sprig
- Extra virgin olive oil 2 ½ tbsp (30 g)
- Black pepper to taste
- Fine salt to taste

To prepare the orecchiette with broccoli and sausage, start by bringing a pot of salted water to a boil. Cut the broccoli into florets and slice them in half, or even quarters if they're too large. Place them in the boiling water and put the lid on the pot. Cook the vegetables for 6-7 minutes, and in the meantime, continue with the rest.

Finely chop the thyme and rosemary and set aside. Make an incision in the sausage and remove the skin, pulling it away gently with your hands, then crumble the sausage meat using the prongs of a fork.

Drizzle some olive oil into a large frying pan and fry the garlic clove, then add the sausage. After a few seconds, add the chopped herbs and deglaze the pan with the white wine. Using a slotted spoon, and without discarding the cooking water, remove the cooked broccoli from the pot of water and add it to the meat a little at a time. Leave everything to cook for 3-4 minutes, then use kitchen tongs to remove the garlic, and add a pinch of black pepper. Bring the water you used to cook the broccoli back to a boil, pour in the pasta, and leave to cook. Once the pasta is cooked, use a slotted spoon to drain it and transfer directly to the broccoli and sausage sauce. Add the last of the orecchiette pasta, along with a ladleful of the cooking water if needed, then stir well to mix the pasta into the sauce thoroughly, adding some black pepper and cooking everything in the pan for a couple of minutes. Your orecchiette with broccoli and sausage is ready to be plated up and served.

Tagliatelle with white ragù
Ingredients:
- **Tagliatelle 250 g**
- **Minced beef 250 g**
- **Fresh sausage 150 g**
- **Bacon 100 g**
- **Celery 60 g**
- **Carrots 60 g**
- **Golden onions 60 g**
- **Garlic 1 clove**
- **White wine 60 g**
- **Extra virgin olive oil 50 g**
- **Rosemary 1 sprig**
- **Sage 3 leaves**
- **2 bay leaves**
- **Black pepper to taste**
- **Salt up to taste**
- **Water to taste**

To prepare the tagliatelle with white ragù, start with the sautéed ingredients. In a saucepan, heat the oil with a clove of garlic and let it brown. Add the finely chopped celery and carrot.
Also add the chopped onion and mix with a spatula. Leave to cook for a few minutes on low heat; in the meantime peel the rosemary and chop it with a knife, then add it to the sautéed mixture. Wash and dry the sage, peel it and chop it finely; add it to the rest of the sautéed vegetables and finally season with two whole bay leaves. Cut the bacon into cubes and brown it together with the vegetables, mixing with a spatula.
Now take care of the sausage: score the external casing lengthwise with a small knife and remove it with your fingers; crumble the sausage.

Add it to the sauce together with the minced meat and cook over high heat, stirring with a spatula to further break them up. Cook everything for a few minutes. Remove the garlic clove and the bay leaves and blend with the white wine.

When the wine has evaporated, continue cooking by adding a ladle of hot water, season with salt and pepper and cook over low heat for about an hour, adding more water if necessary. After the necessary time, put out the fire. When there is half an hour left at the end of cooking, put a pan with plenty of water on the fire to bring to the boil: when it boils, add salt to taste and boil the tagliatelle.

Drain the pasta and transfer it directly into the now ready sauce pan. Mix the pasta well and bind the sauce by adding, if necessary, a little cooking water from the pasta kept aside. Serve your tagliatelle with white ragu still steaming immediately.

Spaghetti Alla Nerano
Ingredients:
- **Spaghetti 320 g**
- **Provolone 150 g**
- **Zucchini 700 g**
- **Basil to taste**
- **Parmigiano Reggiano to grate 30 g**
- **Salt up to taste**
- **Black pepper to taste**
- **Garlic 1 clove**
- **Extra virgin olive oil 30 g**
- **TO FRY**
- **Extra virgin olive oil q.s.**

To make spaghetti alla Nerano, put the zucchini on the fire: wash and trim them, then cut them into thin slices with a mandolin. Heat the olive oil in a large pan, once the oil has reached 150°, the ideal temperature for frying, dip the courgette slices a few at a time so as not to lower the oil temperature, cook for about 5-6 minutes, enough time to brown them. Once cooked, drain them with a slotted spoon and place them on a tray lined with absorbent paper to dry the excess oil. As you cook the zucchini, season them with salt
and basil leaves torn by hand. Keep the zucchini aside, and place a high-sided pot full of salted water on the fire, which will be used to cook the spaghetti. In the meantime, grate the Parmesan and Provolone del Monaco with a grater with large holes. Then cook the pasta which will need to be drained after about 6 minutes of cooking. In the meantime, heat 30 g of extra virgin olive oil in a large saucepan, add the poached garlic to flavor then remove the garlic with kitchen tongs and pour in the previously fried zucchini.

Add a ladle of the pasta cooking water and sauté the zucchini for a few seconds so that they soften slightly and are not dry. After about 6 minutes of cooking the spaghetti, drain them directly into the pan with the sauce, taking care to keep the cooking water.

Add a ladleful of pasta cooking water at a time, as needed, to continue cooking the spaghetti, making them risotto: this will take about 3 minutes. Then turn off the flame. Pour a part of the Provolone del Monaco mixing the spaghetti to melt it and create the cream; once it has been absorbed, go on to pour the grated Parmigiano Reggiano and the remaining provolone cheese

Flavor again with the basil broken up by hand and pour another ladle of the pasta cooking water. Stir and once ready add a sprinkling of ground pepper. Serve your Nerano spaghetti piping hot!

Pasta allo scarpariello
Ingredients:
- Spaghetti 320 g
- Datterino tomatoes 500 g
- Pecorino Romano cheese 30 g - grated
- Parmigiano Reggiano cheese 30 g - grated
- Basil 1 bunch - large
- Fresh chili pepper ½
- Extra virgin olive oil 70 g
- Garlic 1 clove
- Fine salt to taste

To make your pasta allo scarpariello, start by heating a saucepan with water to cook the pasta. Once the water is boiling, add a little salt. Take the Datterino tomatoes, wash them and slice them in half , then take the long fresh chili pepper, trim it and open it up to remove the seeds, before slicing it into strips and chopping it.

Grate the Pecorino Romano and Parmigiano cheeses. Pour the extra virgin olive oil into a large pot and heat. Add the chopped chili and the whole peeled garlic so it will be easier to remove. Fry for around 3 minutes, stirring occasionally, then add the datterino tomatoes, and cook over medium heat for around 10 minutes. Meanwhile, boil the spaghetti until it is cooked al dente. Once the tomato sauce is ready, season with salt, remove the garlic, and add some of the basil leaves. Add a ladleful of cooking water to create a delicious creamy texture. Drain the spaghetti, keeping a couple of ladlefuls of cooking water aside, and pour the pasta directly into the pot with the sauce .

Finish cooking in the pan over medium-low heat, mixing the spaghetti into the sauce and adding cooking water if necessary, so that the sauce is creamy. Turn off the heat and add the grated Pecorino and Parmigiano Reggiano cheeses in several stages, alternating them with more cooking water as needed and stirring constantly so the cheese doesn't go stringy. Flavor again with some basil leaves. Serve the pasta allo scarpariello immediately, adding more fresh basil to each plate.

Tagliatelle with porcini mushrooms
Ingredients:
- **Tagliatella 500g**
- **Porcini mushrooms (clean) 500 g**
- **Butter 50 g**
- **Extra virgin olive oil 35 g**
- **Fine salt to taste**
- **Garlic 1 clove**
- **Parsley 1 sprig**
- **Black pepper to taste**

Cut into slices the porcini mushrooms. In a large frying pan, put in the butter and melt it over very low heat; when it has almost completely melted, pour in the oil , leave to heat slightly over low heat and then pour in the porcini mushrooms and a whole clove of garlic, cleaned or chopped if you prefer (optional).

Season with salt and peppe to taste, then let the mushrooms cook for about 10 minutes . When finished cooking you can remove the garlic clove if you have added it . Once prepared, keep them warm. Then mince the parsley very finely and set it aside.

Bring the water to a boil and salt to taste; cook the tagliatelle.

Then drain them directly into the seasoning while preserving the cooking water. Set the heat to low under the pan with the seasoning and mix the ingredients to combine them. Add the finely chopped parsley 2and, if needed, add a ladle of pasta cooking water to prevent the tagliatelle from being too dry. Then serve the tagliatelle with porcini mushrooms as soon as they are ready!

Pasta alla Norma

- **Ingredients:**
  Pasta 500 g
- **Eggplant 1**
- **Ricotta 150 g - salted**
- **Fine salt to taste**

FOR THE SAUCE
- **Tomatoes 1.5 kg**
- **Garlic 4 cloves**
- **Fine salt to taste**
- **Basil 1 bunch**

FOR FRYING
- **Extra virgin olive oil to taste**

To make pasta alla Norma, first wash and dry the eggplant well, and trim it. Cut it into slices around 8 mm and transfer to a colander.
Sprinkle with salt and leave to drain for at least 15 minutes. In the meantime, turn to the tomatoes: Wash them and remove the stems. Cut in half.
Place in a pot with a pinch of salt, 3 cloves of garlic (you can use fewer if you prefer, but the garlic characterizes pasta alla Norma), and a handful of basil.
Let this cook over low heat for 30 minutes without adding anything else; the tomatoes will release their liquid. After 30 minutes, remove the garlic and basil. Transfer the tomatoes to a food mill fitted with the finest disc and grind them.
Once you've got your purée , transfer it to a pot, add another clove of garlic and a sprig of basil. Let it cook for another 40 minutes, stirring every once in a while.
At this point, you can rinse the eggplant well, drying it with paper towel. Next, pour the extra virgin olive oil in a deep pot and bring it to a temperature of around 170-180°C. Immerse a few slices of eggplant at a time in the oil 16 and turn them every now and then. It will take a few minutes for them to turn nicely golden. At this point, remove the eggplant from the pot with kitchen tweezers and transfer to a tray lined with paper towel. Continue frying the eggplant, and in the meantime, put a pot full of water on the stove, which you'll use to cook the pasta.

Once the sauce is fairly thick, remove the basil, add a spoonful of the oil the eggplant was cooked in and a drizzle of fresh olive oil.

Cook the pasta, drain, and pour into the sauce. Flip the pan quickly to cover the pasta with the sauce.

Transfer the pasta to the plates, add the fried eggplant, plenty of grated ricotta salata, a basil leaf, and then your pasta alla Norma is ready to be served !

Pasta with broccoli
Ingredients:
- **Fresh troccoli 320 g**
- **Broccoli 450 g**
- **Garlic 1**
- **Extra virgin olive oil to taste**
- **Fine salt to taste**
- **Black pepper to taste**

To make pasta with broccoli, start by removing the broccoli florets from the middle stalk; cut them in half if they are very big. Rinse them under running water. Bring some salted water to the boil in a saucepan and add the broccoli as soon as the water starts to boil.
Cook for around ten minutes. In the meantime, brown a garlic clove in a drizzle of oil, in a deep pan. Drain the broccoli and place in a saucepan, save the cooking water for later.
Leave a few whole florets to one side, which you will then add to the finished pasta dish. Add a little water to the broccoli. Add salt and pepper, then cook on a medium-low flame for around 20 minutes, or at least until cooked and a cream starts to form. Add some more water if necessary. Once cooked, remove the garlic clove.
Cook the troccoli until firm to the bite in the same water used to boil the broccoli: bring the water back to the boil and follow cooking times indicated on the package. Add the broccoli left to one side to the sauce. Drain the pasta and add to the broccoli cream.
Add a ladle of cooking water, depending on how creamy the sauce is. Sauté the pasta with the broccoli for a few moments and serve nice and hot ; add pepper to taste. Your pasta with broccoli is ready, buon appetito.

Pasta with sardines
Ingredients:
- **Bucatini pasta 320 g**
- **Sardines 500 g**
- **Wild fennel 180 g**
- **Yellow onions 80 g**
- **Raisins 30 g**
- **Pine nuts 25 g**
- **Chopped almonds 30 g**
- **Salted anchovies 5**
- **Extra virgin olive oil 50 g**
- **Water 70 g- for diluting**
- **Saffron 1 packet - powdered**
- **Fine salt to taste**
- **Black pepper to taste**

FOR THE BREADING
- **Breadcrumbs 30 g**
- **Extra virgin olive oil 2 tbsp**

To prepare the pasta with sardines start by cleaning them if not already cleaned. Cleaning them is very simple, just detach the head and pull them open by sliding your finger between the two parts, so you can gently detach the central bone. During this operation use a trickle of running water to eliminate the waste and clean the sardines at the same time. Keep the clean sardines on a plate. Soak the raisins for about ten minutes. Slice an onion as finely as possible (you can chop it in a mixer for a few moments on pulse to avoid obtaining a mush) and pour it into a pan with the olive oil and anchovies. Cook for about ten minutes over low heat and stir frequently, so that the base lightly fries without burning and the anchovies dissolve.

In the meantime, dilute the saffron in the water stirring with a fork and then pour it into the pan and add the clean sardines.

Then drain and rinse the raisins and pour them into the pan, add the finely ground almonds and whole pine nuts, stir and continue cooking over a low flame for another 10 minutes.

Put a pot on the stove with plenty of water to boil and then add the fennel. If you buy the fennel uncleaned, you can buy 180 g of it so that once cleaned, having removed the leathery parts, you will have 125 g left to use for the recipe. Then rinse the tender part and blanch for a couple of minutes. Drain well, without throwing away the water, letting the fennel cool for a few moments so you can handle it.
Squeeze it well and chop it with a knife, cutting one cut from the other an inch or so (a couple of centimeters) apart. Then put it in a pan, add salt and pepper, and stir to mix well.
Boil the pasta in the same water that you cooked the fennel in. In the meantime, toast the breadcrumbs and pour into a pan with 2 tsp of oil. Mix often to keep from burning and when they are golden brown, turn off the heat.
At this point, the pasta should be cooked al dente, drained and then sauteed briefly in the pan. Place and garnish with the breading: your pasta with sardines is ready, enjoy your meal!

Spaghetti aglio e olio (Spaghetti with garlic, oil and chili pepper)
Ingredients:
- **Spaghetti 320 g**
- **Garlic 3 cloves**
- **Fresh chili pepper 3**
- **Extra virgin olive oil 70 g**
- **Fine salt to taste**

To prepare the garlic, oil and chili pepper spaghetti, start by cooking the pasta in boiling salted water. Cook the spaghetti al dente, and in the meantime prepare the seasoning: peel the garlic cloves, divide them in half and remove the core (the green central part of each clove).
Cut the cloves into rather thin slices. Take the fresh chili peppers, and slice them removing the center. If you prefer less spiciness, you can open them lengthwise and remove the seeds before slicing them. Now pour the oil into a large pan.
Place the pan over very low heat and add the sliced garlic and chili peppers. Continue to fry over very low heat; the chili and garlic should not burn, and should only fry for a couple of minutes.
For even browning without the risk of burning, you can tilt the pan to gather the oil, garlic and chili peppers in one area and allow them to brown evenly. Once the pasta is cooked al dente, you can transfer it directly into the pan and add a ladle of cooking water.
Stir for a few moments to combine the flavors and sauté, then you can plate your garlic, oil and chili pepper spaghetti and serve very hot!

Pasta and zucchini
Ingredients:
- **Pasta 320 g**
- **Zucchini 650 g**
- **Basil to taste**
- **Fine salt to taste**
- **Extra virgin olive oil 1 ½ tbsp**
- **Black pepper to taste**
- **Garlic 1 clove**

To prepare pasta and zucchini, boil water in a large pan and add salt when it comes to a boil. In the meantime, wash and dry the zucchini , trim and grate them with an extra coarse grater. Pour the extra virgin olive oil in a fairly large pan and heat it over low heat together with a peeled garlic clove.

As soon as the oil is hot, add the zucchini seasoned with salt and pepper and let them cook for 5-6 minutes, stirring occasionally; then remove the garlic. In the meantime, cook the pasta in boiling salted water and drain it al dente, keeping a little cooking water.

Pour the pasta directly into the pan with the zucchini and add a little cooking water, sweat for a few moments, stir, then turn off the heat. Add a few fragrant hand-torn basil leaves and your pasta and zucchini is ready to be enjoyed.

Paccheri pasta with calamari
Ingredients:
- **Calamari (squid) 500 g- (cleaned)**
- **Paccheri pasta 320 g**
- **Cherry tomatoes 200 g**
- **Tomato puree 200 g**
- **Extra virgin olive oil to taste**
- **White wine 3 tbsp**
- **Fresh chili pepper 1**
- **Garlic 3 cloves**
- **Parsley 2 tbsp**
- **Fine salt to taste**

To prepare the paccheri pasta with calamari, place a pan with plenty of water to cook the pasta on the stove. Once it's boiling, add salt to taste. Crush the garlic cloves (you can also use whole peeled cloves and remove them after cooking) in a pan with a little oil and let them sweat with the chili pepper for a few minutes over low heat. Add the squid rings with the tentacles and cook over high heat for just 1 minute, so that the squid does not become too tough.

Pour in the white wine and allow it to simmer for a few minutes so that it evaporates. Add the cherry tomatoes and the tomato puree.

Mix and let everything cook over low heat for 5-6 minutes. In the meantime, pour the paccheri pasta into salted boiling water and then drain halfway through cooking (reserving some of the cooking water) and pour straight into the pan with the sauce.

You will need a few ladlefuls of the reserved pasta cooking water to finish cooking the pasta; pour in a little at a time as needed and stir frequently. In the meantime, finely chop the parsley and sprinkle it over the paccheri once cooked. Everything is ready, your paccheri pasta with calamari can be eaten piping hot!

Pasta with bell pepper sauce
Ingredients:
- **Penne Rigate pasta (320 g)**
- **Red peppers (400 g)**
- **Cluster tomatoes (250 g)**
- **Garlic 1 clove**
- **Basil to taste**
- **Extra virgin olive oil to taste**
- **Fine salt to taste**
- **Black pepper to taste**

To prepare the pasta with bell pepper sauce, boil the water for the pasta. In the meantime, wash the peppers, remove the cap, cut them lengthwise, and discard the internal seeds, then dice them.
Coarsely chop the cluster tomatoes. Pour a drizzle of oil into a saucepan and fry the unpeeled garlic. Add the diced peppers and the tomatoes, then season with pepper and basil leaves. Cook over medium heat for about 15 minutes, stirring occasionally.
When the bell peppers are cooked, pour the pasta into the boiling water and cook it for the time indicated. In the meantime, pour the bell peppers and tomatoes into a tall container and blend everything using a hand blender

Transfer the sauce into a pan, or use the same pan in which you cooked the bell peppers, turn the heat to low, add a ladle of the water of the pasta, and then, once the pasta is cooked, drain, and add it directly into the peppers) sauce.
Mix for a few moments to thoroughly coat the pasta, then transfer it to the serving dishes and season with a few more leaves of fresh basil. Your pasta with bell pepper sauce is ready to be served.

Shrimp, zucchini and saffron linguine
Ingredients:
- Linguine 320 g
- Zucchini 300 g
- Red prawns 300 g
- Saffron (1 sachet)
- Shallot 50 g
- Extra virgin olive oil q.s.
- Black pepper 1 pinch
- Salt up to 1 pinch
- Marjoram to taste

To prepare the shrimp, zucchini and saffron linguine, start by cleaning the red prawns: remove the head, remove the shells and extract the intestines, then set them aside in a bowl.

Prepare the bisque: pour a drizzle of oil into a fairly large saucepan and wait for it to become hot, then add the shells and toast them well. When they are browned, pour in 500 g of cold water and cook for 10 minutes. Once the bisque is ready, strain into a bowl and set aside. Now cut the zucchini into cubes. Also chop the shallot and cut the prawns into ½ cm pieces. Heat a drizzle of oil in a non-stick pan and add the prawns. Brown them for a few minutes, then remove them and keep them aside. Put the shallots to stew in the same pan in which you cooked the prawns. Then add the zucchini too. When the zucchini are well browned, add the prawns and turn off the flame. Salt and pepper. Pour a spoonful of bisque into a small bowl and dissolve the saffron powder in it.

Cook the linguine in boiling salted water, keeping the cooking backwards for 2-3 minutes. Drain it in the pan with the sauce and finish cooking by adding the saffron mix and the bisque little by little as the pasta dries. Stir in the end by adding a drizzle of oil, pepper and marjoram leaves. Serve the shrimp, zucchini and saffron linguine piping hot.

Pappardelle with speck and porcini mushrooms
Ingredients:
- **Pappardelle with egg 250 g**
- **Porcini mushrooms 500 g (clean)**
- **Speck (2 thick slices) 150 g**
- **Liquid fresh cream 50 g**
- **Parsley to be chopped q.b.**
- **Garlic 1 clove**
- **Black pepper to taste**
- **Extra virgin olive oil 40 g**
- **Salt up to taste**

Take care of the speck: First cut each slice in half lengthwise and then cut into strips in the other direction. Pour the oil into a pan and add a clove of unpeeled garlic, which you have previously crushed gently.
Add the speck and let it cook for a few minutes until it is crispy and golden brown. In the meantime, cut the porcini mushrooms into slices and if they are too large you can divide them in half. When the speck seems cooked to perfection, remove the garlic and add the porcini mushrooms to the pan. Continue cooking for 6-7 minutes and in the meantime you can cook the pappardelle in abundant salted boiling water to taste. When the mushrooms are slightly wilted, add the cream

and a pinch of black pepper. Since the speck is already quite savory, it will not be necessary to add salt, but adjust according to your taste. Finely chop the parsley and drain.

Pour them directly into the mushroom-based sauce, add the parsley and sauté them for a few moments. Serve your pappardelle with porcini mushrooms and speck, add a final sprinkling of pepper to your liking and serve while still hot!

Main Course

Stuffed eggplants
Ingredients:
- **Eggplant 700 g**
- **Pork 300 g - ground**
- **Tomato puree 300 g**
- **Onions 1**
- **Stale bread 50 g**
- **White wine 60 g**
- **Extra virgin olive oil to taste**
- **Basil 6 leaves**
- **Black pepper 1 pinch**
- **Fine salt 1 pinch**
- **Caciocavallo cheese 175 g**

To make stuffed eggplant, first wash and dry the eggplants. Cut them in half longways, including the stem. Empty the insides of the eggplants. Chop the flesh roughly. Next, dice the onion. Pour some oil into a pan, then add the onion and stew for a few minutes. Add the meat and brown for 3-4 minutes. Deglaze with the white wine, allowing it to evaporate, then add the eggplant flesh. Leave this to cook for 4-5, seasoning with salt and pepper, then pour in the tomato purée (be sure to save around 1¾ tbsp (30 g) for later) and the basil leaves. Turn off the heat. Cut the stale bread into small pieces and then blitz in a food processor.
Grate the caciocavallo using a coarse grater. Add the breadcrumbs and cheese to the pan and stir.
Next, arrange the eggplants in a baking dish, drizzle with oil, season with salt, and then stuff with the filling.
Pour over the tomato purée you set aside before, then dress with a splash of oil and cook in a conventional oven preheated to 200°C for 30 minutes. Once the stuffed eggplant has finished cooking, serve it piping hot.

Oven baked rice
Ingredients:
- Carnaroli rice 375 g
- Tomato puree (1 l)
- Fior di latte mozzarella cheese 300 g
- Parmigiano Reggiano DOP cheese 150 g - for grating
- Onions 1 - medium
- Extra virgin olive oil to taste
- Fine salt to taste
- Black pepper to taste
- Basil 7 leaves
- Water to taste

To prepare oven baked rice, start by dicing the fiordilatte mozzarella into 0.21 inch cubes approximately and leave 2 or 3 slices for the final decoration. Place the cubes in a colander and leave to one side for at least an hour, to drain the excess whey. Prepare the sauce in the meantime. Peel and finely chop the onion.

Add a drizzle of oil to the saucepan, followed by the onion; stir and sweat on a low flame for around 5 minutes. Soften the onion and then add the tomato puree; pour a little water to the emptied bottle to clean it and dilute the sauce. Add salt to taste and leave to cook for at least 40 minutes.

Once the indicated cooking time is up, dilute the sauce with a little hot water if necessary, bring to the boil and add the rice. Cook for the length of time indicated on the packet (usually around 18 minutes) and stir frequently so that it does not stick to the pan. Remove from the heat 2-3 minutes before the end of the cooking time, add 2/3 of the diced fiordilatte cheese and 2/3 of the grated Parmigiano Reggiano , a few hand-torn basil leaves and lastly, pepper to taste.

Stir thoroughly and place in a baking tray. Smooth the surface and sprinkle with the remaining fiordilatte cheese, the grated Parmigiano Reggiano and a few basil leaves. Bake in a static oven preheated to 220°C for around 15-20 minutes; if you want a crust to form on the surface then switch the oven to grill mode and leave the rice inside a few minutes longer. When ready, leave the oven baked rice to rest for 5 minutes before serving.

Roman-style tripe
Ingredients:
- Tripe 1 kg
- Guanciale 100 g
- Pecorino Romano cheese 100 g
- Celery 40 g
- Carrots 80 g
- White onions 90 g
- Extra virgin olive oil 2 tbsp
- Canned tomatoes 400 g
- White wine 3 ⅓ tbsp
- Mint 3 leaves
- Garlic 1 clove
- Fine salt to taste
- Black pepper to taste

To prepare the Roman-style tripe, start by cleaning it, then put it in a colander and rinse it well under running water, then drain. In the meantime, prepare the chopped aromatic mixture by peeling the carrot and cutting it into cubes, do the same with the celery, removing its top leaves, and then the onion, removing the peel. If you do not wish for an intense flavor, remove its core. Then cut the slice of guanciale into cubes. In a saucepan, pour the extra virgin olive oil together with the chopped celery, carrot, and onion, then add the peeled garlic clove, let it season for a few moments over high heat, then add the cubes of guanciale and lastly, the tripe.

Pour the white wine and let it evaporate completely, add salt and pepper, then the crushed tomatoes, stir everything and let it cook for 2 hours, there will be no need to cover or add water, as the tripe will release juices during cooking.

After the first hour of cooking, add the mint leaves and continue cooking. After two hours of cooking, remove the garlic clove, Turn off the heat, add the grated pecorino romano cheese, stir a few moments and serve the Roman-style tripe hot.

Frittata with onions
Ingredients:
- **Medium eggs 6**
- **Red onions 400 g**
- **Marjoram to taste**
- **Extra virgin olive oil q.s.**
- **Salt up to taste**
- **Black pepper to taste**

To prepare the frittata with onions, first peel the onions and cut them into slices about 1 cm thick. Pour the onions into a non-stick pan with a 20 cm base where you have heated a drizzle of oil, add salt and cover with a lid: cook over medium-high heat for 7-8 minutes.

In the meantime, shell the eggs in a bowl, add the salt, pepper and marjoram leaves, then beat with a whisk until the mixture is smooth. When the onions are cooked through but still whole, pour the egg mixture into the pan, making sure all the onions are coated. Cover with the lid and cook over low heat for 6-8 minutes. After this time the frittata will be quite cooked and in shape, cover with a plate and turn the pan upside down to turn the frittata.

Slide the frittata back into the pan and continue cooking for about 3-4 minutes, this time without a lid. Once cooked to perfection, the onion frittata is ready to be served!

Vegetable soup
Ingredients:
- **Fine salt to taste**
- **Beans 200 g**
- **Cauliflower 300 g - cleaned**
- **Water to taste**
- **Carrots 80 g**
- **Black pepper to taste**
- **Pumpkin 250 g- cleaned**
- **Peas 200 g**
- **Red onions 80 g**
- **Celery 60 g**
- **Extra virgin olive oil 50 g**
- **Rosemary 1 sprig**
- **White zucchini 150 g**
- **Potatoes 330 g**
- **Cluster tomatoes 350 g**
- **Leeks 150 g**
- **Bay leaves 2 leaves**

To prepare the vegetable soup, start by washing a drying the vegetables. Now take the pumpkin and peel it using a knife with a large blade.
Remove the seeds and white strings, using a spoon. Now cut it into slices that are equal in size, then dice into 1 cm sized cubes.
Wash and tip the zucchini, cut them into slices and dice them. Now shell the beans,
cut the cauliflower in half, remove the core and cut off the florets; now remove the outermost and greener part of the leeks and cut into thin rings. Peel the potatoes and cut them into slices that are not too thin, then dice. Prepare the tomatoes: remove the stalks, slice and dice them. Lastly, prepare the ingredients for the saut base: finely chop up the onion. Tip and peel the carrots, cut them into strips and finely chop them using a knife.

Finely chop the celery too. To finish off, tie the rosemary sprigs together with the bay leaves to create a bouquet garni. Now all the ingredients for preparing the vegetable minestrone are ready. Take a capacious pot with a lid and add the oil, carrots, celery, onion and leek and gently brown for around 10 minutes, stirring frequently. Once the saut? base vegetables become tender, add the bouquet garni and the beans.

Cover with water: the vegetables must be covered by a finger span of water. Bring to the boil and cook for 2 minutes. Add the pumpkin and repeat the same procedure: add water, cover with a finger span of water, wait for the water to return to the boil and cook for 2 minutes.

Repeat with the potatoes, followed by the cauliflower.

Cover with some more water, cover with the lid and cook for 25 minutes once the soup is brought to the boil. Once the 25 minutes are up, add the zucchini,

peas and the tomatoes, add more water if necessary, add salt and pepper and once brought back to the boil, cook for a further 2-3 minutes.

Remove the bouquet garni. The soup is ready : serve it with a drizzle of oil and some ground pepper to taste.

Sausage and Beans
Ingredients:
- **Sausage 500 g**
- **Dried beans 200 g**
- **Golden onions 70 g**
- **Red wine 50 g**
- **Tomato puree 500 g**
- **Rosemary to taste**
- **Salt up to taste**
- **Black pepper to taste**
- **Extra virgin olive oil q.s.**

To make sausage and beans, start by soaking the beans for 8 hours. The next day, drain the beans, rinse them and then pour them into a large saucepan, cover with cold water and bring to the boil. As soon as the water is at temperature, lower the heat until everything simmers and cook for about 50 minutes; salt only at the end of cooking.

Meanwhile, peel an onion and chop it with a knife, then pour into a pan with the oil and cook over low heat for 6-7 minutes. Then add the sausages and leave to brown for 3-4 minutes, stirring occasionally so as not to burn the bottom. Deglaze with the wine until the alcohol has completely evaporated.

Add the sprigs of rosemary and the tomato puree. Season with salt and pepper and cook for 35-40 minutes on low heat. After the indicated time, drain the cooked beans.

Add them to the sauce and continue cooking for another 10-15 minutes, letting the flavors blend well. At this point your sausage and beans dish is ready, add some chopped rosemary a drizzle of raw oil and serve!

Egg with tomato sauce
Ingredients:
- **Eggs 4**
- **Tomato puree 500 g**
- **Golden onions 1**
- **Parsley to taste**
- **Extra virgin olive oil q.s.**
- **Salt up to taste**
- **Black pepper to taste**

To prepare the eggs with tomato sauce, first peel and slice the onion. Heat a drizzle of oil in a non-stick pan, add the onion and let it brown for a few minutes, then pour in the tomato purée. Season with salt and pepper, stir and cook over low heat for 15-20 minutes.

Meanwhile, chop the parsley and set aside. After the cooking time, break the first egg into a small bowl and create a small space in the sauce with the help of a ladle.

Pour the egg into the sauce and proceed in the same way with the other 3 eggs. Cover with a lid and cook for 5 minutes, just long enough for the egg white to set. At this point, remove the pan from the heat and sprinkle with fresh parsley, then serve the eggs with tomato sauce piping hot!

Ricotta cheese fried balls with sauce

Ingredients:
- Ricotta 350 g
- Cread (140 g) - crumbs
- Parmigiano Reggiano DOP cheese 3 tbsp (100 g) - to be grated
- Eggs 2
- Garlic 1
- Parsley 1 tbsp - to be minced
- Fine salt to taste
- Black pepper to taste

FOR THE SAUCE
- Tomato puree (750 g)
- Garlic 1 clove
- Basil to taste
- Extra virgin olive oil to taste
- Salt to taste
- Black pepper to taste

Before you start preparing the fried ricotta cheese balls with sauce, drain the whey from the ricotta by placing it in a narrow mesh strainer in the refrigerator for at least a couple of hours, preferably overnight. Then proceed as follows: remove the crust of the bread, cut the soft and then finely chop it in the mixer . Meanwhile, take the ricotta cheese and sieve it with a narrow mesh strainer.

Place the chopped crumbs in a large bowl with the sifted ricotta cheese, then add the crushed half clove of garlic and whole beaten eggs.

Add the grated Parmigiano Reggiano, parsley, saltand pepper to taste. Then mix all the ingredients well with a fork.

Mix well until soft but compact. Put a little oil on the palms of your hands and, taking a portion of the dough, form meatballs of about (30 g) each. Continue until you have about 25 pieces. Set aside and proceed with the preparation of the sauce: brown the oil and a clove of garlic in a pan; once the garlic is golden, remove it from the heat.

Add the tomato puree, a pinch of salt and basil leaves , then add pepper to taste. Bring the sauce to a boil over low heat, then add the ricotta meatballs you have prepared, distributing them evenly. Leave to cook for about 10 minutes over low heat. Once the time has elapsed, turn off and serve the ricotta cheese balls with sauce while hot.

Chickpea and pumpkin soup

Ingredients:
- Pumpkin (600 g) - (to be cleaned)
- Precooked chickpeas (400 g) - (drained)
- Chard (100 g)
- Yellow onions (100 g)
- Juniper berries 3
- Bay leaves 2
- Water (1.5 l)
- Extra virgin olive oil to taste
- Fine salt to taste
- Black pepper to taste

To make the chickpea and pumpkin soup, first peel the onion and slice it thinly. Next, take your pumpkin, cut it in half, then remove the seeds from inside, along with the skin; you'll need to end up with (430 g) of clean pumpkin.

Cut the flesh, first into slices and then into cubes. Wash the chard and cut into thin strips.

Pour the olive oil into a pan, then add the sliced onion and the juniper berries. Allow to brown over low heat until the onion has softened. At this point, add the pumpkin, brown over medium heat, and add with a little of the water.

Add the chickpeas, chard strips, salt, pepper and the rest of the water needed for cooking.

Season with the bay leaves, mix everything together, cover with a lid, and cook on high heat for 15 minutes. Once the 15 minutes are up, remove the lid and continue to cook for a further 15 minutes. Remove the bay leaves and juniper berries and serve your soup with a drizzle of uncooked oil and a twist of black pepper. Your pumpkin and chickpea soup is ready to serve.

Potato and bean soup
Ingredients:
- **Dried beans 250 g**
- **Potatoes 3**
- **Smoked bacon 80 g**
- **Carrots 1**
- **White onions 1**
- **Celery 1 rib**
- **Sage 4 leaves**
- **Parsley 1 sprig**
- **Garlic 1 clove**
- **Extra virgin olive oil 4 tbsp**
- **Salt up to taste**
- **Black pepper to taste**

TO GARNISH
- **Grated Grana Padano DOP q.s.**
- **Extra virgin olive oil q.s.**

To prepare the soup, start by soaking the dried beans in cold water for about 10/12 hours. Then cook them for 15 minutes in a pressure cooker with salted water (if you want you can also add a carrot and a leg of celery) or for about 40 minutes in a normal saucepan.
At the end of the cooking, drain them keeping the water. In the meantime, peel the onion, carrot and celery and chop them finely, peel the potatoes and cut them into small cubes, chop half of the smoked bacon.
Put the extra virgin olive oil in a saucepan and add the clove of garlic, the chopped onion, carrot and celery and the sage leaves, let them dry and then add the smoked bacon that you have chopped

and the rest in cubes. When the bacon is browned, add the potato cubes and brown them. Then add 4/5 ladles of the cooking water from the beans and cook over medium heat for about 10 minutes, i.e. until the potatoes are tender, add more cooking water if necessary.

Season with salt, pepper well and if you prefer, remove the clove of garlic which will have released its aroma. Finally, add the cooked beans and leave everything to flavor for another two minutes. Take about half of the soup and chop it finely with an immersion blender. Add the cream thus obtained to the rest of the soup, finally sprinkle with chopped fresh parsley. Serve the potato and bean soup piping hot with grated Grana Padano and a drizzle of raw extra virgin olive oil!

Uova alla contadina (Baked eggs in tomato sauce)
Ingredients:
- **Eggs 4**
- **Tomato puree 300 g**
- **Tomini cheese 30 g**
- **Rosemary 3 sprigs**
- **Extra virgin olive oil to taste**
- **Fine salt to taste**
- **Black pepper to taste**

To make uova alla contadina, first cut the tomino cheese into cubes, then take an ovenproof dish and spread a layer of tomato passata over the base. Add a little oil.

Now add one egg at a time to the pan. We recommend breaking the egg into a small bowl first to make sure you keep the yolk intact. Arrange the 4 eggs side by side and spread the remaining tomato puree over the top, seasoning with salt and pepper.

Add the cubes of tomino cheese and flavor with the rosemary sprigs. Bake in a conventional oven preheated to 180°C for 20-25 minutes, depending on how hard you like your eggs. When your uova alla contadina is done, take the dish out of the oven and serve piping hot.

Zucchini risotto

Ingredients:
- Carnaroli rice 2 (320 g)
- Zucchini 2 (350 g)
- Vegetable broth (1 l)
- White onions (80 g)
- White wine (100 g)
- Butter 3 ½ tbsp (50 g)
- Parmigiano Reggiano DOP cheese ⅔ cup (70 g) - (to be grated)
- Fine salt to taste
- Black pepper to taste
- Extra virgin olive oil - a dash
- Mint 5 leaves

Start with the vegetable broth when making zucchini risotto. Put a pot of clean, unpeeled, and cut seasonal vegetables on the stove. Salt, add pepper grains, and bring to a boil. In the meantime, clean and finely chop the white onion with a knife. Put in a bowl and move to the stove. Pour a drizzle of oil into a saucepan and add the onion. Cook over low heat for about ten minutes, stirring often: it will help make the onion brown. If the bottom dries out, add very little hot broth.

Turn up the heat and pour in the rice letting it toast for a few minutes while stirring continuously and ensuring that the grains do not burn. As soon as the rice has taken on a lighter color, simmer with white wine until reduced.

Let the alcohol evaporate completely, then add a few ladles of simmering broth.

Remember that the risotto should not be mixed much, and the broth should be poured as needed before the rice has completely absorbed it. In the meantime, cut the zucchini, already washed and dried, and grate them with an extra coarse grater. Halfway through cooking, place the zucchini in the risotto, stir,
and continue cooking. Turn off the heat and add the mint leaves, the black pepper by hand, then the butter and grated Parmesan cheese cold from the fridge. Stir and add very little broth to adjust the consistency if needed. Let rest for a few minutes, with the lid on, and then serve your zucchini risotto.

Potato and sausage crumble
Ingredients:
- Red potatoes 600 g
- Eggs 1
- Grana Padano PDO 100 g
- Corn starch 200 g
- Salt up to taste
- Black pepper to taste

FOR THE STUFFING
- Sausage 360 g
- Buffalo mozzarella 550 g
- White wine 50 g
- Shallot 1
- Rosemary 1 sprig

To make the potato and sausage crumble, first place the potatoes in a saucepan with cold water, until covered. Boil them for 30-40 minutes, until they become soft when pierced with the prongs of a fork. Then cut the mozzarella into slices. Place it in a colander placed over a bowl, cover with plastic wrap and let it drain well.

In the meantime, take care of the filling. Peel the shallot and chop it finely. Switch to the sausage. Remove it from the casing and cut it coarsely with a knife.

Also chop the rosemary. Move on to cooking. Pour the shallot into a pan with a drizzle of oil and let it simmer over low heat for 7-8 minutes. Then raise the heat and add the sausage and brown it. Add the rosemary and when it is golden brown, add the white wine.

Add salt and pepper and let the wine evaporate well, then turn off the heat and set aside. Once the potatoes are cooked, drain them and mash them with a potato masher, collecting the puree in a large bowl.

Wait until they are warm. Then add the starch, half the dose of grated Grana, salt and pepper.

Also add the whole egg and work everything with your hands (if you want in the first phase you can work with a wooden spoon) until you get a homogeneous mixture, but still crumbly. Line a 24 cm diameter cake tin with parchment paper and pour half of the dough inside. Use the back of a spoon to press lightly and create a homogeneous base.

Squeeze the mozzarella well and arrange half of it on the potato base, breaking it with your hands. Add the sausage, distribute it evenly, then finish with the remaining mozzarella. Cover with the remaining dough, distributing it well and crumbling it, so as to cover the filling. Drizzle with a drizzle of oil and season with a pinch of pepper.

Add the rest of the parmesan to the surface and cook in a preheated static oven at 200°, on the medium shelf, for 20 minutes. After 20 minutes, continue cooking for 5 minutes with the grill at 240°. When cooked, the salted crumble will be well browned on the surface, take it out of the oven. Let it cool before unmolding and serve it!

Tomato soup
Ingredients:
- Tomato puree 800 g
- Tuscan bread 300 g
- Vegetable broth 1 l
- Extra virgin olive oil 35 g
- Garlic 2 cloves
- Sugar 1 pinch
- Salt up to taste
- Black pepper to taste
- Basil 1 bunch

Cut the bread into thin slices. Then take a dripping pan and after having covered it with baking paper, place the slices of Tuscan bread next to each other without overlapping them. Bake at 200°C for a few minutes. Once removed from the oven, let them cool. When they are warmed, rub the previously peeled garlic cloves on them.

Now take a non-stick frying pan with high edges and place the toasted bread inside. Pour the tomato purée and the vegetable broth inside so that the slices of bread are completely covered. At this point, add the sugar and cook over low heat for 40-50 minutes to allow the liquid to evaporate. Stir from time to time to allow uniform cooking and reduce the bread to a pulp.

Then season with salt and pepper. When cooked, turn off the heat and garnish with basil leaves to give a fresh and intense flavor to your tomato soup which will be so ready to serve in individual bowls or soup plates to drizzle with plenty of olive oil!

Stuffed zucchini
Ingredients:
- Round zucchini 4
- Pork 100 g - ground
- Sausage 100 g
- Eggs 1
- Parmigiano Reggiano DOP cheese (30 g) - grated
- Parsley 1 tbsp
- Black pepper to taste
- Breadcrumbs 20 g
- Fine salt to taste
- Extra virgin olive oil 1 tsp

To prepare the stuffed zucchini, wash the zucchini under running water, dry them with a clean cloth, and cut off the top to form the lid . Score the inner perimeter with a small knife, then make an X in the flesh and remove one segment at a time.

Next, scoop out the inside using a melon baller or teaspoon, creating a shell around (1 cm) thick. This way, you'll have both the lids and the shells ready to be stuffed. Season the insides of the zucchini with salt and bake in the oven at 200°C for 15 minutes.

In the meantime, prepare the filling: Place the ground pork in a bowl and add the sausage, with the skin already removed, and the grated Parmigiano Reggiano cheese.

Then add the chopped zucchini flesh, the egg, lightly beaten, and the chopped breadcrumb. Now add the chopped parsley, season with salt and pepper, and combine the mixture with your hands until it's even.

Grease a deep baking dish with a good glug of oil. Take the (cooked) zucchini and put them in the dish, then fill them to the brim with the stuffing you just made.

Put the lids in the dish as well and bake in a conventional oven preheated to 170°C for around 60 minutes. Once the stuffed zucchini have gone golden and crispy on the surface, take them out of the oven and serve them up, placing the lids on top of the stuffing.

Broad beans and wild chicory
Ingredients:
- Dried peeled broad beans 400 g
- Wild chicory 400 g
- 3 bay leaves
- Extra virgin olive oil q.s.
- Salt up to taste
- Water to taste

To prepare broad beans and wild chicory, first you will have to rehydrate the beans by soaking them in a bowl with plenty of cold water for about 12 hours (you can put them in the evening and then cook them the next day). The next day, drain the broad beans, rinse them under running water, and cook them in a large saucepan, covering them flush with water and adding 2-3 bay leaves.

Close the pot with a lid and cook the broad beans over low heat for at least 2 hours, adding hot water if necessary in case they dry out. During these two hours the beans will release a froth that you will eliminate with a slotted spoon. In the meantime, wash the chicory well under running water and let it drain, then clean it, removing the hardest part, the white one in the lower part that holds the leaves together, with a knife. Remove even the most damaged leaves, keeping only the most beautiful ones. Blanch the chicory quickly in boiling salted water for a few minutes, stirring with a wooden spoon. As soon as they are well kept, drain them and keep aside.

Meanwhile, the broad beans will have finished cooking: they will be ready when, stirring constantly with a wooden spoon, they will fall apart easily, until you have a coarse-textured purée. Salt the broad beans and, once ready, compose the traditional dish of broad beans and chicory divided in half: place the broad beans on one side of the plate and the chicory on the other. Season everything with a drizzle of extra virgin olive oil, better if a good Apulian oil, and serve the broad beans and wild chicory accompanying them with slices of bread!

Meat

Steak pizzaiola
- **Sliced veal (400 g)**
- **Tomato puree (400 g)**
- **Garlic 2 cloves**
- **Oregano to taste**
- **Extra virgin olive oil to taste**
- **Fine salt to taste**
- **Black pepper to taste**

TO DECORATE
- **Basil to taste**

To prepare the steak pizzaiola, start with the sauce: heat the oil in a pan and add the crushed garlic cloves. After a couple of minutes, pour the tomato puree and a drop of water used to rinse the jar. Simmer for about 15 minutes over low heat.
In the meantime, prepare the meat: make small cuts on the edges of the slices where there is some fat to prevent them from curling during cooking, then transfer the slices on a sheet of parchment paper. Cover with another sheet and beat them lightly, being careful not to tear the meat; you will need to obtain a uniform thickness of about 3-4 mm.
When the sauce has reduced, flavor with oregano, salt and pepper, then remove the garlic.
Dip the slices of meat in the sauce (if they are too big you can cut them in half) and let them cook 2 minutes per side. Garnish with a few basil leaves, if you wish, and immediately serve your steak pizzaiola!

Veal Milanese (Breaded veal cutlet)
Ingredients:
- Veal loin 1 kg (slices)
- Eggs 4 - large
- Breadcrumbs 300 g
- Clarified butter 300 g
- Salt to taste

FOR THE POTATOES
- Grated potatoes 500 g
- Clarified butter 100 g
- Rosemary 1 sprig
- Fine salt to taste
- Black pepper to taste
- Garlic 1 clove

Using a meat pounder, beat the the slice of meat slightly, so that the thickness is evened out but without reducing it. Use a knife to remove the extra connective tissue, which would make the cutlet shrink during cooking. Set aside the meat and prepare the eggs. Break them into a bowl and mix them slightly with a whip, without breaking them up too much. If they're small, add another one. Put the breadcrumbs into a large bowl. Take the cutlets by the bone and first dip them in the breadcrumbs, then dip them in the eggs 1and again in the breadcrumbs, pressing well with your hands so that the breadcrumbs stick better. Make a double breading by dipping the cutlets again in the eggs and again in breadcrumbs, pressing well but without flattening the meat too much. Repeat this operation for all the cutlets, then using the flat side of the blade of a knife, tap the slices to even out and set the breadcrumbs. Finally, with the dull edge of the blade, make a sort of grid on the ribs by first pressing horizontal lines and then vertical. Repeat the same for all the others and start preparing the potatoes. Wash the potatoes with a little water and baking soda, then dry them. Then get your vegetable slicer and a bowl full of water. Make slices about 2-3 mm thick and gradually transfer them into the bowl filled with water; this way they will release some starch but will not oxidize. Put some water in a pan, salt it and bring it to a boil. Then drain the potatoes and pour them into the water. Blanch them for about 90 seconds a half minutes then drain them again and cool them slightly under cold water jet. This precooking will reduce the cooking time in butter. Dry the potatoes with a dish towel and in the meantime heat a large saucepan. Add the clarified butter and let it melt. Then add a lightly crushed poached clove of garlic to the potatoes, a sprig of rosemary and let it all brown over a high flame, stirring occasionally. In the meantime, take another larger pan, which will be used to cook your cutlet and melt the butter. As soon as it is hot but not too hot, place the cutlets, making sure that the part with the lines is in contact with the pan. After about 4 minutes, the cutlets will be well browned, then turn them and with a spoon collect some cooking fat and sprinkle it on the rib bone; this way there will be no bloody streaks and you will get a clear bone. Cutlets will have to cook for about another 4 minutes, this time depends on the thickness of the cut and you will want a pinkish meat inside. Potatoes will have the same cooking time; when they are cooked, you can salt them and season them with a little pepper. Drain the potatoes on a sheet of absorbent paper, remove the garlic and blot them with another sheet to remove the excess fat, even if it is very little due to the type of potatoes chosen.

When cutlets are ready, using a pair of tongs, transfer them to a plate with absorbent paper and again with a sheet of paper gently dab, to eliminate the excess fat. At this point everything is ready, all you have left to do is put them on a plate. Place the potatoes on the side of the plate, near the cutlet and season with maldon salt. Serve your Milanese cutlet hot.

Roasted rabbit
Ingredients:
- **Rabbit in pieces 1,2 kg**
- **Rosemary 4 sprigs**
- **Salt up to taste**
- **Black pepper to taste**
- **Vegetable broth 150 g**
- **Potatoes 800 g**
- **Red onions 120 g**
- **Thyme 4 sprigs**
- **White wine 40 g**
- **Garlic 1 clove**
- **Bay leaf 1**
- **Extra virgin olive oil 70 g**

Chop the rosemary, then transfer half of it into a pan where you have poured 40 g of oil and add the peeled clove of garlic.
Add a bay leaf and let it all flavor over low heat for 2-3 minutes. At this point, raise the heat and add the pieces of rabbit, let them brown on both sides for 3-4 minutes, add salt and pepper and blend everything with the white wine. Once the alcoholic part has evaporated, add a ladle of broth and cook over low heat for another 5-6 minutes. In the meantime prepare the potatoes, peel them and cut them into rather large chunks. Also cut the onion into slices and transfer everything into a bowl, flavored with the chopped rosemary needles and previously kept aside, the thyme leaves, salt and pepper. Drizzle with 20 g of oil and mix potatoes and onions to make them flavor evenly. Transfer everything to a large pan, oiled with about 10 g of oil, so that the potatoes and onions are well distributed. Then also arrange the previously browned pieces of rabbit. Add the remaining vegetable broth and cook the rabbit together with the potatoes in a preheated static oven at 200° for 40 minutes. Once out of the oven, serve your rabbit still steaming in the oven!

Tasty chicken salad
Ingredients:
- Chicken breast 600 g - fillets
- Green olives 2 ¼ tbsp (30 g) - pitted
- Pickles 60 g
- Red peppers 200 g
- White celery 170 g
- Carrots 150 g
- Parmigiano (in flakes) 100 g
- Fine salt to taste

FOR THE DRESSING
- Black pepper to taste
- Mustard 1 tbsp (15 g) - delicate
- Fine salt to taste
- White wine vinegar 1 tbsp (20 g)
- Extra virgin olive oil 100 g
- Mayonnaise 120 g

To prepare the tasty chicken salad, start by beating the chicken slices with a meat tenderizer, between two sheets of baking paper to break down the fibers of the meat without tearing it. Then cook on a hot grill and turn only when the meat is completely white and has the typical grill marks. Then turn and add a pinch of salt to the cooked part. Meanwhile, cook the other side for the same amount of time. It will take about two minutes, but the time may vary depending on the thickness of the chicken fillets, so avoid poking the meat with a fork or the juices will come out and the chicken will be too dry. When the meat is well cooked, remove it from the grill and season it with salt immediately, to allow the heat to melt the salt. Place the chicken breasts on a plate and let them cool.

In the meantime, clean the vegetables: take the pepper and remove the inner seeds, then julienne it, peel and trim the carrots and cut them into strips too. Slice the celery ribs, pickles, and pitted green olives crosswise. And finally cut the cheese into flakes.

In the meantime the meat will have cooled down, cut it into strips and prepare the dressing: put the mayonnaise in a bowl, add the mustard, white wine vinegar, salt and pepper.

Finally, pour in the olive oil, mix the ingredients and set aside. Now take a large bowl, add the chicken and all the previously cut ingredients: peppers, celery , carrots, pickles, cheese, olives and stir.

Then add the dressing, stir again and cover with plastic wrap ; let it rest in the fridge for at least an hour. After this time the flavors will have blended thoroughly and you can enjoy your tasty chicken salad.

Veal scalloppini with white wine and parsley
Ingredients:
- Veal (8 slices)
- Parsley 2 tsp
- Butter (80 g)
- Flour 00 to taste
- Dry white wine (100 g)
- Vegetable broth (70 g)
- Fine salt to taste
- Black pepper to taste

To prepare the white wine and parsley scalloppini, prepare the vegetable broth and keep it warm. Clean the parsley, remove the leaves , then finely chop it and set it aside. Cut 8 slices from the piece of meat, moisten them with very little water and start beating them with a meat tenderizer. Proceed by squeezing and stretching: the meat will thin without tearing. At this point, melt the butter over medium-high heat in a sufficiently large pan,
when the bottom is hot and the butter is melted, quickly flour the slices of meat and place them in the pan. Let them brown for a few moments on one side and then on the other, turn with tongs. Then blend with the white wine and let the alcohol evaporate.
When the broth has evaporated, add a pinch of salt and pepper and let the seasoning sink in for a couple of minutes over medium heat. Gently jiggle and shake the pan and then turn the slices. Turn off the heat, flavor with the previously chopped parsley and your white wine and parsley scalloppini are ready. Enjoy your meal!

Baked pork knuckle with potatoes
Ingredients:
- **Pork shank 1 800 g**
- **Small potatoes 500 g**
- **Carrots 1**
- **Celery the coast 1**
- **Small onions 1**
- **Garlic 1 clove**
- **Salt to taste**
- **Pepper as needed.**
- **Extra virgin olive oil 60 g**
- **Sage to taste**
- **Juniper the berries 4**
- **Rosemary 2 sprigs**
- **Water 150g**
- **Red wine 50 g**
- **2 bay leaves**

To prepare the baked pork shank with potatoes, start by rinsing and drying the aromatic herbs. Take the rosemary which you will then chop very finely together with the juniper berries and sage. Switch to the potatoes: rinse them under plenty of running water and cut each one into four pieces if large or two if small, without removing the peel. Make sure you get potatoes of the same size to help them cook evenly later.
Cut the ingredients for the sauté into chunks: add the carrots, garlic, celery and onion to the blender.
Operate the blades of the mixer until you obtain a finely chopped mixture which you will pour into a pan with a thick bottom and high edges: let it dry over a very low heat with the oil. While preparing the sauté, remove the visible fat from the pork shank.

When the sauce is ready, add the shin to the pan. Brown it well on all sides, turning it several times in the pan with a kitchen spatula: the shank will release a little liquid during cooking. Season with salt and pepper. Then flavored with the chopped herbs.

Finally add the bay leaves. Mix the smells so that the shin absorbs the perfumes. Deglaze with the red wine and let the alcoholic part evaporate, then pour in the water: the shank must never remain dry to prevent the meat from drying out.

Add the potatoes and cook over medium heat for 10 minutes, covering with a lid: the potatoes should soften and be tender, without falling apart, the water should dry. Remember to turn the shin while it is cooking with the aid of kitchen spatulas to promote uniform cooking. Never use forks to turn it so as not to pierce the meat.

Once the cooking time has elapsed in the pan, transfer the shin, the potatoes and the cooking juices into an ovenproof dish in such a way as to fill it completely with the ingredients. Bake in a preheated static oven at 200°C for at least 40-45 minutes (or in a convection oven at 180°C for about 30-35 minutes: however, be more careful that the meat does not dry out). If you notice that during cooking in the oven the shin gets too dry, add more water and turn it occasionally so that it cooks evenly. However, the cooking time may vary slightly depending on the size of the shank you are cooking. For greater precision, measure the temperature of the meat with a probe, which must be between 75° and 85°. At the end of cooking, the potatoes should also be very tender. Once the cooking time has elapsed, remove the dish from the oven and enjoy your pork knuckle in the oven with potatoes still hot!

Palermitan Cutlet
Ingredients:
- Chicken breast 400 g
- Breadcrumbs 130 g
- Pecorino to grate 30 g
- Extra virgin olive oil 50 g
- Parsley 2 g
- Salt up to taste
- Black pepper to taste
- Lemons (optional) to taste
- Mint (optional) to taste

To prepare the Palermitan cutlet, start with the meat. If you use chicken breast, carefully remove the fat parts and the central bone from the whole breast. Then with a sharp knife cut into slices of about 1 centimeter. Then beat them with the special hammer or a meat tenderizer to soften the meat and reduce its thickness. Then transfer the slices of meat onto a plate, brush them with oil on both sides and set them aside while you continue with the preparation.

Then prepare the breading: wash the tuft of fresh parsley. Dry it and finely chop the leaves. In a large bowl, put the breadcrumbs and add the chopped parsley. If you like, you can also add a few leaves of chopped fresh mint. Then add the grated pecorino to the mixture.

To flavor the breading, add the salt and pepper and mix everything together. Now you can pick up the meat set aside and pass it in the breading slice by slice, pressing well with your hands to make the mixture adhere

Heat the grill well over medium heat and cook the meat for minutes, turning it a couple of times halfway through cooking until the slices of meat are well grilled on both sides. If you prefer, you can cook the cutlet in a preheated static oven at 190° for about 15 minutes (if a convection oven at 170° for about 10 minutes). The Palermitan cutlet will then be ready to be served piping hot. You can grate the untreated lemon zest and squeeze the juice before serving, accompanied with a salad, crunchy vegetables or baked potatoes to your taste!

Ligures rabbit
Ingredients:
- Rabbit 1.5 kg
- Taggiasca olives 100 g
- Onions 1
- Rosemary 1 sprig
- Garlic 2 cloves
- Thyme 1 tbsp
- Extra virgin olive oil about 5 tablespoons
- Meat broth to taste
- 3 bay leaves
- Salt up to taste
- Pine nuts 2 tbsp

First, cut the rabbit into at least a dozen pieces, remembering to keep the head, liver and kidneys aside.

Once this operation is finished, put the olive oil in a large saucepan, heat it, and let the chopped onion and garlic wither over a low heat; add the rabbit and brown it, then add the bay leaves, thyme (or marjoram) and the chopped rosemary needles. Cook until the rabbit has taken on a nice golden colour.

Let it cook for a few minutes and then add the glass of red wine, let the wine evaporate, then add the Taggiasca olives. If you like them, you can add the kidneys and liver of the rabbit.

Then add the pine nuts, mix everything well and then cover the rabbit with a lid and cook for about an hour until the rabbit becomes tender (the meat should detach easily from the bone). From time to time add a ladleful of stock to the pot and cook over low heat. Serve the rabbit by sprinkling it with plenty of cooking sauce and enjoy your meal!!

Chicken rolls
Ingredients:
- **Chicken breast 8 slices**
- **Cooked ham 120 g**
- **Spinach 500 g**
- **Fontina cheese 200 g**
- **White wine 80ml**
- **Extra virgin olive oil q.s.**
- **Salt up to taste**

To prepare the chicken rolls, start by boiling the fresh spinach in boiling salted water for a few seconds. Once blanched, stop cooking in water and ice, drain them well, squeeze them to remove all the water using a cloth, finally chop them finely with a knife.

Lightly beat the chicken breast slices with a meat tenderizer to make them thinner and more regular, then salt them. Place the cooked ham cut to size and two thin slices of fontina cheese on each slice of meat.

Finally stuffed with a spoonful of boiled spinach. Then start rolling the chicken tightly starting from one end towards the other, fixing it at the end with a toothpick; keep it up for all the rolls. Heat the oil in a non-stick pan and arrange the rolls. Brown over high heat on all sides.

When they are well browned, add the white wine. Let the wine evaporate, cook the rolls for about 15 more minutes over low heat (cooking times will depend on the thickness of the meat); If the meat gets too dry during cooking, add some hot water. When the chicken rolls are ready, serve them piping hot!

Chicken breast with bell peppers
Ingredients:
- **Chicken breast 600 g**
- **Red peppers 300 g**
- **Yellow peppers 300 g**
- **Peeled baby plum tomatoes 400 g**
- **Butter 3 tbsp**
- **Shallot 1**
- **White wine 3 tbsp**
- **Water 1 - ladleful, hot**
- **Flour 00 to taste**
- **Extra virgin olive oil to taste**
- **Fine salt to taste**
- **Black pepper to taste**

To make the chicken breast with bell peppers, start by peeling the shallot and chopping it finely. Wash the red and yellow peppers, slice them in half, then remove the stalk and inner seeds.

Slice the peppers into strips and set aside. Heat the olive oil in a large pan and pour in the chopped shallot. Sauté for 1 minute, then add a ladleful of hot water (or vegetable stock) and simmer for a further 3 minutes over low heat. Once the shallot has softened, add the peeled baby plum tomatoes and bell pepper slices, season with salt and pepper to taste, cover with a lid, and cook over medium heat for 25 minutes. Meanwhile, melt the butter in a pan over very low heat, and flour the chicken breast slices. Once the butter begins to sizzle, lay the slices to brown on each side for a few minutes over medium heat, then deglaze with white wine and allow to evaporate. Cook for a few minutes, just long enough to brown the meat. Once the bell pepper and tomato sauce is ready, add the browned chicken breasts.

Cover with a lid, and cook for another 5 minutes over medium heat before removing the lid and continuing to cook for a further 5 minutes over low heat to thicken the sauce a little. Your chicken breast with bell peppers is ready to be served hot!

Pork stew
Ingredients:
- **Pork loin 800 g**
- **Potatoes 450 g**
- **Celery 1 rib**
- **Carrots 1**
- **White onions 1**
- **Rosemary 2 sprigs**
- **Butter 20 g**
- **Dark beer 800 g**
- **Salt up to taste**
- **Black pepper to taste**
- **Flour 00 (for flouring) 50 g**
- **Garlic 1 clove**

To make the pork stew, start by cutting the loin into cubes of a couple of centimeters, then flour them on all sides and set aside. Meanwhile, wash and peel the vegetables for the sauté: the carrot, celery and onion, then chop them finely with a knife.

Now chop the rosemary needles with a knife, melt the butter in a large saucepan, then pour the mixture for the sauté and also squeeze in a clove of garlic. To finish, flavor with the chopped rosemary and let the sautéed mixture simmer over a moderate heat for about 5 minutes and then add the pork. Brown the meat for at least 5 minutes and then sprinkle it with the beer,

let it evaporate and then cover with the lid, add salt and pepper and continue cooking for 40 minutes. Meanwhile, peel the potatoes. Cut them into cubes as large as those of meat.

After 40 minutes of cooking the meat, add the potato cubes and continue cooking for another 30 minutes with the lid on, enough time to cook the potatoes too and create a delicious creamy sauce. Once ready, serve the pork stew piping hot.

Chicken strips Sorrento style

Ingredients:
- **Chicken breast 500 g**
- **Tomato puree 300 g**
- **Mozzarella cheese 100 g**
- **Shallot 1**
- **Basil 4 leaves**
- **Flour 00 to taste - to dust**
- **Parmigiano Reggiano DOP cheese 3 tbsp (20 g) - grated**
- **Extra virgin olive oil to taste**
- **Fine salt to taste**
- **Black pepper to taste**

To prepare the chicken strips alla sorrentina, begin with the sauce. Peel a shallot and chop it finely. Add to a pan with a drizzle of extra virgin olive oil and cook for a few minutes over low heat, stirring often to stop the shallot from burning. Add the tomato puree, salt to taste, and add a ladle of water.

Cover and cook over medium heat for 20 minutes. Meanwhile, prepare the chicken. Cut the breast into strips about ½ inch (1 cm) thick and then into irregular pieces about 2 inches (5 cm) long.

Coat the chicken strips in flour and place them on a baking sheet lined with parchment paper. Heat some oil in a frying pan and then sear the chicken by cooking over high heat for 2-3 minutes, turning occasionally. When the strips are golden brown, season with salt, and then add the tomato sauce. Cook for another 2 minutes and then turn off the heat. Add the diced mozzarella and the basil leaves, torn up by hand. Season with ground black pepper and mix everything together. Pour into a casserole dish , sprinkle the surface with grated Parmigiano cheese. Broil in a preheated oven at 240°C under the broiler for 8-10 minutes or however long it takes for the mozzarella to melt and form a lightly browned crust on the surface. Your chicken strips alla sorrentina are ready to serve. All you have to do now is get them to the table piping hot.

Creamy chicken breast
Ingredients:
- Chicken breast 1 kg
- Extra virgin olive oil 40 g
- Lemons 1
- Garlic 1 clove
- Fine salt 1 tbsp
- Black pepper 1 tsp
- Smoked paprika 1 tsp
- Rosemary 1 sprig

FOR THE CREAM
- Butter 20 g
- Flour 00 20 g
- Whole milk 200 g
- Fine salt 1 tsp
- Nutmeg 1 tsp
- Rosemary 1 sprig

To prepare the creamy chicken breast, remove the fat and bones from the chicken breast and divide it in half. With a sharp knife, make incisions on the surface of the chicken, without going all the way, obliquely on both sides.
In this way the aromas will penetrate the meat better. In a bowl, season the chicken with half the oil, salt,
pepper, paprika and lemon zest.
Massage the chicken, trying to get the seasoning to penetrate through the cracks in the cuts. In a pan, heat the oil with the rosemary and garlic. Add the chicken. Cook over medium-high heat until the bottom is colored, it will take about 6-7 minutes.
Meanwhile, squeeze the lemon juice. Turn the chicken and still keeping the flame medium-high, pour in the lemon juice, cover with a lid and cook on the other side for 6 or 7 minutes.
Remove the garlic and rosemary from the pan and transfer the cooked chicken to a separate plate.

In the same pan, pour the butter and let it melt. Add the flour and toast it, stirring with a whisk.

Pour the milk at room temperature several times, always mixing with the whisk, and thicken. Season with salt, nutmeg and rosemary.

Put the chicken back in the pan, cover with the lid and continue cooking for another 2 minutes. Garnish the creamy chicken breast with lemon zest and rosemary to taste and serve.

Bolognese Cutlet
Ingredients:
- **Veal loin (4 slices of 200 g each) 800 g**
- **Breadcrumbs 200 g**
- **Flour 00 100 g**
- **Eggs 2**
- **Butter 50 g**
- **Raw ham 300 g**
- **Parmigiano Reggiano DOP (to be grated) 170 g**
- **Meat broth 250 g**
- **FOR THE DRESSING**
- **Tomato puree 100 g**

To prepare the Bolognese cutlet, prepare the meat broth (or vegetable broth even if the sauce will be lighter at that point); then start beating the slices of meat with a meat mallet to make them thinner (you can also use a sheet of baking paper to spread over the meat so as not to risk breaking the fibers); then prepare three low and wide containers: beat the eggs in one; in the other place the sifted flour and in the third the breadcrumbs. Dip the slices of meat one at a time, first in the flour turning it on both sides to coat it thoroughly. Then in the egg, finally roll them in the breadcrumbs, making sure they are completely covered. For cooking you will have to adjust according to the size of the slices or the pan; we advise you to cook 1 or 2 slices at a time if you use a pan that is not very large, in order not to risk reusing the butter too many times. Then melt the butter in a pan and once melted, place the slices. Brown on one side, then flip to the other. Once they are well browned on both sides, place the slices of ham and sprinkle with grated Parmesan. Once seasoned, sprinkle the slices with meat broth (one ladle for each cutlet) and cook with the lid on for 5-6 minutes; when they're ready, filter the cooking liquid from the pan in which you cooked the cutlet and transfer it to a saucepan. Then add 20 g of Parmesan and thicken over high heat.

You are now ready to serve: if you wish, you can garnish the serving dish with simple tomato sauce, then place the cutlet and season with the broth reduction. Your bolognese cutlet is ready to be served!

Veal and sausage stuffed peppers
Ingredients:
- Bell peppers 4 (1100 g) - large

FOR THE FILLING
- Veal ⅔ lb (300 g) - ground
- Sausage ⅓ lb (150 g)
- Stale bread 1 cup (100 g) - ((crumb)
- Grana Padano DOP cheese ½ cup (50 g) - grated
- Provolone cheese ½ lb (200 g)
- Whole milk ⅔ cup (150 g)
- Eggs 2
- Parsley ⅓ cup (10 g) - chopped
- Fine salt to taste
- Black pepper to taste

FOR BAKING AU GRATIN
- Grana Padano DOP cheese 3 tbsp (20 g) - grated
- Provolone cheese ¾ oz (20 g) - grated

FOR GARNISHING
- Basil to taste

To make the meat and sausage stuffed peppers, first cut the stale bread into small cubes, then place the cubes in a bowl and cover them with the milk. Press the bread cubes lightly so they absorb the milk well. Now move on to the peppers: Wash and dry them.

Cut off the tops and remove the pith and seeds. Take the tops, cut around the stem to remove it, and then cut the remaining part of the pepper into small pieces.

Place the ground veal in a large bowl, then remove the casing from the sausage and place the sausage meat in the bowl as well. Take the bread that's been soaking in the milk and squeeze out the milk well.

Add the bread to the meat and knead thoroughly. Next, grate the provolone cheese and add this and the grated Grana Padano to the bowl, and knead again using your hands. Now pour in the two eggs and the diced pepper, and knead again.

Season with salt and pepper and add the chopped parsley. Knead everything well until you get an even mixture. Take the peppers, arrange them in a baking dish and fill them to the top with the meat and sausage filling. Press down with the back of a spoon to ensure the filling is stuffed in well. Pour over a drizzle of oil and cook the peppers on the middle rack of a conventional oven preheated to 350°F (180°C), for 40 minutes. After 40 minutes have passed, remove the peppers from the oven, sprinkle them with the grated Grana Padano and provolone cheeses. Return the peppers to the oven, placing them under the broiler at 465°F (240°C) for 3-4 minutes. Once the cheese has melted, remove them from the oven, garnish with basil leaves and serve.

Fish and SeaFood

Risotto with scampi cream
Ingredients:
- Carnaroli rice 320 g
- Scampi 1.2 kg
- Extra virgin olive oil 50 g
- Shallot 60 g
- Garlic 1 clove
- Salt up to taste
- Black pepper to taste
- Liquid fresh cream 45 g
- Lemons 1
- Thyme to taste

FOR THE SHELLFISH CARTOON
- Shallot 40 g
- Brandy 30 g
- Extra virgin olive oil 30 g
- Parsley 1 sprig
- Water 1.2l
- Scampi heads and shells
- Garlic 1 clove
- Peppercorns to taste
- Salt to taste
- Tomato paste 1 tbsp

To prepare the scampi cream risotto, start by cleaning the scampi. First, remove the head from them, then with the help of scissors, cut the part of the belly and gently extract the carapace. Remove the dark stringy part on the back, i.e. the intestine, with pliers. At this point, keep the pulp aside and use the scraps to prepare the shellfish stock, which will be used to cook the risotto.

Cut the shallot into slices and pour it together with the oil and the crushed garlic into a pan. Let everything brown over high heat and add the scampi scraps, wait a few minutes, stirring occasionally, and blend with the brandy.

Once all the alcoholic part has evaporated, add the parsley, then add the water, the coarse salt, the peppercorns

and lastly the tomato paste, stir and cook over a moderate heat for 30 minutes. Once the shellfish stock is ready you can filter it through a sieve. Now take care of the scampi cream: pour 20 g of oil into a pan together with a clove of garlic and let it brown over a moderate heat, then remove it and add the cleaned scampi. Let them brown on both sides for a couple of minutes, add salt and blend with the lemon juice. Take some scampi that will be used for the cream; keep the others aside to decorate the dishes.

Pour the scampi into a container with a high edge, add a ladleful of stock, the fresh cream and blend with the immersion blender to obtain a cream. At this point take care of the risotto, finely chop the shallot and transfer it to a pan where you have poured the remaining part of the oil. Let it brown gently, with a ladle of comic strip

then add the rice and let it toast for a few minutes, stirring often with a wooden spoon. Once the rice has changed color slightly, start adding a ladleful of stock. Mix everything together and cook the rice adding more stock a ladle at a time, allowing the liquid to be absorbed before adding more. When cooked, stir in the scampi cream

flavored with the grated lemon zest and thyme leaves, serve garnishing the dish with the prawns kept aside previously. Your scampi cream risotto is ready to be tasted!

Sea bream in crazy water
Ingredients:
- 1 sea bream (800 g) clean
- Cherry tomatoes 300 gr
- Parsley a tuft
- Garlic 4 cloves
- Extra virgin olive oil 2 tbsp
- Salt to taste.
- Pepper as needed.
- Half a glass of water
- Half a glass of white wine

Put a pinch of salt, a clove of garlic and a couple of parsley leaves inside the belly. Take a baking dish (or a baking tray), sprinkle the bottom with extra virgin olive oil, then place the sea bream on it. Cut the cherry tomatoes into wedges or cubes and add them to the baking dish together with the two remaining sliced garlic cloves, the parsley leaves, the salt and pepper (or fresh chilli if you like), the water and the white wine; the liquids must not completely cover the sea bream but remain less than half the height of the fish. Bake in a preheated oven at 220° for about 20-25 minutes: to make sure that the fish is cooked you should try to tear off the caudal fin: if it comes off easily the sea bream will be cooked, otherwise, if it resists, cook the fish for a few more minutes.

When the sea bream in crazy water is cooked, remove the pan from the oven, place the sea bream on a plate, remove the skin and divide the sea bream into fillets, eliminating all the bones (the large central one and the lateral ones) and the head. Once the 4 fillets have been obtained, place them in a serving dish, sprinkling them with the cooking juices and serve immediately. If you prefer cooking in a pan, proceed in the same way, cooking over a flame by placing a lid on the pan used.

Prawn guazzetto
Ingredients:
- Prawns (600 g) - (12 pieces)
- Peeled tomatoes (400 g)
- Water 1 cup (200 g)
- Brandy ¼ cup (50 g)
- Extra virgin olive oil 2 ½ tbsp (30 g)
- Garlic 1 clove
- Fresh chili pepper 1
- Parsley to taste
- Fine salt to taste
- Black pepper to taste

To prepare the prawn guazzetto, start by cleaning the prawn: Remove only their outer shell and take out the dark vein (the digestive tract) by pulling gently with the blade of a knife or toothpick. Leave the head and tail attached and place the prawn on a tray. Take the fresh chili pepper, remove the inner seeds, and cut it into thin strip. Heat the olive oil in a frying pan, add a whole peeled clove of garlic and the sliced chili pepper. When the oil is hot, place the prawns in the pan alongside one other without overlapping, brown on both sides for a minute, then douse with the brandy. Tilt the pan so that the liqueur catches fire and let it flambé until the flame goes out on its own. Add the peeled cherry tomatoes. and dilute the sauce with water. Season with salt, cover with a lid, and continue cooking for about 4-5 minutes. Using tongs, remove the garlic clove, then crush some of the cherry tomatoes with a fork and continue cooking the prawns for another 10 minutes.

Wash, dry, and finely chop the parsley. Once cooked, turn off the heat, garnish the prawns with the parsley and serve the dish piping hot.

Cod Vicentina

Ingredients:
- Stockfish (spider type, soaked for about 3 days) 1 kg
- White onions 300 g
- Desalted salted sardines 40 g
- Flour 00 to taste
- Coarse salt to taste
- Whole milk 180 g
- Grana Padano PDO 20 g
- Black pepper to taste
- Extra virgin olive oil 180 g
- Parsley to taste

To prepare the Vicenza-style cod, the stockfish you will use must already have been soaked for about 3 days and dried overnight. Then first of all chop the onion and desalt the sardines, rinsing them carefully under water. Then pour them into a pan together with the chopped onion add a generous drizzle of oil, mix everything and cook for about 50-60 minutes over low heat until the sardines have melted and the onions are well dried and you have obtained a sort of amber-coloured cream.

Now switch to cod, spider variety. Take the tenderloin soaked, boned and opened with the skin intact. Then stuff with part of the onion mixture, spreading it only on one half, season with coarse salt and a pinch of freshly ground pepper.

Finally sprinkle with flour, you'll need just a veil. Close the cod as if it were a sandwich and cut into pieces about 6 cm wide.

Equip yourself with a saucepan (choose one of a size that allows you to have the pieces of cod close together) and spread about half of the remaining onion mixture on the bottom. Arrange the pieces of stockfish vertically inside the pan. The pieces will have to be arranged next to each other. Cover with the remaining onion, sprinkle again with a little flour, add a pinch of coarse salt, pepper, Grana Padano and pour over all the milk.

Then add the oil slowly until the cod is completely covered. At this point let everything cook for about 4-5 hours on low heat, trying to touch it as little as possible during cooking. If you prefer, you can cover with a lid, but leave a part uncovered to let the steam escape. After 5 hours the cod will be soft, white and not too flaky (in large chunks), the scent will be intense. Finally, add the chopped parsley, mix everything together and serve with slices of polenta, as tradition dictates.

Sea bass in a herb salt crust
Ingredients:
- **Fine salt (400 g)**
- **Sea bass (550 g)**
- **Coarse salt (500 g)**
- **Sage 6 leaves**
- **Thyme 6 sprigs**
- **Parsley 1 bunch**
- **Dill 2 bunches**
- **Bay leaves 4**
- **Rosemary 3 sprigs**
- **Egg whites (105 g)**
- **Garlic 1 clove**
- **Lemons 1**

To make sea bass in a herb salt crust, start by scaling the fish with a scaler or the back of a knife so as not to damage the meat. Rinse thoroughly under running water. Pour the herbs and the peeled garlic clove into the bowl of a blender. Chop the herbs and transfer them to a bowl. Alternatively, chop all the herbs with a knife. Grate the lemon zest and add it to the chopped herbs.

Stuff the belly of the sea bass with a spoonful of herb mix. Meanwhile, pour the egg whites into a bowl and whip them until stiff with a hand whisk.

Gently mix the herbs. Stir, add the fine and coarse salt a little at a time and mix everything together.

Spread a sheet of parchment paper on a dripping pan and then lay a thin layer (about 1.5 cm) of the mixture obtained. Then place the sea bass on the bed of salt and cover it with the salt mixture, pressing it gently to make the dough adhere well.

Line a baking tray with a sheet of baking paper and place a thin layer (about 1.5 cm) of the mixture on top.

Then place the sea bass on the bed of salt and cover with the salt mixture, pressing gently to make the mixture adhere well and making sure that the fish is entirely covered. Cook the sea bass in its herb salt crust in a preheated static oven at (200°C) for 30 minutes. Once the fish is cooked, remove it from the oven and let it rest for a few seconds. Then, take a small hammer or meat tenderizer, crack the salt crust, fillet the fish, and serve hot!

Pan-fried cod fillet
Ingredients:
- Cod fillet (4 fillets) 600 g
- Pine nuts 30 g
- Clarified butter 80 g
- Flour 00 50 g
- Salt up to taste
- Black pepper to taste
- Parsley to be chopped 10 g
- Water 150g

To prepare the cod fillet in a pan, first toast the pine nuts over a moderate heat for 2-3 minutes until they are golden brown; so keep them aside. In the meantime, also chop the parsley, which will be used later. Pour the clarified butter into a pan and let it melt over low heat.

Meanwhile, pour the flour into a baking dish, salt and pepper. When the butter is completely melted, start flouring the cod fillets, raise the heat and place them in the pan.

Quickly continue to bread the other fillets and gradually arrange them in the pan. Leave to cook for a couple of minutes over high heat, in order to obtain a golden crust, then turn the fillets using a kitchen spatula and continue cooking for another 2 minutes. Then transfer the cod fillets to a plate and keep them warm.

Pour the 150 g of water into the same pan where you have just cooked the cod and cook over high heat for a few seconds until you obtain a creamy sauce; then add the chopped parsley, mix everything together and season with salt and pepper. Let the water evaporate completely: it will take about 4-5 minutes. At this point, transfer the fillets to a serving dish; then with a spoon take the sauce from the pan and place it on the fillets. Top with the toasted pine nuts and your pan-fried cod fillet and serve while still hot.

Seafood salad
Ingredients:
- **Mussels 1 kg - clean**
- **Clams 750 g clean**
- **Octopus 700 g clean**
- **Shrimps 500 g clean**
- **Squid 400 g- clean**
- **Carrots 2**
- **Celery 2 ribs**
- **Garlic 1 clove**
- **Bay leaves 4 leaves**
- **Parsley to taste**
- **Ground black pepper to taste**
- **Coarse salt to taste**

FOR THE DRESSING
- **Lemon juice 3 tbsp**
- **Extra virgin olive oil 3 tbsp**
- **Parsley to taste**
- **Fine salt to taste**
- **Black pepper to taste**

Cook the octopus: Chop the celery and carrots roughly and add them to a pot filled with plenty of water, together with the parsley and bay leaves. Add the peppercorns as well and bring to a boil. Then immerse the entire octopus in the water, cover the pot with a lid , and leave it to cook for 30-35 minutes over medium heat, skimming off any residue that forms on the surface of the water from time to time. Cut into rings the squid.

At this point, check on the octopus: Prick it in the middle with a fork and when it's ready, it will be tender but still firm. Transfer the cooked octopus to a colander and let it cool, then remove the vegetables from the cooking water and add the squid. Boil for around 4-5 minutes, depending on the size.
Pour in the shrimp, too, and blanch for 30 seconds, then drain the squid and shrimp and set aside.

Add a drizzle of oil to a pot and brown a clove of garlic in it. Then add the mussels and clams and cover the pot with a lid .

Cook over high heat for 5 minutes, just enough time for them to open. Drain the cooking liquid into a bowl – you can use it in other recipes. Discard any mussels and clams that are still closed and remove the open ones from their shells and place in a bowl; be sure to keep a few in the shells to use as garnish. Take the octopus, which should have cooled by now, and clean it, first cutting across the head at eye level to remove them.

Remove the insides from the head and the beak on the underside, in the middle of the tentacles. Cut the tentacles into ¾-inch pieces and place in a large bowl.

Lastly, prepare the citronette dressing: Place the oil and lemon juice in a small bowl, then chop the parsley and add it to the bowl as well. Season with salt and pepper and emulsify with a fork.

Take the bowl with the octopus and add the shelled mussels and clams, squid, and shrimp.

Dress with the citronette emulsion and stir well. Garnish with the whole mussels and clams you set aside, and then serve up your delicious seafood salad!

Stewed cod
Ingredients:
- Desalted cod 500 g
- Yellow onions 200 g
- Flour 00 100 g
- Tomato puree 600 g
- Extra virgin olive oil 3 tbsp
- Salted capers 3 tbsp (30 g) - (to be disalinated)
- Taggiasca olives 6 tbsp (60 g)
- Oregano 1 tbsp - dried
- White wine 3 tbsp
- Black pepper to taste
- Fine salt to taste
- Parsley to taste

To prepare stewed cod, start by desalinating the capers: rinse them thoroughly under running water. Now check there are no bones in the fish. Run your fingers along the surface of the cut of fish and if you find any, remove them with pincers. Now cut the cod into 4 pieces, each around 1.2 inches in size, without removing the skin, as it will keep the fish intact during cooking. Lastly, peel and thinly slice the onion. Heat a saucepan on the stove. Add the oil and then the onion; brown on a low flame, stirring occasionally, for around 4-5 minutes. Once softened, leave the onion to one side, without gathering up the oil too and quickly dredge the cod pieces with flour. Be sure to remove any excess flour.

Turn the flame up and add the cod pieces and cook for 1-2 minute per side: turn the pieces over when golden. Add the white wine, simmer and reduce, then turn the flame down a little and add the tomato puree. Add the onions to the condiment, followed by the olives and desalinated capers, flavor with the oregano and lastly, add a pinch of salt and pepper. Stir delicately, put the lid on and cook for around 40 minutes on a low flame. Your stewed cod is now ready, all you need to do is add some fresh parsley to taste and enjoy it with a few slices of bread.

Drowned octopus

Ingredients:
- **Octopus (already cleaned) 1 kg**
- **Peeled tomatoes 800 g**
- **Dried chilli to taste**
- **Garlic 1 clove**
- **Parsley 1 sprig**
- **White wine 50 g**
- **Extra virgin olive oil 40 g**
- **Salt up to taste**
- **Black pepper to taste**

Put the peeled garlic in a large pan, together with the oil and the dried chilli pepper. Heat well for 1-2 minutes, also tilting the pan so that the oil can be flavored well with the garlic and chilli pepper, but being careful not to let them burn. At this point, pour the octopus and let them burn for 2-3 minutes over high heat, turning them from time to time with the help of tongs. Deglaze with the white wine and, again with tongs, turn the octopuses and let them cook for a couple more minutes. Add the peeled tomatoes and the sprigs of parsley, then salt and pepper.

Cover the pot with a lid, and cook over low heat for 30-40 minutes, depending on the size of the octopuses. To check if they are cooked, test them by piercing them with a fork: if they are tender it means that they are perfectly cooked. Remove the garlic, always using kitchen tongs; the poached octopus are ready to serve!

Baked sea bass
Ingredients:
- Sea bass (clean) 800 g
- Onions 1
- Carrots 2
- Celery 3 ribs
- Garlic 1 clove
- Bay leaf 1
- Cherry tomatoes 250 g
- Parsley to taste
- Extra virgin olive oil q.s.
- Salt up to taste
- Black pepper to taste
- Basil to garnish q.s.

To prepare the sea bass in the oven, start by cleaning the vegetables. Cut the onion, carrots and celery sticks into coarse pieces, then cut the cherry tomatoes in half and chop the parsley. Pour the vegetables onto the baking tray, grease, season with salt and pepper. Cook the vegetables in a preheated static oven at 180° for about 10 minutes.

In the middle of the sea bass, pour a pinch of salt and a bay leaf, arrange the sea bass on the dripping pan, grease the surface of the fish and cook for 15 minutes in the oven. Once ready, add a few basil leaves and the baked sea bass is ready to be enjoyed.

Baked cod fillets
Ingredients:
- Cod fillet 400 g
- Breadcrumbs 50 g
- Lemons (juice and zest) 1
- Flaked almonds 15 g
- Thyme 3 sprigs
- Extra virgin olive oil 40 g
- Salt up to taste
- Black pepper to taste

To prepare the cod fillets, first take care of the breading. Pour the breadcrumbs into a bowl, add the thyme, lemon zest and juice.
Then add the flaked almonds, salt and pepper and mix everything together.
Now take care of the cod fillets: remove the bones present with kitchen tweezers, to check their presence, caress the fillets with your hands to feel where they are present. Arrange the fillets in a bowl, spread over half a dose of olive oil and the almond breading that you have prepared previously.
Massage the fillets so that the breading adheres to all sides. Now take a baking dish, drizzle the bottom with the remaining olive oil and place the breaded cod fillets inside.
Add the rest of the breading and proceed with cooking: cook the fillets in a preheated static oven at 200° for 15-20 minutes or until the fillets form a crispy crust on the surface. When cooked, take the pan out of the oven and serve the cod fillets hot in the oven.

Cuttlefish with peas
Ingredients:
- Peas 500 g
- Clean cuttlefish 1 kg
- White onions 1
- Extra virgin olive oil 4 tbsp
- Salt up to taste
- Parsley to taste
- Vegetable broth to taste
- Peeled tomatoes 500 g
- White wine 50 g
- Black pepper to taste

Remove the tentacles, remove and cut them into small pieces.
Cut the cape into rather wide strips. Heat the olive oil in a large saucepan, pour in the chopped onion and simmer over medium heat for about 10 minutes, adding hot vegetable broth as needed to avoid letting the onion dry out too much.
When the onion is very soft and transparent, add the cuttlefish, salt and pepper. The cuttlefish could release water so you can raise the flame to dry them. When they have lost their water, pour in the white wine and let it evaporate. Finally add the peas
the peeled tomatoes previously crushed and deprived of the stalk; add a ladleful of broth and continue cooking over low heat for 15/20 minutes. Meanwhile, wash, dry and chop the parsley. When the cuttlefish with peas are soft, turn off the heat, flavor with fresh parsley and serve immediately.

Mediterranean salmon fillets
Ingredients:
- **Salmon 800 g**
- **Cherry tomatoes 350 g**
- **Dried oregano 1 sprig**
- **Extra virgin olive oil 30 g**
- **Salt up to taste**
- **Garlic 1 clove**
- **Pitted black olives 70 g**
- **Pickled capers 5 g**

To prepare the Mediterranean salmon fillets, start by washing the cherry tomatoes, then dry them and cut them into 4. Transfer them to a large bowl, add the peeled and halved garlic and the chopped dried oregano. Add the oil, salt, mix everything and cover with transparent film. Leave the tomatoes to macerate for about 1 hour at room temperature.
After this time, take the salmon steak and remove any bones with tweezers and remove the skin if present; then tagliatelle into 4 fillets of equal thickness. Pick up the cherry tomatoes, remove the garlic and transfer them to a lightly greased baking dish.
Arrange the salmon fillets on top of the cherry tomatoes and with a teaspoon, take some tomatoes and arrange them on top of the salmon. salt, pepper, add the black olives and capers. Bake in a preheated static oven at 180° for about 15 minutes (if you want to use the convection oven, cook at 160° for about 10 minutes). After this time, take out of the oven and serve your Mediterranean salmon fillets still hot!

Lemon and shrimp risotto

Ingredients:

- Carnaroli rice 2 cups (350 g)
- Vegetable broth 4 ¼ cups (1 l)
- Black pepper to taste
- Chives to taste
- Lemon juice 1
- Butter 2 ¼ tbsp (40 g)
- Lemon peel 1 -
- White wine 1 glass -
- Shrimps 1 lb (400 g) - shelled
- Fine salt to taste

To prepare lemon and shrimp risotto, start by heating a pot filled with water on the stove. As soon as the water comes to the boil, add a pinch of coarse salt. Now add the shelled shrimps and wait a couple of minutes before draining.

Place them on a cutting board. Coarsely chop around half of the shrimps and leave the rest to one side for decorating later. Now remove the zest of half a lemon and chop it with a knife, or grate it. Squeeze the juice from the lemon and leave to one side.

Now prepare the rice. Place 1 tbsp of butter in a pan and when it starts to melt add the rice. Add the rice once the butter has fully melted, so that it does not brown excessively. Stir with a wooden ladle and leave the rice to toast for a few minutes. Once well toasted, add the white wine, simmer and reduce.

Add the lemon juice and stir some more. Wait a few moments before adding a ladle of broth. Continue adding broth when necessary, until the rice is fully cooked. Stir occasionally, so that the rice does not stick to the bottom of the pan.

Once cooked, add the previously coarsely chopped shrimps. Add the lemon zest. Stir some more, season with salt and pepper.

Remove from the heat and add the remaining 1.25 tbsp of butter. Gently stir to cream the risotto, gently moving the pan all the while. Once the risotto is nice and creamy, portion it out onto plates. Once ready to serve, garnish with the remaining shrimps and a little lemon zest. Add a pinch of black pepper, some finely chopped chives, and serve.

Dessert

Carnival Tortelli
Ingredients:
- Whole milk 210 g
- Butter 100 g
- Flour 00 300 g
- Sugar 100g
- Lemon zest 1
- Eggs 4
- Yolks 2
- Baking powder for cakes 8 g
- Salt up to 1 pinch

TO FRY
- Peanut oil to taste
- **TO SPRINKLE**
- Sugar to taste

To prepare the Tortelli di Carnevale, pour the milk into a pan, add the cut butter, the sugar, the grated lemon zest and the salt. Bring the mixture to the boil, stirring with a wooden spoon.

When it has reached a boil, remove the pan from the heat and pour in the sifted flour together with the baking powder and mix vigorously. Then put the pan back on low heat and keep stirring for 2-3 minutes until the mixture is smooth. Transfer the mixture into a bowl and leave to cool. When it has cooled, add one egg at a time to the mixture, mixing well until the egg is completely absorbed, then proceed in the same way with the other eggs, being careful not to add the next egg if the previous one is not has been fully incorporated; at the end you will have to obtain a smooth and fluid compound. Pour some seed oil into a pan with high edges and bring it to a temperature of 160°-170°. The tortelli will have to fry slowly so as not to suddenly darken while keeping the inside raw, therefore, before frying one, do a test with very little batter: it will have to brown slowly. When the oil is ready, scoop out a quantity of dough the size of a walnut with a spoon.

With another spoon, slide the dough into the oil, turn the tortello to make it brown and puff up equally over the entire surface. Once golden, drain the tortelli with a slotted spoon.

Place the tortelli on a tray lined with paper towels to dry the excess oil, then roll them in the caster sugar. Your Carnival tortelli are ready to be enjoyed!

Chestnut and chocolate tart
Ingredients:
- Flour 00 3 (380 g)
- Eggs 2
- Butter (90 g)
- Brown sugar (150 g)
- Fine salt 1

FOR THE FILLING
- **Chestnuts (500 g)**
- **Brown sugar 3 tbsp**
- **Rice milk (160 g)**
- **Dark chocolate (135 g)**
- **Cow's milk ricotta cheese ¼ cup (60 g)**
- **TO SPRINKLE**
- **Powdered sugar to taste**

To make the chestnut and chocolate tart, first prepare the pastry. We've decided to use a mixer, but you can also make it by hand like in the video recipe. First, pour the brown sugar, cold butter cut into pieces, and the salt into the bowl of a stand mixer fitted with the flat beater attachment. Turn the mixer on briefly to combine the ingredients and then add the whole eggs.

Turn the mixer on again to combine everything well and then pour in the flour and work the dough for around 3 minutes. Once the dough is smooth, transfer it to a pastry board.

Work it to shape it into a small mound, wrap it in plastic wrap, and leave in the fridge for 30 minutes to firm up. In the meantime, turn to the chestnuts: Make an incision in them with a sharp knife (this will allow you to peel them more easily after cooking), place them in a pot with water on the stove, and cook for 20 minutes from when the water is boiling.

Once finished cook in, let them cool a little and peel them; you'll get around (400 g) of chestnuts. Put the peeled chestnuts in the bowl of a food processor, chop them roughly, and set aside. Chop the dark chocolate as well, using a knife. Now you can start to make the cream: Pour the rice milk and sugar into a saucepan, then add the chestnuts, stir, and bring to a boil. At this point, remove the pan from the heat and add the dark chocolate immediately.

Stir so that it melts completely, then add the ricotta. Stir again with a whisk and then place it in the fridge for 10 minutes.

Go back to the pastry and divide it into two parts, one larger than the other: Roll out the larger part on a lightly floured pastry board, to a thickness of about ¼ inch (4-5 mm). Use this disc to line a cake pan with an 8-inch (20-cm) diameter and trim around the edge with a knife. At this point, fill the crostata with the chestnut cream, leveling the surface well with a spatula.

Now roll out the other part of the pastry, again to a thickness of around ¼ inch (4-5 mm), lay it across the top of the cake pan, and trim around the edge. Next, using a dough scraper, stretch the pastry across so it's spread out well, and pinch it to make the two layers of dough stick together and seal it.

Bake on the middle rack of a conventional oven preheated to 180°C, for around 40 minutes. When it's finished baking, take the chestnut and chocolate tart out of the oven, let it cool, and then dust with powdered sugar and serve.

Italian Meringue
Ingredients:
- **Sugar (250 g)**
- **Water (50 ml)**
- **Egg whites (125 g)**
- **Fine salt 1 pinch**

To make Italian meringue, pour the water into a heavy-bottomed saucepan, add the sugar and cook over low heat, stirring to dissolve it. Immerse the food thermometer, which will indicate the temperature to be reached, i.e. 120° C. When the temperature of the syrup reaches 115° C, place the egg whites in a stand mixer equipped with a whisk (or use an electric blender) and whip them at medium speed. When the syrup has reached 120° C, lower the speed of the stand mixer (to prevent the syrup from dispersing on the walls of the bowl), pour half of the syrup into the egg whites and then increase the speed again. Wait a few seconds and keep pouring the syrup slowly, without pouring it directly onto the whisk. Continue to whip until the meringue has cooled down completely.

The meringue mixture must be very dense, smooth, and shiny and can only be cooked when it is completely cold. Pour the meringue into a pastry bag, choosing the nozzle according to your intended use, and form the meringues by squeezing the mixture on a baking tray lined with baking paper. You can create classic cloud meringues using a wide star-shaped nozzle.

You can form the shells by using a star-shaped nozzle, swirls by rotating while squeezing the meringue with a smooth nozzle. Draw the outline on baking paper with a pencil to make it easier. Bake the meringues in a static oven preheated to 60-70°C and let them dry for at least 4 hours leaving the oven door slightly ajar, in order to avoid any condensation that would prevent them from drying properly (humidity is a bitter enemy of meringues). Once cooked, turn off the heat and leave the meringues in the oven with the door ajar, and let them cool and dry completely for at least a couple of hours.

Orange donut
Ingredients:
- **Flour 00 250 g**
- **Sugar 170 g**
- **Butter 150 g**
- **Orange juice 130 g**
- **Orange zest 1**
- **Eggs 3**
- **Baking powder for desserts 16 g**

TO DUST
- **Powdered sugar to taste**

To prepare the orange donut, first melt the butter in a saucepan and let it cool. In the meantime, pour the sugar into a large bowl (or into the cup of a stand mixer fitted with a whisk), add the grated orange zest and the eggs, then start working with the electric whisk until you obtain a light and frothy mixture.

Sift the flour into the bowl and operate the whisk again to incorporate it. At this point, also pour in the orange juice and the warmed melted butter, always continuing to work with the whisk.

Finally, add the yeast and mix everything together. Pour the compound obtained into a donut mold with a diameter of 24 cm, which you will have buttered and floured.
Level the surface with a spatula and cook in a static oven at 170° for about 45 minutes. Once cooked (always do the toothpick test), let the donut cool in the mold before turning it out of the mold and dusting it with icing sugar to taste: your orange donut is ready to be enjoyed!

Crostata amalfitana (Lemon custard and sour cherry tart)
Ingredients:
- **Flour 00 2 300 g**
- **Eggs 2**
- **Butter 150 g**
- **Sugar 150 g**
- **Lemon peel 1**
- **Fine salt ½ tsp (3 g)**
- **Baking powder 1 tsp**

FOR THE CREAM
- **Black cherries in syrup 120 g**
- **Whole milk 370 g**
- **Egg yolks 4**
- **Sugar 150 g**
- **Flour 00 40 g**
- **Lemon peel 1**

TO GARNISH
- **Powdered sugar to taste**

To prepare crostata amalfitana (lemon custard and sour cherry tart), pour the flour, baking powder and the cold, chopped butter into the bowl of a food processor fitted with a spatula. Mix for a few minutes, then add the sugar. and the salt. Start the machine again to obtain a floury and crumbled mixture, then flavor with the rind of half a lemon and pour in the eggs, knead until the dough is compact and well-blended. Then put the dough on the work surface, knead it lightly with your hands into a loaf and cover with plastic wrap. Let it rest in the fridge for at least 1 hour.
In the meantime, prepare the custard: pour the yolks and sugar into a small saucepan, stir with a spatula and then add the flour.
Mix until smooth and thick, then set aside. Now pour the milk into a saucepan, flavor it with lemon zest and heat it on the stove.
When it starts to boil, pour a small amount on the egg mixture, stirring with a spatula, then add the rest and blend. Transfer the saucepan over the heat and let the cream thicken over medium heat, stirring continuously, until it is creamy and thick. Transfer the cream into a bowl, fill a larger bowl with ice cubes and place the cream on top.

Cover it with plastic wrap, this way it will cool down quickly without losing color and texture. Once it's cold, let it cool in the fridge for an hour. Once the necessary time has passed, take 2/3 of the shortcrust dough and roll it out with a rolling pin to a thickness of about 1/8 inch (3 mm). Transfer the sheet obtained to a 9 1/2-inch (24 cm) round mold, preferably with a removable bottom. Make the pastry stick well to the bottom and sides, then cut off the excess dough around the top.

Fill the tart with the cream and spread it evenly with a spatula. Drain the sour cherries from their syrup and scatter them over the cream.

Take the rest of the dough and the pieces of dough, roll them out with a rolling pin to a thickness of 1/8 inch (3 mm) and cut out strips about 1/3-inch (1 cm) wide. Lay the strips on the tart in a slanted direction, overlapping them to create a lattice pattern. Cut off the excess dough around the edges with a knife.

Once you have finished decorating, bake the tart in a static oven on the middle shelf at 180°C for 35 minutes. When it is cooked, remove the crostata amalfitana (lemon custard and sour cherry tart) from the oven, let it cool down, then unmold it and serve it dusted with powdered sugar.

Almond crumble (Sbrisolona)
Ingredients:
- **Flour 00 (200 g)**
- **Corn flour (100 g)**
- **Almond flour (200 g)**
- **Butter (200 g) - soft but still malleable**
- **Sugar (200 g)**
- **Eggs (100 g)**
- **Almonds (40 g) - (coarse to be chopped)**
- **Maraschino (30 g)**
- **Powdered yeast for sweets 2 tsp**
- **Vanilla bean 1**
- **Fine salt ⅓ tsp (2 g)**

To prepare the almond crumble you will need unpeeled almond flour . Place the flour 00, yeast and corn flour on the work surface with the almond flour. Create the classic mound. In the middle, place the butter, salt, eggs and sugar . Start working the ingredients placed in the middle with your hands. Add the maraschino and coarsely chopped raw almonds. Keep kneading with your hands, and add the seeds from the vanilla bean. Work the dry ingredients in a cross shape, bringing the ingredients from the outside to the inside, handling and mixing them with the rest.

You will obtain a homogeneous consistency in a few moments. Now transfer the dough to a baking sheet lined with baking paper and push it down with your hands. Place in the freezer to let the dough cool for at least 4 hours. As soon as the dough is rigid, you can prepare the crumbs. Place a cooling rack with 1/2 inch (1 cm) square holes on a bowl, cut the dough into pieces and crumble it by passing it through the grater 16. This way you will obtain big crumbs. Take a flared aluminum mold measuring 13 inches (32 cm) on the surface and 11 inches (28 cm) on the bottom; place a circle of baking paper inside and pour the crumbs in.

Spread them gently without pressing. Cook in a static oven preheated to (170°C) for 45 minutes until golden brown. Remove from the oven and let cool before removing it from the mold and serving.

Grandma's ring cake
Ingredients:
- Flour 00 (500 g)
- Sugar (300 g)
- Butter (250 g) - room temperature
- Whole milk (250 g) - room temperature
- Eggs 5 - room temperature
- Raisins 6 tbsp
- Candied orange 5 tbsp
- Oranges 1 - (the peel and the juice)
- Lemon peel 1
- Vanilla bean 1
- Powdered yeast for sweets 1 tbsp

FOR THE MOLD AND SOFTENED RAISINS
- **Butter to taste**
- **Flour 00 to taste**

FOR GARNISHING
- **Powdered sugar to taste**

To prepare grandma's ring cake, start by making sure that all the ingredients taken from the refrigerator are at room temperature, otherwise they will not bind together. Grate the lemon and orange peel and leave to one side, then cut the orange in half, squeeze out the juice and filter it in a container. Now rinse the raisins and leave them to soak in the orange juice.

In the meantime filter the flour and the yeast in a bowl, then stir. Before you continue, butter and flour a 9 inch diameter ring cake mold that is 3.5 inches tall and switch the oven on. Now that everything is ready, start with the preparation: place the softened butter in a bowl, add the citrus peel,
the seeds of the vanilla bean and beat with a whisk while gradually adding the sugar, a little at a time.

After around 5 minutes add the eggs one at a time 10 and continue to whisk all the while. Beat for a few more minutes until the mixture is frothy and homogeneous. Lastly, gradually add the flour and the yeast a little at a time, using a spoon. Continue to beat with the whisk all the while, gradually add and temper the milk. Switch off and remove the whisk. Drain the raisins and sprinkle with a little flour.

Remove any excess flour and add the raisins to the candied orange peel. Now pour 1/3 of the mix into the mold and spread half of the raisins and candied peel over it. Repeat with 1/3 of the mix and the remaining part of the raisins and peel.

Lastly, cover with the remaining 1/3 of the mix. Smooth the surface and the cake is ready to be baked. Bake in a static oven preheated to (180°C) for around 60 minutes; check that it is done by performing the toothpick test. Once baked, leave the grandma's ring cake to fully cool before removing from the mold and sprinkling with the powdered sugar to taste!

Snowflakes
Ingredients:
- Manitoba flour 250 g
- Flour 00 2 250 g
- Sugar 80 g
- Whole milk 300 g- at room temperature
- Fresh brewer's yeast 1 tbsp (10 g)
- Butter 2 tbsp (30 g) - at room temperature
- Fine salt ½ tsp (4 g)
- Vanilla bean ½

FOR THE WASH
- Egg yolks 1
- Whole milk 1 tbsp (15 g)

FOR THE RICOTTA FILLING
- Cow's milk ricotta cheese 150 g
- Fresh liquid cream 150 g
- Powdered sugar 3 tbsp (25 g)
- Lemon peel ½

FOR THE MILK FILLING
- Whole milk 200 g
- Sugar 60 g
- Cornstarch 2 ½ tbsp (20 g)
- Wildflower honey ½ tbsp (10 g)
- Vanilla bean ½

To make the snowflakes, first dissolve the yeast in the milk at room temperature. Then combine both flours, the milk containing the dissolved yeast, sugar, and the seeds taken from half a vanilla bean in the bowl of a stand mixer. Knead everything at medium speed for a couple of minutes to form a smooth mixture. When the dough starts to stick to the dough hook, add the soft butter a little at a time.

Start the mixer again. When the butter is nicely absorbed, add the salt and carry on working the dough until it's well-blended, which will take about five minutes.

Then transfer the dough to a lightly floured surface and roll it into a ball with your hands. Transfer back to the bowl of the stand mixer, cover with plastic wrap and leave to leaven for about one and a half hours at room temperature (25-26°C).

The dough will not double in volume during this time, but it will grow a little. Transfer to a work surface, take a portion, and cut it into (30 g) pieces. You should have 28 pieces in total by the time you've used up all the dough.

Shape each portion by rolling it on the work surface to make a perfect ball. Gradually place the balls on a baking sheet lined with parchment paper, spacing them well apart to leave room for them to expand a little more. Cover with plastic wrap and leave to rise for another hour and a half, again at room temperature.

Meanwhile, prepare the ricotta filling. Pour the whipping cream into a bowl and whip with a hand mixer until stiff, then place in the fridge. In another bowl, soften the ricotta using a spatula (or whisk), then add the powdered sugar and the grated lemon peel, and carry on beating until the mixture is smooth and even. Now add the ricotta to the whipped cream that cooled in the refrigerator, and fold into the mixture using the spatula, working from the bottom up. When the ricotta filling is ready, cover the bowl with plastic wrap and keep it in the refrigerator. Now make the milk filling. Pull the milk and sugar into a small saucepan. Place on the heat and stir to dissolve the sugar. Add the honey and the seeds from the vanilla bean.

Then add the cornstarch, stirring with a spatula to dissolve and beating continuously with a whisk to prevent lumps from forming. Cook the sauce for a few minutes until it thickens enough to coat the spatula.

Transfer to a wide, shallow bowl, cover with plastic wrap, and leave to cool, first at room temperature, then in the fridge. When the balls have risen, beat the egg with the milk for the wash in a small bowl and gently brush the surface of the balls with the resulting mixture. Bake in a conventional oven preheated to 180°C for about 18 minutes, until the balls are golden brown. In the meantime, take the milk filling, which will now be cold, and beat with a whisk until smooth.

Add to the ricotta filling and stir gently from the bottom upwards to ensure it does not separate. Transfer the mixture to a pastry bag with a long soft plain piping ti. Place back in the refrigerator until ready to use. As soon as the snowflakes are golden brown, take them out of the oven and let them cool down. Then use a plain piping tip to gently pierce the base and squirt in the filling, squeezing the pastry bag continuously. Transfer one by one to a baking sheet, then dust with powdered sugar before serving.

Bonet

Ingredients:
- Macaroons 200 g
- Bitter cocoa powder 35 g
- Yolks 1
- Whole milk 500 g
- Sugar 150g
- Eggs 4
- Salt up to 1 pinch
- Liqueur 2 tbsp

FOR THE CARAMEL
- Sugar 150g
- Water 50 g

TO DECORATE
- Macaroons to decorate q.b.

To prepare the bonet, start with the caramel: pour 50 g of water into a saucepan, then 150 g of sugar, heat over the heat without stirring, until the mixture turns amber. Once ready, pour the caramel into a 22x8 cm loaf pan and keep it aside.

Pour the eggs, yolk and sugar into a bowl, mix with a whisk.

Sift the cocoa, add a pinch of salt, then crumble the amaretti biscuits. Flavor with the liqueur, then pour in the milk, stirring several times. The dough is ready.

Pour everything into the mould. Cook in a bain-marie in this way: take a large baking dish that can hold the bonet mold, then fill it with water enough to reach 2-3 cm from the base of the mold. Place in the oven and bring to a temperature of 150°, static mode. Once at temperature, open the oven and insert the bonet mold into the pyrophile. Then cook for about 50-60 minutes. Once ready, open the oven and carefully remove the mold from the pan.

Let cool completely at room temperature. Once cold, to make it easier to unmold the bonet, heat the base just barely (with a torch, a lighter or even on gas if you have no alternative), be careful not to bring the flame too close and it takes just a few seconds: turn it over a cutting board or platter. Decorate with whole amaretti biscuits and serve your homemade bonet immediately.

Almond pastes
Ingredients:
- Whole peeled almonds 250 g
- Sugar 250 g
- Egg whites 2
- Almond flavoring ½ tsp

TO GARNISH
- Candied cherries to taste
- Whole almonds to taste

To prepare the almond paste, place the peeled almonds and sugar in a mixer fitted with steel blades and blend until they are reduced to a powder. Remember that this step should last a few minutes to prevent the almonds from overheating and releasing their oil.

Add the egg whites and the almond aroma and blend again to mix everything. The dough will be ready when it is compact but soft to the touch, so transfer it into a very resistant sac-à-few with a 10 mm lined nozzle.

Line a baking tray with parchment paper which you can fix better by squeezing a little dough into the 4 corners of the pan. Form small piles with a diameter of 3 cm and about 2 cm high and garnish part of them with the candied cherries cut in half and part with the whole almonds. At this point, place the dripping pan in the refrigerator and leave the almond paste to cool for at least 7 hours (or even better overnight), covered with plastic wrap. After this time, take the pan back and cook in a preheated fan oven at 180° for about 15 minutes, placing the pan on the middle shelf. Be careful not to overcook them, otherwise they won't be soft enough inside: they will still have to be a little pale. Once baked, let it cool and serve your almond pastries!

Pears Cake
Ingredients:
- **Williams pears 760 g**
- **Flour 00 225 g**
- **Cane sugar 170 g**
- **Very soft butter 120 g**
- **Eggs 2**
- **Whole milk 100 g**
- **Rum 15 g**
- **Lemon juice ½**
- **Baking powder for cakes 8 g**

TO DUST
- **Powdered sugar to taste**
- **Cinnamon powder to taste**

To prepare the pear tart, wash the pears and dry them. Then, without peeling them, remove the stem and base, divide them in half and remove the core with the help of a small knife.

Cut them into thin slices. In a bowl, combine the sliced pears and 50 g of brown sugar. Squeeze the juice from half a lemon
and wet the pear slices. Mix and add the rum too, then keep aside. Move on to the dough: pour 100 g of cane sugar into a bowl, add the very soft butter.

Work with the whisk for a couple of minutes, then add the eggs one at a time.

Combine the sifted flour and baking powder in a bowl, then always work with a whisk and when the flour and baking powder are almost completely absorbed, add the milk. Work again with the whisk to obtain a homogeneous mixture without lumps. Take 1/3 of the pears and keep it aside; pour the remaining 2/3 of pears into the mixture and mix. Grease a 22 cm diameter and 6.5 cm high springform pan and pour the mixture into it.

Decorate with the pear slices kept aside; sprinkle the surface with the remaining 20 g of brown sugar and cook in a preheated static oven at 180° on the central shelf for 30 minutes. Subsequently, without opening the oven, set the cooking for another 30 minutes in ventilated mode, always at 180°. Remove the pear cake from the oven and let it cool completely before unmolding it. Mix the icing sugar with ½ teaspoon cinnamon and sprinkle the pear cake on top before serving.

Stracciatella cake
Ingredients:
- Medium eggs 3
- Flour 00 200 g
- Corn starch 75 g
- Sugar 200g
- Seed oil 100 g
- Liquid fresh cream 100 g
- Dark chocolate 150 g
- Baking powder for desserts 16 g

To prepare the stracciatella cake, start by chopping the chocolate with a knife and keep it aside. Then go on to sift the powders, then pour the flour, cornstarch and baking powder into a container fitted with a strainer.

Continue breaking the eggs at room temperature in the cup of a planetary mixer fitted with a whisk and operate while pouring the sugar. Let it whip until the mixture has become clear and frothy, then add the sifted powders to the mixture. Add one spoonful at a time: then add the next one only when the previous one has been completely absorbed. Dilute by pouring the cream at room temperature
and when it's absorbed, slowly add the seed oil. As soon as the dough is ready, remove the cup from the planetary mixer and add the chopped chocolate, mix it delicately with a spatula with a movement that goes from the bottom to the top and then pour it into a buttered and floured 24 cm cake tin.

You just have to cook the dessert in a preheated static oven at 180° for 40 minutes. Once it has cooled, let it cool completely on a serving plate and finally serve your stracciatella cake. If you prefer, you can decorate with icing sugar.

Amor Polenta (Polenta sponge cake)
Ingredients:
- Eggs 1
- Egg yolks 2
- Sugar 2 ½ tsp
- Fine salt ¼ tsp
- Vanilla bean 1
- Lemon peel 1
- Almond flour (68 g)
- Flour 00 3 tsp
- Baking powder 1 tsp
- Fioretto corn flour 2.5 tsp
- Butter (125 g)

FOR THE BUTTER AND ALMOND MIX
- Butter 3 tsp
- Almond flour 2 tbsp

To make amor polenta, first prepare the butter and almond mix: put 1 tablespoon of butter and 2 tablepoons of almond flour in a mixer. Blend to obtain a homogeneous mixture and set aside. Then melt 125 g of butter over very low heat and let cool.

Whip the egg together with the sugar in a large bowl with electric whisks, then continue to whip the egg yolks and the seeds taken from the vanilla bean.

Add the grated rind of an untreated lemon, salt, and the almond and butter mix.

Once you have whipped the mixture, move on to the dry ingredients: pour the almond flour, baking powder, corn flour and 00 flour into a bowl, then sift it on a sheet of baking paper.

Add the sieved dry ingredients to the whipped mixture and incorporate them evenly. Pour in the melted butter and stir again gently to obtain a homogeneous and uniform mixture. Now butter and flour a traditional 8x3 inch (20x7.5 cm) amor polenta mold and pour in the mixture. Bake it in a static oven at 165° C for 60 minutes. Once cooked, let it cool before removing the mold, and sprinkle with powdered sugar: your amor polenta is ready to be enjoyed!

Part 3
Appetizer, snack and side

Mussels marinara
Ingredients:
- Mussels 1,5 kg (clean)
- Garlic 2 cloves
- Parsley to chop 1 tuft
- White wine 50ml
- Extra virgin olive oil 5 tbsp

In a non-stick pan put five tablespoons of oil and two crushed cloves of garlic (or whole if you wish to then remove them) and lightly brown. Then add the mussels, when they begin to open, pour in the white wine and add two tablespoons of chopped parsley. Finally, cover everything with a lid and let all the mussels open. When the mussels are all open, leave them on the fire for a few more minutes so that the sauce is further flavored and once ready, serve the mussels marinara immediately.

Eggplant Cutlets

Ingredients:
- Round black eggplants 500 g
- Coarse salt 50 g

FOR THE CLASSIC VERSION
- Eggs 1
- Breadcrumbs 50 g
- Salt up to 1 pinch

FOR THE VEGAN VERSION
- Chickpea flour 50 g
- Water 75 g
- Breadcrumbs 25 g
- Foil corn flour 25 g
- Black pepper 1 pinch
- Salt up to 1 pinch

FOR THE PECORINO VERSION
- Eggs 1
- Breadcrumbs 25 g
- Pecorino to grate 25 g
- Sweet smoked paprika 1 pinch
- Black pepper 1 pinch
- TO FRY
- Seed oil 800 g

To prepare the eggplant cutlets, start by preparing the eggplants: wash them, trim them on both sides and cut them into slices about 1.5 cm thick, until you get 12 slices. Arrange all the slices on a wire rack and sprinkle each slice with coarse salt. Let them drain, at room temperature, for about an hour. For this phase it is advisable not to let the eggplants rest for more than 1 hour and a half otherwise they will become soaked in salt.

After this time, wash each slice well under running water in order to remove the excess salt and dry them well with a clean cloth or kitchen paper. Then heat the seed oil in a saucepan, using a kitchen thermometer, and start preparing the vegan batter: pour the chickpea flour into a bowl, pour the water slowly, stirring with a whisk to prevent it from form lumps. Salt and pepper lightly and mix again.

Now in another bowl, pour the breadcrumbs and the foil cornmeal, and mix well to mix the two ingredients well. Take a slice of eggplant and dip it in the batter of water and chickpea flour and then in the mixture of breadcrumbs and cornmeal first on one side and then on the other. Do the same thing for 4 slices of eggplant taking care, after having breaded each slice, to place them delicately on a plate on which you have put some baking paper.

Now move on to the second breading, the classic one: beat an egg in a bowl and salt it lightly, then proceed to breadcrumb one slice of eggplant at a time by dipping it first in the beaten egg and then in the breadcrumbs.

Repeat the operation to make the double breading: after dipping the slice in the breadcrumbs, dip it again in the egg, and then again in the breadcrumbs. Do the same thing until you get 4 slices of eggplants, which you will place on the plate with the baking paper. It's the turn of the third breading: pour the Pecorino into a bowl and add the breadcrumbs. Add the sweet smoked paprika and a sprinkling of pepper (you can avoid the salt because the pecorino is already tasty on its own), then mix everything well. In a bowl, beat an egg and proceed to coat the eggplant slices with breadcrumbs, first dipping them in the egg and then in the mixture of breadcrumbs and Pecorino first on one side and then on the other. Also in this case you will make a double breading: then go back to dip the eggplant in the egg and then again in the breadcrumbs and cheese. Continue until you have 4 slices of eggplants with this last breading, always arranging them on the plate once breaded. At this point check the oil: when it has reached a temperature of 170 degrees you can start frying your eggplant cutlets. Start with cutlets with vegan breading, so that they don't come into contact with animal derivatives during frying.

Dip the eggplants in the oil four at a time, fry them for 2-3 minutes and turn them well on both sides with the help of tongs. Once they are perfectly browned, put them on a plate with kitchen paper, so that they lose the excess oil. Continue to fry all the other eggplant slices, those with the classic breading and those with Pecorino: they all have the same cooking time. Arrange them on a plate, keep them divided by type of breading and serve. Your eggplant cutlets are ready to be enjoyed!

Supplì on the phone
Ingredients:
- Rice 500 g
- Minced beef 150 g
- Mozzarella 200 g
- Dried mushrooms 50 g
- Medium eggs 2
- Tomato puree 400 g
- Meat broth 1 l
- Grana Padano PDO 120 g
- Half onions
- Butter + 50 g for creaming 30 g
- White wine 100ml
- Extra virgin olive oil 2 tbsp
- Salt up to taste
- Black pepper to taste

FOR BREADING AND FRYING
- Breadcrumbs to taste
- Eggs 2
- Peanut oil to taste

Melt the butter with the oil in a pan, add the chopped onion and the minced meat, then let it brown; add the previously soaked, squeezed and minced mushrooms.

Let it brown for another 5 minutes and then blend with the wine and add the tomato puree. Add salt and pepper and cook over medium heat until the sauce has reduced and thickened.

When the sauce is ready, add the rice and, stirring often, cook the rice adding, when needed, some meat broth until the rice appears dry and compact.

Turn off the heat and add the butter and grated parmesan; mix well and then add the two beaten eggs. Stir until all the ingredients are incorporated and blended well, then pour the mixture onto a large flat plate and let it cool completely.

In the meantime, cut the mozzarella into small pieces and put it to drain in a colander, so that it loses the excess water. When the rice is cold, form the supplì by taking a little of the mixture with wet hands and giving it an oval shape: insert a couple of small pieces of mozzarella inside and in the center of the supplì, then close well. Do this until you run out of ingredients.

Once you have obtained all the supplì, dip them in the beaten egg and then in the breadcrumbs, making sure that the breadcrumbs adhere to all sides.

Then fry the rice balls in abundant hot oil (at least 180°) turning them several times over the entire surface, which must be more than golden. The supplì must float in the oil, which must therefore be abundant. Put the rice balls on a sheet of absorbent paper to drain and serve piping hot.

Peppers with breadcrumbs
Ingredients:
- Red peppers 2
- Yellow peppers 2
- Extra virgin olive oil q.s.
- Stale breadcrumbs q.b.
- Pecorino to grate 40 g
- Capers 1 tbsp
- Oregano to taste
- Garlic 1 clove

To prepare the peppers with breadcrumbs, wash and dry the peppers well, cut them in half, remove the stalk and the internal seeds, then cut them into strips 2-3 cm wide. Cook the peppers in a pot with plenty of extra virgin olive oil for 15-20 minutes. In the meantime, prepare the crumb-based sauce: with the help of a mixer, chop the stale bread,
then transfer it to a bowl and add the grated pecorino, the capers, a clove of minced garlic and
the oregano. Mix well to mix all the ingredients, then add the mixture to the peppers and cook for 20 minutes over medium heat, covering with a lid. When the peppers are almost ready, remove the lid and let everything cook, raising the heat to toast the bread. The peppers with breadcrumbs are ready: let them cool down and serve them as a side dish, or as a tasty appetizer; they are also excellent eaten cold.

Potatoes with Tropea onions
Ingredients:
- **Potatoes 930 g**
- **Tropea red onions 240 g**
- **Extra virgin olive oil 60 g**
- **Salt up to taste**

First peel the potatoes, then cut them into slices about 3 mm thick. Then peel the onion and do the same thing: first cut it in half and then into slices less than half a cm thick.

Pour the oil into a pan, let it heat up then add the potatoes. Season with salt. Cover with the lid and cook for 8 minutes, without ever stirring or moving the pan. After the indicated minutes, move the lid, add the onions and cover again with the lid. Cook for another 20 minutes, shaking the pan from time to time to prevent them from sticking to the bottom.

Then remove the lid and continue cooking for another 15 minutes over medium heat. You won't have to stir the potatoes very often at this stage. To obtain well-intact potatoes you will only have to skip them a couple of times, otherwise you can mix them gently with a wooden spoon. When cooked, remove the potatoes with a slotted spoon and transfer them to a serving dish. It will not be necessary to use blotting paper. Serve the potatoes with onion while still hot.

Tramezzini
Ingredients:

INGREDIENTS FOR 8 COOKED HAM SANDWICHES
- Sliced Edamer 60 g
- Bread for sandwiches 170 g
- Pitted black olives 50 g
- Curly lettuce 30 g
- Copper tomatoes 80 g
- Sliced cooked ham 60 g
- Mayonnaise 50 g

INGREDIENTS FOR 8 TUNA SANDWICHES
- Capers 40 g
- Curly lettuce 30 g
- Copper tomatoes 80 g
- Pitted green olives 12
- Bread for sandwiches 170 g
- Tuna in oil 150 g
- Mayonnaise 50 g

INGREDIENTS FOR 8 VEGETARIAN SANDWICHES
- Bread for sandwiches 170 g
- Sliced Edamer 50 g
- Copper tomatoes 80 g
- Curly lettuce 30 g
- Medium eggs 1
- Pickled gherkins 30 g
- Mayonnaise 50 g

To make the ham sandwiches, start by preparing all the ingredients you will need to fill it: wash and clean a head of lettuce, divide it into leaves and set them aside, then take the tomatoes, wash them and cut them into thin slices. Finally, cut the black olives into rounds and put them in a small bowl.

At this point, start composing your sandwiches. Spread the mayonnaise on two slices of bread, then take one and arrange it on top, in order: the ham in slices, the salad leaves,
sliced tomatoes, more ham, sliced Edamer cheese
and finally the olives cut into slices. Cover with the other slice of bread, then wrap everything in plastic wrap and place in the refrigerator to rest for at least an hour. In this way the sandwiches will be further flavored and tastier.
After the necessary time, take your sandwich and cut it in half, so as to form two squares, then cut each square along the two diagonals, to give the classic triangle shape of the sandwich.

TUNA SANDWICHES

To make the tuna sandwiches, start by preparing the cream: drain well 50 g of tuna taken from the total dose and shell it with the help of a fork. Put the mayonnaise in a bowl, then add the tuna and mix everything with the help of a whisk, it must be a creamy mixture. At this point, take two slices of bread, spread them with the cream, and place a handful of capers on each side. On one of the two slices, place the salad leaves and tomato slices on top.

Now put the remaining drained tuna, the green olives cut in half and cover with the other slice of bread. Put the bread in the refrigerator to rest for about an hour, covered with plastic wrap, then proceed to cut it following the procedure described above.

VEGETARIAN SANDWICHES

To prepare the vegetarian sandwiches, spread two slices of bread with mayonnaise, then take one and place the salad leaves on top. Continue to compose the sandwiches by putting the sliced tomato, the sliced cucumber, the sliced Edamer cheese, then spread again with a spoonful of mayonnaise. At this point put the hard-boiled egg cut into slices and cover with the other slice of bread. Wrap everything in plastic wrap 6 and leave to rest in the refrigerator for about an hour. After the necessary time, proceed to cut the sandwich as described above.

Zucchini with mint and vinegar
Ingredients:
- Zucchini (500g)
- Extra virgin olive oil (70g)
- White wine vinegar 3 tbsp
- Garlic 2 cloves
- Mint to taste
- Fine salt 1 tbsp
- Black pepper to taste

FOR FRYING
- Vegetable oil to taste

To make your zucchini with mint and vinegar (alla scapece), start by topping, tailing, and washing the zucchini. Next, cut them into rounds approximately 3 mm thick, transfer to a colander, and sprinkle with 1 tbsp of fine salt. Stir and cover with a dish towel, leaving the liquid to drain from the vegetables for at least 30 minutes.

After 30 minutes, rinse the zucchini under running water, then leave them to dry thoroughly on a dish towel. Next, prepare the zucchini dressing: Pour the oil into a bowl, add the white wine vinegar, add salt, emulsify it all together, then add the previously washed and chopped mint, the peeled and chopped garlic cloves, pepper to taste, and mix everything together.

Heat some oil for frying and fry a few zucchinis at a time, for around 5 minutes, until golden brown. In the meantime, prepare a wide, shallow casserole dish in which you'll spread the first layer of dressing.

As you drain the zucchini, pour them hot into the casserole dish, and layer them with alternating layers of the dressing. Serve your zucchini alla scapece once they've cooled completely (at least a couple of hours) or even while still slightly warm.

Carrots Milk
Ingredients:
- Carrots 800 g
- Whole milk 300 ml
- Salt up to taste
- Water 150ml
- Butter 30 g
- Flour 00 20 g
- Nutmeg powder ¾ tsp

To prepare the carrots with milk, wash and peel the carrots, then cut them into slices about 3 mm thick.
Melt 30 g of butter in a large, shallow saucepan, then add the flour, mix and then add the milk, water,
the nutmeg and salt: mix well with a whisk to avoid the formation of lumps and as soon as the liquid in the pot starts to boil, add the sliced carrots. Let the carrots cook in milk gently until they are tender but not mushy and the cooking liquid has thickened and dried a lot. Before the end of cooking, season with salt if necessary and then serve the carrots in hot and creamy milk. If you like, you can sprinkle them with chopped parsley.

Neapolitan pasta fritters
Ingredients:
- Bucatini pasta (500 g)
- Cooked ham (150 g) - (for chopping into cubes)
- Frozen peas (75 g)
- Garlic 1 clove
- Extra virgin olive oil to taste
- Peanut seed oil (1.5 l)
- Fine salt to taste

FOR THE BÉCHAMEL SAUCE
- Flour 00 (200 g)
- Butter (130 g)
- Whole milk (1 l)
- Fine salt to taste
- Nutmeg to taste
- **FOR THE BATTER**
- Water 1 (325 g)
- Flour 00 1 (200 g)

To make the Neapolitan pasta fritters, start with the béchamel sauce. Heat the milk in a saucepan, and in the meantime, melt the butter in a pot. As soon as the butter has melted, add the flour all at once and whisk until the mixture thickens up. Don't worry if it condenses quickly. Next, dilute with the hot milk, pouring it in a little at a time and making sure that no lumps form. Once the mixture is well diluted, add salt and nutmeg and continue cooking until you get a nice thick cream. Transfer it to a bowl, cover with plastic wrap, and leave to cool at room temperature.

Move on to the filling Cut the ham into slices, strips, and finally ¼-inch (0.5-cm) cubes. Next, crush a clove of unpeeled garlic and put it in a frying pan together with a drizzle of oil. Allow the flavor to develop for a few minutes over medium heat, then add the ham cubes and peas.

Sauté for a minute or two, season with salt, remove the garlic, and set aside. At this point, you can cook the pasta in salted boiling water; be sure to drain it when there are 2-3 minutes of cooking time left. Pour the pasta out onto a lightly greased work surface, then add a drop of oil and mix it in quickly so you don't burn yourself. Cut the pasta roughly with a knife and leave to cool.
When all the ingredients are at room temperature, pour the béchamel sauce over the pasta. Mix together well with your hands and then take a handful. Make a little indentation in the middle of the pasta mixture and fill with a handful of peas and ham. Close the pasta around the filling and then press it down inside of a 3-inch (8-cm) food ring mold to form a medallion. Alternatively, you can also shape the medallions by hand. Carefully lift the medallions using a small spatula and arrange them on a tray lined with parchment paper. Remove the ring mold and repeat the process so you get around 15 medallions. Once they're all ready, leave to cool in the fridge for at least an hour or until they've firmed up nicely.
Next, heat the oil for frying and prepare the batter. Pour the flour into a bowl and slowly add the water to it while whisking. Season with salt and continue whisking until you get a smooth batter without any lumps, and then dip the first medallion in.
Drain the excess batter and plunge into the boiling oil. You can add other medallions, too, but no more than 2 or 3 at a time. This way, the oil temperature will remain hot at 350°-375°F (180°-190°C). After 3-4 minutes, they should be nice and golden, so drain on paper towel and continue cooking the others. Now your Neapolitan pasta fritters are ready! Buon appetito!

Cauliflower balls
Ingredients:
- Cauliflower 650 g
- Potatoes 150 g
- Medium eggs 1
- Grana Padano PDO to grate 50 g
- Thyme 4 sprigs
- Salt up to taste
- Black pepper to taste

FOR BREADING AND FRYING
- Breadcrumbs 130 g
- Medium eggs 2
- Peanut oil 700 g

FOR THE ACCOMPANYING SAUCE
- Sour cream 250 g
- Chives 5 threads

To prepare the cauliflower balls, start with the potato: rinse it and then boil it for about 30-40 minutes depending on the size (you can shorten the time using a pressure cooker). In the meantime, proceed to cleaning the cauliflower: remove the outer leaves, the part of the stem and remove the florets with your hands.
Then separate them further always with your hands. Put a pot full of water on the fire and when it starts to boil, add the cauliflower and boil it for about ten minutes.
After 10 minutes, drain the cauliflower well and let it cool. At this point, transfer it to the container of a mixer equipped with blades and operate the blades until the cauliflower is reduced to a cream. Then transfer it to a large bowl.
When the potato is cooked too, drain it and mash it directly in the bowl with the cauliflower cream (if you use a potato masher, there will be no need to peel it). Add the thyme leaves to the lightly beaten egg and mix everything together.

Then add the grated Grana Padano, salt and pepper and mix to make the mixture uniform.

At this point, take about 25 g of the mixture and form your cauliflower balls; gradually place them on a tray lined with parchment paper. You will get about 35. Now take care of breading the meatballs by first passing them in the egg

and then in the breadcrumbs, gradually placing them on another tray. Heat the peanut oil in a deep pan until it reaches a temperature of 170° (to be measured with a cooking thermometer) and start frying a few meatballs at a time,

until they are well browned; it will take a few minutes. Once cooked, drain them from the oil using a slotted spoon and transfer them to a plate lined with absorbent paper. Continue with the frying of the other meatballs. Then take care of preparing the accompanying sauce: finely chop the chives and add it to the sour cream placed in a bowl, together with a pinch of black pepper. Mix everything together and serve your sour cream together with the freshly fried cauliflower balls!

Stuffed mozzarella roll
Ingredients:
- **Mozzarella cheese 600 g**
- **Prosciutto crudo 90 g**
- **Cluster tomatoes 200 g**
- **Arugula 20 g**
- **Water 100 g**
- **Fine salt to taste**

To make this stuffed mozzarella roll, start by placing the mozzarella in a bowl (preferably one just a little bigger than the mozzarella), together with the water it comes in, and add more water until the mozzarella is completely covered. Then microwave at 900 W for 7 minutes to melt the mozzarella. In the meantime, wash and thinly slice the cluster tomatoes, and prepare the arugula and prosciutto slices. Once the mozzarella has softened, use a spoon to transfer it to a sheet of parchment paper. Place another sheet on top, then roll out the mozzarella with a rolling pin. This step should be done as quickly as possible, since mozzarella tends to solidify quickly, making it difficult to roll out. Try to obtain a thin rectangle a few millimeters thick and measuring around 14" x 10" (35 x 25 cm). Gently remove the upper sheet of parchment paper, season with salt , and fill the rectangle with the sliced prosciutto.

Next, dress with the slices of cluster tomato and the arugula, and finally add another layer of sliced prosciutto. Using the parchment paper to help you, roll the whole thing up, holding tightly as you roll up the filling. Once ready, leave the roll to rest in the refrigerator wrapped in the parchment paper for at least 10 minutes. After this time, remove the parchment paper and cut the roll into rounds of about 1" (2.5 cm) thick. Your stuffed mozzarella roll is ready to be served as an appetizer!

Chickpeas Salad
Ingredients:
- Precooked chickpeas 300 g
- Yellow peppers 100 g
- Round courgettes 100 g
- Datterini tomatoes 100 g
- Red onions 80 g
- Cucumbers 50 g
- Feta cheese 60 g
- Mint 12 g
- Lemons 1
- Extra virgin olive oil 20 g
- Salt up to taste
- Black pepper to taste

To prepare the summer chickpea salad, start by washing and drying all the vegetables. Cut the pepper into thin strips. Cut the tomatoes in half.
Switch to the zucchini: trim it and cut it into slices; from these you get sticks. Trim the cucumber and, without peeling it, cut oblique slices that are not too thick.
Peel and cut the red onion into thin slices. Finally, prepare the salad dressing by pouring the fresh mint leaves together with the oil into the bowl of a mixer. Blend with the immersion blender
and add the lemon juice. Mix and transfer to a bowl. Drain the precooked chickpeas and pour them into a fairly large bowl, then add all the other ingredients one by one: the courgettes, red onions and peppers, cucumbers and cherry tomatoes. Then flavored with the grated lemon zest and seasoned with mint oil, salt and pepper to taste.
Stir and add the finishing touch: crumbled feta. One last stir and your summer chickpea salad is ready to be enjoyed!

Friggitelli in a pan
Ingredients:
- **Friggitelli peppers 600 g**
- **Garlic 2 cloves**
- **Extra virgin olive oil 25 g**
- **Water 25g**
- **Salt up to taste**

To prepare the friggitelli in a pan, first wash the friggitelli thoroughly under running water, leaving them whole and with the stem intact, and dry them with a sheet of kitchen paper. In a rather large pan, heat the extra virgin olive oil and brown the poached garlic for 3-4 minutes over moderate heat, then add the friggitelli. Briefly sauté the friggitelli over high heat, turning them often, then lower the heat, pour in the water and cover with a lid. Cook the friggitelli for about 10 minutes until they are wilted.

When the friggitelli are wilted, remove the garlic from the pan, add salt and turn off the heat: your friggitelli in the pan are ready to be served!

Lentil stew
Ingredients:
- Dried lentils (500 g)
- Tomato puree (1 l)
- Extra virgin olive oil to taste
- Carrots 1
- Celery 1 rib
- Yellow onions ½
- Garlic 1 clove
- Bay leaves 3
- Rosemary to taste
- Sage to taste
- Fine salt to taste
- Black pepper to taste

To make the lentil stew, start with the vegetable mixture. Trim the carrot and chop into cubes of around 1/8" (4 mm). Do the same with the celery and onion. Next, chop the onion again to cut it into even smaller dice. Tie the aromatic herbs together with some string to form a small bunch. Add a good glug of oil to a large pot, followed by the chopped vegetables and an unpeeled clove of garlic. Let this brown over low heat for 5-7 minutes, until the vegetables are very soft. Rinse the lentils well under running water, then add them to the pot, along with the bunch of herbs.

Now add the tomato purée. Fill the container the purée was in with water to rinse it, adding this water to the pot slowly until the lentils are covered. You'll need around 1 1/4 cups (300 ml) of water. Stir and then leave to cook over low heat, covered, for 45-60 minutes. While the lentils are cooking, you'll need to stir them every once in a while and add more water when they start to get dry; in total, you should add around another (500 ml) of water. After 45 minutes have passed, taste the lentils to check the consistency and whether you need to cook them for longer.

Toward the end of the cooking time, adjust with water as needed. Season with salt and pepper, remove the bunch of aromatic herbs and clove of garlic. Serve the lentils hot or warm, finishing off the plates with a drizzle of olive oil and chopped rosemary and pepper to taste.

Meatballs with cheese and eggs
Ingredients:
- Stale bread (crumb only) 75 g
- Pecorino cheese 200 g
- Eggs 2
- Parsley 10 g
- Black pepper to taste
- Salt up to taste

TO FRY
- Sunflower seed oil to taste

FOR THE SAUCE
- Tomato puree 300 g
- Extra virgin olive oil q.s.
- Salt up to taste
- Garlic 1 clove
- Basil to taste

First prepare the tomato puree. Pour a drizzle of oil into a saucepan, add a clove of garlic and let it brown for a couple of minutes over low heat. Then add the puree, mix and cook for about twenty minutes, always on a low flame and stirring occasionally.
In the meantime, prepare the dough for the cacio e ova balls. First, chop the parsley, then cut the stale breadcrumbs. Then transfer to a blender and blend until crumbs are obtained.
Transfer the bread crumbs into a bowl, add the grated Pecorino cheese 8 and the eggs.
Also add the parsley, pepper and salt.
Work vigorously with your hands for a few minutes, until you have obtained a homogeneous mixture. Form the meatballs, taking a portion of the dough and roll it up in your hands. In everything you will get.

Heat plenty of seed oil until it reaches a temperature of 160°-170°. Dip a few pieces at a time and cook for a couple of minutes, until they are golden brown. Drain and transfer them to a tray lined with kitchen paper.

At this point the sauce will also be cooked, add the meatballs inside, cook for another ten minutes and turn off the heat. Add some basil leaves, remove the garlic and serve your meatballs!

Sautéed cabbage
Ingredients:
- Cabbage 600 g
- Taggiasca olives 50 g
- Golden onions 50 g
- Extra virgin olive oil 3 tbsp
- Vegetable broth 100ml
- Salt up to taste
- Black pepper to taste

To prepare the cabbage in a pan, first peel the onion, chop it finely and keep it aside. Switch to the cabbage. Remove any more damaged outer leaves, wash it well under running water and cut it in half with a sharp knife.
Then cut it into strips, leaving out the hardest central part which will be thrown away. In a fairly large pan, pour the extra virgin olive oil and the onion. Let it wither over medium heat and add the cabbage.
Pour in the hot broth, cover with the lid and cook for 10 minutes, stirring several times. Remove the lid, season with salt.

Add some pepper, pour in the Taggiasca olives and continue cooking until the broth has evaporated. Serve the cabbage hot and with a generous sprinkling of pepper.

Zucchini Trifolate
Ingredients:
- **Zucchini 800 g**
- **Garlic 2 cloves**
- **Parsley to chop 2 tbsp**
- **Salt up to taste**
- **Black pepper to taste**
- **Extra virgin olive oil 40 g**

Wash and trim the zucchini, then dry them and cut them into slices at least 2 mm thick. Place the oil and garlic (1 or 2 cloves as you prefer) in a non-stick pan and brown them, remove it from the pan after 5 minutes and add the zucchini over high heat
covering the pan with a lid and stirring occasionally. A few minutes before the Zucchini Trifolati are ready, add the salt, stirring and the chopped parsley, mix well and serve.

Pasta

Spaghetti with tomato sauce
Ingredients:
- **Spaghetti (320 g)**
- **Peeled tomatoes (800 g)**
- **Extra virgin olive oil 2 tbsp**
- **Garlic 1 clove**
- **Basil to taste**
- **Fine salt to taste**

To make spaghetti with tomato sauce, start by preparing the sauce. Pour the extra virgin olive oil in a pan with the peeled and halved garlic clove, so you can remove the core and make the scent more delicate. Cook for 2 minutes over high heat, add the peeled tomatoes and salt.

Cover with a lid and cook for at least 1 hour over very low heat: the sauce should simmer gently. Mix it from time to time. After this time, remove the garlic and pass the tomatoes through a sieve to obtain a smooth and homogeneous puree.

Pour the sauce back into the pan, turn the heat to very low and add the basil leaves. After a few minutes, turn off the sauce and keep it warm. All you have to do now is cook the pasta in plenty of boiling salted water.

Drain the spaghetti al dente directly into the sauce and stir for a few moments over high heat to mix everything together. Your spaghetti with tomato sauce is ready, all you have to do is serve it, garnished with fresh basil to taste!

Pasta alla cenere (pasta with Gorgonzola and black olive sauce)
Ingredients:
- Rigatoni (320 g)
- Gorgonzola cheese (180 g)
- Black olives 40 g - (pitted)
- Whipping cream (120 g)
- Fine salt to taste
- Black pepper to taste

To make pasta alla cenere, start with the olives. Place them in an immersion blender cup and pulse to chop roughly. You could also chop them roughly using a knife.

Next, bring a pot of salted water to a boil to cook the pasta and, while you're waiting for it to boil, prepare the Gorgonzola. Remove the crust and cut the cheese into small cubes, then transfer to a pan together with the light cream.

Turn the heat to low and let the cheese melt, stirring constantly with a wooden spoon. Now cook the pasta; you'll need to drain it 2-3 minutes before the time stated on the package. As soon as the pasta is drained and ready, pour it directly into the cheese sauce. Add a ladleful of pasta cooking water and finish off the cooking in the pan, stirring frequently. Once the pasta is fully cooked, add the olive pâté and stir well to blend. Dish up your pasta alla cenere and serve with a good grind of black pepper. Buon appetito!

Pasta alla zozzona (Carbonara, amatriciana and cacio e pepe pasta)

Ingredients:
- Rigatoni (320 g)
- Guanciale (200 g)
- Sausage (250 g) - (pork only)
- Pecorino Romano cheese 9 tbsp (60 g) - to be grated
- Canned cherry tomatoes (350 g)
- Extra virgin olive oil to taste
- Egg yolks 4

TO MIX IN
- Pecorino Romano cheese 6 tbsp (40 g)

To prepare pasta alla zozzona, boil some water to cook the pasta and add salt. Take the guanciale, slice it and cut it into strips. Then remove the sausage from its casing
and cut it into chunks. Pour a drizzle of oil into a pan and add the sausage and guanciale, leaving them to brown for about 15 minutes over medium-low heat, stirring occasionally.

When they are well browned, add the cherry tomatoes to the pan and cook for another 10 minutes with the lid on.

Pour the egg yolks into a bowl and add 9 tbsp (60 g) of grated Pecorino Romano cheese. Mix them well to create a cream. Boil the pasta then add a ladle of the pasta's cooking water to the mixture of egg yolks and Pecorino cheese to thin out the resulting cream. Drain the pasta al dente and pour it into the pan with the dressing, mix well and remove from the heat. Pour in the mixture of Pecorino cheese and egg yolks, stir well, and mix in another 6 tbsp (40 g) of Pecorino before serving your pasta alla zozzona (carbonara, amatriciana and cacio e pepe pasta)!

Spaghetti and meatballs
Ingredients:
- Spaghetti (320 g)
- Tomato puree (700 g)
- Shallot (20 g)
- Garlic 1 clove
- Extra virgin olive oil 2 tbsp
- Fine salt to taste

FOR 42 MEATBALLS
- Pork (100 g) - minced
- Sausage (100 g)
- Mortadella (80 g) - in a single slice
- Wholegrain bread (50 g) - stale and crust-free
- Parmigiano Reggiano DOP cheese (50 g)
- Parsley 2 tsp (5 g) - finely chopped
- Eggs 1
- Nutmeg to taste
- Black pepper to taste
- Fine salt to taste

Start by making the sauce. Finely chop the shallot and brown on a low flame. Now peel the garlic too, add it to the shallot and cook for at least 6-7 minutes.

Add the tomato puree, then the salt and pepper; leave to cook for at least 40 minutes, with the lid on. As the sauce cooks, prepare the meatballs: Place the crust-free stale wholegrain bread in a mixer together with the mortadella.

Slice into the sausage with a sharp knife to remove the casing and finely chop it. Finely chop the parsley too.

Place the minced pork , soft part of bread with mortadella, sausage and the parsley in a large bowl. Add salt and pepper to taste.

Flavor with the grated nutmeg, add the egg and grated cheese.

Now mix the ingredients thoroughly by hand. Cover and leave to rest in the refrigerator for around 15 minutes. Then take the meatball mix and roll into 0.35 oz balls, you should make 42 in total. When the sauce is ready, remove the garlic and carefully add the meatballs to the sauce. Leave to cook for another 30 minutes, on a low flame.

Lastly, bring the water to the boil, add salt and then the pasta; drain when firm to the bite and finish cooking it in the sauce. Now your spaghetti and meatballs is ready.

Pasta with zucchini carbonara sauce
Ingredients:
- Farfalle pasta (320 g)
- Zucchini (200 g)
- Egg yolks 5
- Pecorino cheese (100 g)
- Extra virgin olive oil to taste
- Fine salt to taste
- Black pepper to taste
- **TO GARNISH**
- Pecorino cheese to taste

To make the pasta with zucchini carbonara sauce, first wash and trim the zucchini, then cut into sticks and dice. Meanwhile, bring a saucepan full of salted water to a boil, which you will use to cook the pasta. Heat some olive oil in a frying pan.

Add the zucchini and brown for around 6-7 minutes over high heat; they should remain crunchy. Pour the egg yolks and Pecorino cheese into a bowl and whisk.

Add one ladleful of cooking water from the pasta and stir to get a creamy mix. In the meantime, cook the pasta for the time stated on the package.

Season the browned zucchini with salt and pepper, and when the pasta is ready, transfer it directly into the frying pan using a slotted spoon. With the heat off, add the egg yolk and cheese mix.

Stir to combine, then serve the pasta with zucchini carbonara sauce, garnishing the dishes with Pecorino shavings to taste.

Pasta with green peas
Ingredients:
- Ditaloni Striped 320 g
- Whole fresh peas to be shelled 1 kg
- Fresh spring onion 100 g
- Extra virgin olive oil 30 g
- Grated Parmigiano Reggiano DOP 30 g
- Black pepper to taste
- Salt up to taste

To make the pasta and peas, boil water in a large pot and salt it when it boils: you will then need it to cook the pasta. Meanwhile, shell the peas and collect them in a bowl, then take the spring onion, remove the base, divide it in half lengthwise, then slice each half, in this way it will be more practical to cut it. Pour the olive oil into a pan, let it heat up and then pour the freshly sliced spring onion, pour over a ladle of the pasta cooking water and let it simmer for about 10-15 minutes or until it becomes soft (if it dries out too much add more cooking water). Once the spring onion has stewed, add the shelled fresh peas, salt and pepper and add another ladle of cooking water; cook for about 10 minutes.

Now boil the pasta for just 5 minutes (or half the time indicated on the package) because it will then finish cooking in the pan with the peas. Then drain the pasta with a slotted spoon directly into the pan with the peas, cook the pasta by adding the cooking water little by little, taking care to wait for the liquid to be well absorbed before adding more. It will take about 5 minutes. When cooked, flavor with grated Parmigiano Reggiano, stir to flavor, salt and pepper to taste. Your pasta and peas is ready, serve it piping hot!

Salmon pasta
Ingredients:
- **Egg Tagliatelle 320 g**
- **Smoked salmon 400 g**
- **Liquid fresh cream 200 g**
- **Brandy 50 g**
- **Golden onions ½**
- **Parsley to be chopped q.b.**
- **Extra virgin olive oil q.s.**
- **Black pepper to taste**

To prepare the pasta with salmon, first bring a pot of water to the boil to cook the pasta and add salt to the boil. Cut the salmon into strips; do not reduce the salmon into too small pieces otherwise they will fall apart in the pan. Peel and finely chop the onion, then chop the parsley as well.

Heat the oil in a pan and fry the onion, then add the salmon and raise the heat. After sautéing the salmon for a few minutes, pour in the brandy and let it evaporate completely, then turn off the heat. At this point the water will have come to a boil, so add salt and cook the tagliatelle for the time indicated on the package. Meanwhile, pour the cream into the pan with the salmon, always with the heat off. When the tagliatelle are cooked, drain and transfer them directly to the pan.

Turn the heat back on and mix everything well to reduce the sauce. Complete with chopped parsley and a grind of pepper and serve your smoked salmon pasta right away!

Tagliatelle with radicchio and speck
Ingredients:
- **Tagliatelle pasta (250 g)**
- **Radicchio (400 g)**
- **Speck (180 g)**
- **Fresh liquid cream 7 tbsp**
- **Tomato puree 3 tbsp**
- **Shallot (30 g)**
- **Extra virgin olive oil 2 tbsp**
- **Fine salt to taste**
- **Black pepper to taste**

To prepare tagliatelle with radicchio and speck, start by chopping all the ingredients you'll need. Start with the shallot: peel and finely chop it with a knife. Then cut the speck into sticks of the same length and thickness, so that they cook evenly. Lastly, prepare the radicchio by removing the outermost leaves.

Cut it in half lengthwise, cut away the tough part of the stalk and then slice the radicchio into thin strips.

Leave the shallot to sweat on a low flame in a non-stick pan, with a drizzle of oil, for 4-5 minutes. Add the strips of speck and cook for another 4 minutes. Add the milk and the tomato puree.

Add salt and pepper to taste, cook for 6-7 minutes, to thicken. In the meantime, cook the pasta in boiling salted water, remove half way into the cooking time and finish cooking directly in the saucepan, together with the sauce. In this way you'll create a more intense flavor and enhance the creaminess of this dish.

Once cooked, add the radicchio julienne and stir. The tagliatelle with radicchio and speck are ready now, simply enjoy them while they're still piping hot!

Spaghetti with tuna
Ingredients:
- Spaghetti 320 g
- Tuna in oil (drained) 150 g
- Peeled tomatoes 400 g
- Extra virgin olive oil q.s.
- Salt up to taste
- Black pepper to taste
- Basil to taste
- Onions ½

To prepare spaghetti with tuna, start by heating a pot full of water on the stove, add salt to taste when it boils: it will be used for cooking the pasta. Drain the tuna fillet from the conservation oil. Meanwhile, peel the onion, slice it thinly. Heat the olive oil in a pan and add the sliced onion. Let it dry over a low heat for a few minutes, stirring frequently; fray the tuna with your hands and add it to the pan when the onion is softened and let it brown for a couple of minutes, stirring constantly. Now, mash the peeled tomatoes with a fork and pour them into the pan with the tuna; let the sauce cook for about 10 minutes.

Meanwhile, boil the spaghetti, cook them al dente: in the cooking time of the pasta, the sauce will also be ready. Drain the spaghetti directly into the pan with the tuna, season with ground pepper, turn off the heat and add fresh basil leaves. Mix and serve your tuna spaghetti piping hot!

Spaghetti with anchovies and breadcrumbs
Ingredients:
- Spaghetti 320 g
- Anchovies in oil 30 g
- Extra virgin olive oil 20 g
- Breadcrumbs 70 g
- Garlic 3 cloves

To prepare the spaghetti with anchovies and breadcrumbs, put a pan of water on the stove and bring to the boil (you don't have to add salt): it will then be used to cook the pasta. Meanwhile, pour 10 g of extra virgin olive oil into a pan, then add the whole peeled garlic cloves and the anchovy fillets drained from the conservation oil. Take out a ladle of hot water and pour it into the pan, so you can dissolve the anchovies in the best possible way. It will take about 10 minutes so stir often.

Meanwhile, pour 10 g of extra virgin olive oil into a separate pan, then add the breadcrumbs to toast it and mix everything until the crumbs are golden brown; keep aside the breadcrumbs.

At this point, cook the pasta in the now boiling water; you can add very little coarse salt if you prefer, since anchovies are very tasty. Cook the spaghetti for only 5 minutes. Once the time has elapsed, remove the garlic cloves from the sauce pan and drain the pasta by dipping it directly into the pan.

Risotto the spaghetti by pouring the cooking water as needed, stirring occasionally to cook evenly. When the pasta is ready, turn off the flame and add a part of the panure and then mix. If necessary, add a little more cooking water, then serve your spaghetti with anchovies and breadcrumbs and garnish with a final sprinkling of breadcrumbs.

Pasta With Swordfish
Ingredients:
- Linguine Pasta 320 g
- Garlic 1 clove
- Taggiasca olives 70 g
- Swordfish 300 g
- Cherry tomatoes 250 g
- Extra virgin olive oil 40 g
- Salt up to taste
- Black pepper to taste

To prepare the pasta with swordfish, start by washing the cherry tomatoes, then cut them into 4 parts and keep them aside. Take the swordfish steak, remove the skin using a sharp knife and divide the steak in half if it is too thick. At this point, first cut it into strips and then cut them into cubes of about 1 cm each.

Put a pot full of water, salted to taste, on the fire and bring it to the boil, it will be used for cooking the pasta. Pour the olive oil into a pan, add a clove of garlic and let it brown for a couple of minutes (if you prefer a more delicate flavour, you can poach it). Remove the garlic, add the tomatoes,
add salt and pepper and let the cherry tomatoes fry for a couple of minutes; then add a ladle of water (now hot) which will be used to cook the pasta and also add the pitted olives.
If the bottom gets too dry, add another ladle of cooking water and cook for another 2 minutes. Meanwhile, throw the spaghetti into the boiling water and while the pasta is cooking, add the swordfish cubes to the sauce, mix everything together and cook for 5 minutes, adding another ladle of cooking water.
Drain the pasta al dente directly into the sauce and toss it together with the sauce before serving!

Pasta and potatoes
Ingredients:
- Ditalini 250 g
- Yellow-fleshed potatoes 700 g
- Thyme to taste
- Extra virgin olive oil 30 g
- Salt up to taste
- Black pepper to taste
- Shallot 40 g
- Rosemary to taste

To prepare the pasta and potatoes, first peel the potatoes, then wash and dry them carefully with a clean tea towel and cut them into cubes.

Clean the shallot and chop it finely, then chop the rosemary too. Boil a pot with plenty of water, to be salted when it boils, which will then be used to boil the pasta and to lengthen the sauce. Heat the extra virgin olive oil in a pan, add the chopped shallots and rosemary and let them brown for a few minutes, being careful not to burn them. Now add the diced potatoes and cook them, stirring often and adding a ladle of boiling water at a time when necessary; it will take about 20 minutes. When the potatoes are almost cooked, season with salt and pepper. In the meantime, the water for cooking the pasta will have come to a boil, so cook it, then drain it al dente directly into the pan with the potatoes,

mix well and finish cooking by adding a little pasta cooking water as needed: combining pasta and potatoes in the same pan will create a delicious cream thanks to the starch released by the pasta and potatoes. Finally, season with a few thyme leaves and pepper to taste, turn off the heat and season with a drizzle of raw extra virgin olive oil. Your pasta and potatoes is ready to be enjoyed while still hot!

Spaghetti with mussels
Ingredients:
- Spaghetti (320 g)
- Mussels (1.5 kg clean)
- Tomato puree (350 g)
- Extra virgin olive oil (70 g)
- Garlic 2 cloves
- Parsley 2 tbsp - minced
- Black pepper to taste

Pour the oil into a large saucepan together with a peeled clove of garlic and let it season for 1-2 minutes over low heat. As soon as it is hot enough, remove the garlic, and add the mussels and cover immediately. Cook for 2-3 minutes, so that the mussels can open completely. While cooking, shake the pan from time to time to stir. Before draining the mussels, place them in a sterile gauze-lined colander, which will act as a filter, collecting any impurities and sand residue.

Then shell them, keeping some for the final decoration of the dish if desired. Wash and dry the parsley, then finely chop it and pour it into a pan with a little oil and a clove of garlic, and cook for 1-2 minutes.

Add some shelled mussels, so as to further flavor the base and, after 1-2 minutes remove the garlic and add the tomato puree together with some cooking liquid from the clams.

Cover with a lid and leave to simmer for 20 minutes. In the meantime, put a pot with plenty of water on the stove, as soon as it boils, salt and cook the pasta. When the pasta has 2-3 minutes left to cook, add the shelled mussels and the previously drained spaghetti. Toss the pasta by adding the remaining liquid from the mussels and when it is cooked, add the pepper and make sure the salt is right. All you have to do now is plate and serve your spaghetti with mussels.

Paccheri with scampi and shrimp cream
Ingredients:
- Paccheri 320 g
- Scampi 600 g
- Prawns 450 g
- Leeks 1
- Parsley 1 sprig
- Water 2 litres
- Tomato puree 180 g
- Fresh chilli 1
- Shallot 1
- Garlic 1 clove
- Salt up to taste
- Black pepper to taste
- Extra virgin olive oil q.s.
- White wine 50 g

To prepare the paccheri with scampi and prawn cream, wash and slice the leek. Continue with cleaning the crustaceans. Remove the head, remove the shells and remove the intestine (the black thread present on the back of scampi and prawns). Keep the pulp aside.

In a saucepan, pour the leek, the shellfish heads and shells and a few sprigs of parsley.

Cover with water and boil for at least 1 hour and a half. When cooked, strain the fumet and pour it into a tall pan that will be used to cook the pasta.

In a pan, heat a drizzle of oil with a clove of garlic, add scampi and prawns, brown for a few moments for 2-3 minutes over high heat, then pour in the white wine.

Let it evaporate and then turn off the heat, remove the shellfish from the pan and set aside. Chop the pepper.

Peel and chop the shallot. Pour a drizzle of oil, the chilli pepper and the shallot into the pan in which you cooked the shellfish. Stew by lengthening with a ladle of broth.

Bring the comic to the boil and cook the paccheri here, you will have to adjust according to the instructions on the package. While the paccheri are cooking, pour the tomato puree into the pan with the sautéed vegetables. Salted.

Season with pepper to taste. Drain the paccheri directly into the pan with the sauce. Continue cooking the paccheri.

Then take care of the cream: in a tall glass, pour half of the shellfish, a ladleful of stock and 40 g of oil.

Blend everything with the immersion blender to obtain a cream. Add the shellfish cream.

Finally add the remaining prawns and scampi. Season with chopped fresh parsley and serve the paccheri with scampi cream and hot prawns.

Pasta Alla Carrettiera
Ingredients:
- Spaghetti 500 g
- Pecorino (to be grated) 200 g
- Parsley 1 sprig
- Fresh chilli 1
- Garlic 1 clove
- Extra virgin olive oil q.s.
- Coarse salt to taste

To prepare the pasta alla carrettiera, pour the water into a large saucepan, add salt to taste and bring to the boil. Then chop a sprig of parsley and fresh chilli.

Peel the garlic clove, remove the internal green sprout and mince it; then grate the Pecorino.

In a large bowl, pour the minced garlic and chilli pepper, plenty of olive oil and salt to taste.

Mix the emulsion with a fork. Meanwhile, when the water is boiling, boil the spaghetti, then drain them al dente, reserving the cooking water, and put them back in the bowl with the oil, garlic and chilli pepper mixture.

Quickly mix the spaghetti and add the grated pecorino and a ladle of cooking water.

Add the parsley, mix again and serve the pasta alla carrettiera piping hot.

Main Course

Risotto with porcini mushrooms and saffron
Ingredients:
- Porcini mushrooms 400 g
- Saffron 1 sachet
- Vegetable broth 1 l
- White onions 60 g
- Rice 320 g
- Grana Padano PDO 150 g
- Garlic 3 g
- Parsley to be chopped 5 g
- White wine 60 g

To prepare the porcini and saffron risotto, start making the vegetable broth; once ready, dedicate yourself to cleaning the porcini mushrooms. With the help of a small knife, remove the excess earth from the stem, then clean them with a damp cloth. At this point cut the porcini mushrooms into thin slices.

Pour the oil into a pan, add the garlic clove and let it brown over a low heat. Add the porcini mushrooms and cook for a few minutes, stirring frequently and very gently so as not to break them. Towards the end of cooking, add salt, sprinkle with finely chopped parsley and continue cooking for another 5 minutes over low heat.

Keep the mushrooms aside and prepare the risotto. Peel the onion, chop it finely and transfer it to a pan together with a drizzle of oil. Let it brown gently, then add the rice and let it toast, stirring frequently.

Once the rice has changed colour, deglaze it with the white wine, add a ladle of stock and continue cooking, stirring often and adding more stock as needed. Pour the saffron into a glass and dilute it by adding a ladle of hot broth.

Add the saffron to the risotto only towards the end of cooking and keep stirring to mix it well. Once the rice is cooked, season with salt and pepper, turn off the heat, stir in the parmesan and finally add the porcini mushrooms. Stir once again and serve your risotto with porcini and saffron still steaming!

Asparagus Omelette
Ingredients:
- Asparagus 800 g
- Eggs 6
- Leeks 1
- Black pepper to taste
- Grana Padano PDO 3 spoons
- Smoked scamorza cheese 150 g
- Chives for chopping 1 tbsp
- Butter 40 g
- Extra virgin olive oil 3 tbsp
- Salt up to taste

To prepare the asparagus omelette, start by washing the asparagus, remove the white and harder part of the stem. Then boil them for about 15 minutes by placing them in salted water. When they are cooked, drain them and cut them into small pieces. Then clean the leek, removing the tougher outer leaves, wash it and cut it into thin slices, which you will place in a pan in which you have melted the butter.

Soften the leek, then salt and pepper and add the asparagus pieces; cook everything for a few minutes, until the asparagus no longer loses the cooking water. At this point add salt, then turn off the heat and let the vegetables cool down. Beat the eggs in a bowl, add the ground pepper, the grated cheese,
warm vegetables, diced smoked provola and chives (or parsley); mix the ingredients well together. In a non-stick frying pan, place the oil and heat it, then add the egg mixture and cook the omelette for 2-3 minutes on a cheerful but not high heat, then place a lid over the frying pan and lower the heat slightly so that even the inside of the omelette cooks evenly. When the sides of the omelette begin to become golden brown, turn it over with the help of the lid; also brown the other surface of the omelette and then slide it onto a serving plate. Serve immediately by dividing it into wedges.

Grilled Parmigiana
Ingredients:
- Eggplants 8
- Garlic 1 clove
- Mozzarella 400 g
- Pecorino to grate 100 g
- Parmigiano Reggiano DOP to grate 200 g
- Basil to taste
- Extra virgin olive oil q.s.
- Red onions ½
- Tomato puree 1,5 l

To make the grilled eggplants parmigiana, start by preparing the tomato sauce: wash, peel and cut the onion and garlic into cubes and fry them in four tablespoons of extra virgin olive oil. When they are golden, add the tomato puree and cook over medium heat until the sauce is quite thick. Finally, season with salt and add a few chopped fresh basil leaves, then turn off the heat and set the sauce aside.

Now take care of the eggplantss: trim them, wash them and cut them into slices about 1 cm thick, lengthwise, using a slicer if you have one, so as to obtain more regular slices of the same thickness (if you don't have one feel free to use a mandoline or a knife). Heat a non-stick plate very well and grill the eggplants for about 10 minutes.

Then grease a non-stick baking dish with extra virgin olive oil, then sprinkle the bottom with a few spoonfuls of sauce and start to compose a first layer of eggplant slices, arranged side by side, slightly overlapping. Pour more tomato sauce evenly over the eggplants,

sprinkle with the Parmigiano Reggiano and pecorino and finally cover with the slices of mozzarella. Once the first layer has been made, continue following the same procedure for the following layers as well, until all the ingredients are used up: arrange the eggplant slices,

the tomato sauce, the Parmigiano Reggiano and the pecorino cheese, the slices of mozzarella
and finally the eggplants again, and so on. The last layer must consist of only tomato and grated Parmesan. Lastly, add a drizzle of oil and place the grilled eggplant parmigiana to cook in a static oven at 180° for about an hour, or until the tomato has formed a golden crust. The grilled eggplant parmigiana is ready: let it rest for at least 10 minutes before serving, so it will compact a bit and can be cut and served more easily. Enjoy your meal!

Pumpkin lasagna
Ingredients:
- Green Lasagne egg pasta ½ lb (200 g) - (15 sheets)
- Smoked scamorza cheese 1 lb (400 g)
- Fior di latte mozzarella cheese ½ lb (200 g)
- Grana Padano DOP cheese 1 cup (100 g) - grated
- Extra virgin olive oil to taste
- Sage to taste
- Black pepper to taste

FOR THE BÉCHAMEL SAUCE
- Whole milk 1 ¼ cup (1 l)
- Butter ½ cup (100 g)
- Flour 00 ¾ cup (100 g)
- Nutmeg to taste
- Fine salt to taste

FOR THE PUMPKIN
- Pumpkin 4 lbs (1.8 kg)
- Garlic 3 cloves
- Rosemary to taste
- Fine salt to taste
- Black pepper to taste
- Nutmeg to taste
- Extra virgin olive oil 2 tbsp (25 g)

To make the pumpkin lasagna, start with the béchamel sauce. Pour the milk into a saucepan and add the nutmeg, salt, and black pepper. Bring to a boil.
In the meantime, add the butter cut into cubes in another large pot and let it melt. Once the butter has melted, add the flour all at once. Stir quickly with a whisk until you get a nice golden roux. Next, add the warm milk, continuing to whisk. Cook until the béchamel has thickened, then set aside. Now move on to the pumpkin: Peel it and remove the inner seeds. Then cut it into ½-inch (1-cm) cubes. You should end up with nearly 850 g of cubes.

Next, add some oil to a pot along with the chopped sprig of rosemary, a peeled, crushed garlic clove and add this to the pot, too. Allow the flavors to develop over medium heat and then add the pumpkin cubes. Season with salt, pepper, and nutmeg. Stir well, let the pumpkin brown and then cover with a lid. Lower the heat and leave to cook for 15-20 minutes. There's no need to add water or broth because the pumpkin will release its own water, which will be enough to soften it, although remember to check to make sure it doesn't dry out too much due to the heat being too high. It's a good idea to stir it once in a while, in any case. The pumpkin will be nice and soft once it's cooked: If you can mash it easily with a wooden spoon, that means it's ready. While the pumpkin is cooking, cut the scamorza cheese into small cubes.

Then do the same thing with the fiordilatte cheese. As soon as the pumpkin is ready, pour half of it into the béchamel and mix well. Now assemble the lasagna: Pour a thin layer of béchamel and pumpkin into a 9x13-inch (20x30-cm) baking dish, then cover with 3 sheets of lasagna arranged side by side, and finally add another layer of pumpkin béchamel. Add some of the diced scamorza, then some of the mozzarella, a sprinkling of Grana Padano, and some diced pumpkin. Cover with another layer of lasagna sheets. Repeat these steps until you've made 5 layers.
Cover the final layer of pasta well with béchamel, cheese, and pumpkin, finishing off with some sage leaves. Add some pepper, a drizzle of oil, and cook in a conventional oven preheated to 180°C, for around 30 minutes. If the surface of the lasagna doesn't look very golden toward the end of the cooking time, put it under the broiler for a few minutes. Let your pumpkin lasagna rest for a few minutes between taking it out of the oven and dishing it up.

Cheesy rice-stuffed eggplant
Ingredients:
- Eggplant 900 g
- Carnaroli rice 300 g
- White wine 3 tbsp
- Shallot 1
- Extra virgin olive oil 2 ½ tbsp
- Tomato puree 400 g
- Coarse salt 1 pinch
- Vegetable broth 500 g
- Parmigiano Reggiano DOP cheese 150 g
- Scamorza (provola) cheese 120 g
- Basil to taste
- Fine salt 1 pinch
- Black pepper 1 pinch

FOR FRYING
- Peanut seed oil 800 g

To prepare your cheesy rice-stuffed eggplant, first make the vegetable broth that you will need later on for the rice. Meanwhile, prepare the eggplants by washing them, drying them with paper towel, trimming them, and cutting them in half lengthwise. Take a small knife with a sharp blade and make an incision between the skin and the flesh. Continue making this incision, following the outline of the eggplant and applying slight pressure to separate the flesh from the skin without breaking it. Cut the flesh into cubes and fry them in plenty of hot oil. The recommended temperature for dry frying is 340-350°F (170-180°C) (use a thermometer to measure this). Once the eggplant cubes are nicely browned, drain them and place them on a paper towel. Salt to taste. Fry the eggplant skins that you put aside earlier separately in the peanut oil. As soon as they're golden brown, drain them on a tray using paper towels.
Set the eggplants aside while you prepare your rice. Finely chop the shallot and gently fry in a pan with the oil. Once it has softened, add the rice and toast for a few minutes, stirring frequently.

Once the rice has changed color, deglaze with the white wine, then add the tomato puree and a pinch of salt. Stir, then add the hot broth a little at a time until the rice is cooked. This should take around 20 minutes.

Once the rice is ready, add the Parmigiano Reggiano cheese, reserving around 50 g to sprinkle over the eggplant. Stir, then transfer the rice to a bowl. Tear the basil leaves and add them together with the eggplant cubes to the bowl.

Arrange the fried eggplant skins in a casserole dish and start layering your filling. First, add 1 tablespoon of rice, then a slice of scamorza cheese, followed by another tablespoon of rice.

Finish by sprinkling the eggplant with the reserved Parmigiano Reggiano cheese and broil at 460°F (240°C) for around 4-5 minutes. Remove from the oven and serve your cheesy rice-stuffed eggplant hot.

Four-cheese dumplings
Ingredients:
- **Gnocchi 500 g**
- **Gorgonzola cheese (150 g)**
- **Parmigiano (100 g)**
- **Fontina cheese 3 ½ oz (100 g)**
- **Emmentaler cheese 3 ½ oz (100 g)**
- **Heavy cream 1 cup (250 g)**
- **Black pepper to taste**

Cut the Gorgonzola cheese into small pieces. Do the same with the Parmigiano, Fontina and Emmentaler cheese. Heat the cream in a saucepan, then pour all the cheeses in chunks and cook over low heat for 20 minutes, stirring frequently to prevent lumps from forming and to help the cheese melt.

Once the 4-cheese sauce is ready , you can boil the gnocchi in plenty of water; cook them for 2-5 minutes and as soon as they rise to the surface, drain them with a skimmer and pour them into the pan with the 4-cheese sauce. Mix very gently so as not to break them, season with black pepper to taste and serve immediately your four-cheese gnocchi.

Ligurian-style stuffed zucchini
Ingredients:
- Zucchini (700 g)
- White onions (60 g)
- Eggs 2
- Stale bread (40 g)
- Salted capers 1 tbsp
- Pine nuts 2 ½ tbsp
- Parmigiano Reggiano DOP cheese (50 g) - for grating
- Extra virgin olive oil 2 tbsp
- Black pepper 1 pinch
- Anchovies 2 tsp
- Whole milk (60 g)
- Tuna in oil (150 g) - drained
- Thyme to taste
- Breadcrumbs (60 g)

To prepare Ligurian-style stuffed zucchini, first wash the zucchini and boil them according to their consistency: if they are firm, you can leave them in boiling water for about 6-7 minutes. If they are a bit soft, then you can reduce the time by 1-2 minutes. Drain the zucchini and put them in a bowl with ice so they cool quickly without losing the beautiful bright green color. When they are cold, remove the ends of the zucchini, then cut them in half lengthwise and empty them with a corer; set them aside for a moment. In the meantime, cut the stale bread into cubes.

Pour it into a bowl and add the milk, then let it soften. Clean and cut the onion first horizontally, and then vertically. Then chop finely and move to the stove.

Heat the oil together with the onion and anchovies in a frying pan, let the anchovies melt, stirring often with a spatula, then add the zucchini pulp. Toss for a few minutes on high heat and transfer it to a bowl. Meanwhile, toast the pine nuts in another pan, ensuring that they do not burn.

Now that everything is ready, prepare the dough: in the blender pour the drained tuna, toasted pine nuts and the washed capers. Add the soaked bread and blend it all together until a homogeneous mixture is obtained. Add the mixture to the base of onions, anchovies and zucchini. Also add the grated Parmesan cheese, the beaten eggs and then season with salt, pepper and thyme, then add the breadcrumbs and mix well with a spatula. Grease a baking pan that can hold the zucchini then stuff them with the mixture and place them inside the baking pan.

Dust the surface with breadcrumbs and bake in a preheated oven in grill mode at 250° C for about 10-12 minutes. Once cooked, wait 5 minutes before serving your Ligurian-style stuffed zucchini.

Bean soup
Ingredients:
- Dried Borlotti beans (200 g)
- Dried cannellini beans (200 g)
- Black eyed peas (200 g)
- Cluster tomatoes (250 g)
- White onions (200 g)
- Carrots (150 g)
- Celery 2 stalks - (with the leaves)
- Garlic 2 cloves - unpeeled
- Tomato paste 2 tbsp
- Water 8 cups (2 l)
- Aromatic herbs to taste - (rosemary, thyme, sage, bay leaves, marjoram)
- Extra virgin olive oil to taste
- Fine salt to taste
- Black pepper to taste

To make bean soup, start by soaking the cannellini beans, borlotti beans and black eyed peas separately at room temperature for at least 8 hours. Drain the beans once the soaking time is up, place them in cold water and boil for 45 minutes, or until they are done. Place the black eyed peas in a separate saucepan because they may cook in less time, whereas the borlotti and cannellini beans can be cooked together. Prepare the rest of the ingredients in the meantime: dice the celery sticks, then finely chop the leaves. Dice the carrots too. Do the same with the onion and the tomatoes. Lastly, tie the aromatic herbs together with some cooking twine. Place the vegetables in a large saucepan with a drizzle of hot oil , then add the unpeeled garlic clove and the bouquet garnish .
Brown the vegetables for a couple of minutes, then add the black eyed peas, the cannellini and borlotti beans. Add the tomatoes too . Cover with water, then add the finely chopped celery leaves. Add salt, pepper, and bring to the boil. Now cook on a medium flame for around an hour.

Season with the tomato paste half way through the cooking time. Once cooked, remove the garlic and the bouquet garni, then add salt to taste if necessary. Serve your bean soup garnished with a drizzle of raw oil and a grating of pepper!

Stuffed artichokes
Ingredients:
- Artichokes 8
- Eggs 1
- Salt up to 5 g
- Black pepper 3 g
- Vegetable broth 100 g
- Breadcrumbs 50 g
- Parmigiano Reggiano DOP to grate 50 g
- Garlic 1 clove
- Parsley 2 g
- Ground beef 300 g
- Thyme 2 sprigs

TO SPRINKLE
- Breadcrumbs 10 g
- Parmigiano Reggiano DOP to grate 10 g
- Extra virgin olive oil 10 g

To prepare the stuffed artichokes, put a saucepan on the stove with the salted water you will need for the vegetable broth. Then proceed with cleaning the artichokes; the first important operation is to rub your hands with lemon to prevent the substances inside this vegetable from blackening your hands (alternatively you can wear latex gloves). Browse the artichoke, i.e. remove the toughest outer leaves, and go on up to the more tender ones. Once you reach the heart, remove the stem.
Trim the artichokes, then slightly spread the leaves, exerting a slight pressure outwards, and remove the "beard" with a teaspoon.
As you prepare them, place the clean artichokes in a bowl with cold water and lemon juice to prevent them from blackening. Continue with the preparation of the meat-based filling: place the minced meat in a large bowl with the grated cheese and the whole egg; season with salt and pepper, then finely chop the parsley and add it to the meat together with the thyme leaves.

Crush the garlic clove and finally add the breadcrumbs; mix everything with your hands vigorously in order to mix the ingredients well.

Put a saucepan with plenty of salted water on the fire and boil the artichokes for 10 minutes; once ready, drain them and let them cool on a tray. Then gently fill the artichokes with 3 teaspoons of the meat filling you have prepared, being careful not to break them. Once finished, distribute the stuffed artichokes in a cake tin or ovenproof dish next to each other and sprinkle them with the vegetable broth. Finish by distributing a sprinkling of breadcrumbs and a drizzle of olive oil on the surface; cook them in a preheated static oven at 180° for 25 minutes (or at 160° for 15 minutes if in a convection oven), finally put them under the grill for 5 minutes to obtain a crispy browning on the surface. When they are ready, take them out of the oven and serve your stuffed artichokes.

Aosta Valley fondue
Ingredients:
- **Fontina cheese 400 g**
- **Whole milk 400 g**
- **Yolks 4**
- **Butter 30 g**
- **Black pepper to taste**

To prepare the Valdostana fondue, first remove the external rind of the fontina cheese, then slice it thinly. Transfer the cheese into a rectangular baking dish and pour the milk on top.

Cover with cling film and leave in the fridge overnight. After the rest time in the fridge, drain the cheese from the milk through a strainer and keep the milk aside. Melt the cheese over medium heat, stirring with a wooden spoon.

. At this point pour the yolks one at a time, and mix continuously. Add the cold butter and continue mixing. Pepper the Valdostana fondue to taste and mix again.

At this point, pour about 100 g of the milk kept aside, adjust the dose according to the consistency of the fondue which must not be too liquid or too compact. In total, cooking will take about 30 minutes. Once ready, pour the fondue into a pan, sprinkle again with pepper and serve the Valdostana fondue immediately.

Florentine trippa
Ingredients:
- Tripe 1 kg
- Peeled tomatoes 1 kg
- White onions 2
- Carrots 2
- Celery 2 ribs
- Extra virgin olive oil q.s.
- Parmigiano Reggiano DOP (to be grated) 100 g
- Salt up to taste
- Black pepper to taste

To prepare the Florentine tripe, start with the sautéed vegetables: trim and peel the carrot, cut it into strips and then finely chop it. Peel and then finely chop the celery as well. Switch to the onion: remove the outer layer then make cuts without going all the way both horizontally and vertically.
This way you can grind it effortlessly and evenly. Pour the olive oil into a pan, then add the mince: the onion and carrot and celery to follow.
Take the tripe (already washed and cleaned by your butcher) and cut it into strips. Add it to the pan when the fried mixture is wilted and well flavoured.

Let it flavor for about ten minutes, turning from time to time. Add the peeled tomatoes, break them up a bit with a wooden spoon, stir.
Cover with lid and cook for another 20 minutes on moderate heat. Remove the lid, salt and pepper. Once the bowl is ready, before removing from the heat, add the grated Parmigiano Reggiano DOP and mix. If necessary, cook again to let the sauce shrink a little, because the tripe should not be soupy. Once ready, you can serve your Florentine-style tripe on a plate and serve it piping hot with crusty bread and more grated Parmigiano Reggiano DOP to taste.

Risotto with Gorgonzola
Ingredients:
- Shallot 1
- Vegetable broth 1 l
- Dry white wine 100ml
- Butter 20 g
- Grana Padano PDO to grate 30 g
- Black pepper to taste
- Carnaroli rice 350 g
- Gorgonzola 150 g

To prepare the risotto with gorgonzola, start by peeling the shallot and chopping it very finely, then let it dry over low heat in the butter that you have melted in a pan. When the shallot is well wilted, add the rice and toast it for about 2 minutes, until it starts to become transparent, then blend with the white wine.

Add a ladleful of broth and proceed with cooking the risotto, adding broth every time the risotto dries out. When the risotto is almost done cooking, stir in the chopped gorgonzola and the grated parmesan. Remove from heat and pepper to taste. Serve the gorgonzola risotto immediately!

Rice salad
Ingredients:
- Rice (300 g)
- Tuna in oil (200 g) - drained
- Cluster tomatoes (150 g)
- Caciocavallo cheese (150 g)
- Cooked ham (100 g) - diced
- Peas (80 g)
- Red peppers (75 g)
- Yellow peppers (75 g)
- Black olives (80 g) - pitted
- Pickles (80 g)
- Chives to taste
- Fine salt to taste

To make a classic rice salad, place a pot full of salted water on the stove. Once it is boiling, pour in the peas and blanch them for about 3 minutes. Once the peas have been drained, pour the rice into the same water. Cook the rice 2-3 minutes less than the cooking time indicated on the package.

In the meantime, prepare the seasoning: wash the peppers, remove the stem, seeds and internal filaments, cut them first into strips and then into cubes and place them in a large bowl where you will collect all the other ingredients. Wash and cut the tomatoes in half, dig out the pulp with a teaspoon and cut them into cubes. Dice the baked ham. Also cut the caciocavallo cheese into cubes and cut the pickles and pitted olives into rounds. When about 2-3 minutes are left before it finishes cooking, drain the rice and let it cool by placing it on a cold tray (previously stored in the refrigerator) in order to facilitate cooling.

Flavor the seasoning with chives cut into small pieces, add the peas and rice that will have cooled in the meantime. To finish, add the crumbled tuna and the baked ham, adjust the salt and stir with a spoon. Cover the bowl with plastic wrap and let sit in the refrigerator until serving so it will be cold and the flavors will have blended together.

Lasagne with sausage ragu
Ingredients:
- Lasagna sheets (250 g)
- Grana Padano DOP cheese 5 tbsp
- Thyme to taste - (fresh)
- Oregano to taste - (fresh)

FOR THE BÉCHAMEL SAUCE
- Whole milk (1 l)
- Butter 7 tbsp (100 g)
- Flour 00 (100 g)
- Nutmeg to taste
- Fine salt to taste

FOR THE SAUSAGE RAGU
- Sausage (800 g)
- Tomato puree (450 g)
- Celery 1 stalk
- Onions 1
- Carrots 1
- Red wine 1 glass
- Extra virgin olive oil to taste
- Fine salt to taste
- Black pepper to taste

To make the lasagne with sausage ragu, first peel the carrot, onion, and celery and chop them roughly. Add a couple of tablespoons of olive oil to a frying pan, then add the chopped vegetables and brown over high heat for at least 5 minutes. Meanwhile, take the sausage, make an incision in the skin and remove it carefully using your hands. Once the vegetables have turned golden brown, add the sausage to the pan, increase the heat, and break up the sausage using a wooden spoon. Let it brown for about 5 minutes. Then, pour in the red wine and simmer until it evaporates completely. Next, add the tomato puree, season with salt and pepper, and stir to combine. Cover the pan with a lid and cook for about 10 minutes.

In the meantime, start making the béchamel sauce: Pour the milk into a saucepan, season with salt and add the nutmeg, then bring to a boil. Melt the butter in another small saucepan, then sprinkle in the flour, stirring quickly using a whisk. Next, add the hot milk and, stirring continuously, cook the béchamel until it has thickened.

Once the ragu is ready, all you have to do is assemble the lasagne. Spread a little béchamel on the bottom of a 9x13 inch (20x30 cm) pan and arrange the lasagne sheets on top. Cover with the sausage ragu, another layer of béchamel,

and a tablespoon of grated Grana Padano cheese. Repeat these steps another five times, alternating the direction of the lasagne sheets each time.

Once you've put the final layer of pasta in place, cover with the remaining ragu sauce, béchamel, and Grana Padano. Bake in a conventional oven preheated to 425°F (220°C) for 20 minutes, then switch to broil mode at the highest setting and cook for another 3 minutes.

When the lasagne with sausage ragu is golden brown, take it out of the oven, decorate with oregano and thyme leaves, and serve!

Lentils and sausage
Ingredients:
- Dried lentils 250 g
- Tomato puree 250 g
- Sausage 450 g
- White wine 50 g
- Water 500 g
- Celery 1 rib
- Carrots 1
- Onions ½
- Rosemary 2 sprigs
- Sage 4 leaves
- Salt up to taste
- Black pepper to taste
- Extra virgin olive oil 30 g

To make the lentils and sausage, first prepare the sauté by finely chopping the carrot, celery and onion. Heat the oil in a thick-bottomed pan, preferably cast iron. Pour the trite for the sauté and let it simmer over low heat for 10 minutes or until it is well stewed. Meanwhile, rinse the lentils under running water and then leave them to drain in a colander. In the meantime, remove the sausage from the casing, pressing on one side to let the meat come out in order to keep the sausages whole. Chop the sage and rosemary until you get a fine and aromatic mince. When the sauté is well stewed, add the sausages
and flavored with the chopped herbs, let it brown over medium heat for 3-4 minutes, then add the white wine. Let the wine evaporate and then add the well-drained lentils.
Pour the tomato puree and water, stir to mix the ingredients well. Cover with the lid and cook everything for 40 minutes on low heat. After this time, remove the lid, add salt and pepper and continue cooking for another 40 minutes without the lid. When cooked, garnish with a few sprigs of fresh rosemary and serve the lentils and sausage piping hot.

Fish and Seafood

Mediterranean sea bream
Ingredients:
- **Bream (2 pieces clean) 700 g**
- **Extra virgin olive oil 30 g**
- **Salt up to taste**
- **Black pepper to taste**
- **Garlic 2 cloves**
- **Pitted black olives 100 g**
- **Cherry tomatoes 200 g**
- **Thyme to taste**
- **Salted capers 1 tbsp**

Stuff each sea bream with the herbs: the sprigs of fresh thyme, 1 peeled garlic clove each and finally salt and pepper.
Take a baking dish, drizzle the bottom with olive oil, place the two stuffed sea bream, then wash the cherry tomatoes and cut them in half,
distribute them in the baking dish around the two sea breams, then rinse the capers thoroughly under running water to remove the excess salt and add them to the sea breams, also add the pitted black olives, scented with a couple of sprigs of fresh thyme
and drizzle the sea breams with a drizzle of olive oil; season last with salt. Now cook the Mediterranean sea bream in a preheated static oven at 200° for 25-30 minutes. When cooked, take the Mediterranean sea bream out of the oven and serve it with the cherry tomatoes and olives!

Baked stuffed squid
Ingredients:
- Squid 1 (600 g)
- Potatoes (200 g)
- Bread (90 g)
- Whole milk (90 g)
- Fresh scallion 1
- Parmigiano Reggiano DOP cheese 1 ½ tbsp (10 g)
- Marjoram to taste
- Fresh turmeric 1 ¼ tbsp (9 g)
- Eggs 1
- Extra virgin olive oil (10 g)
- Fine salt to taste
- Black pepper
- FOR THE ACCOMPANYING SAUCE
- Natural plain yogurt (130 g)
- Whipping cream 2 tsp (10 g)
- Dill to taste
- Extra virgin olive oil to taste

To prepare the stuffed squid, start with the potatoes. Place them in a saucepan with cold water and cook for around 20-30 minutes from boiling. Once they're ready (make sure they can be pierced easily with a fork), allow them to cool, then peel and set aside. Next, remove the crust from the bread, cut the bread into chunks, and soak the chunks in the milk. Clean the squid by removing the head and the side "wings" with a knife. Rinse the squid thoroughly, both outside and inside, to remove any impurities. Chop up the wings and the tentacles, and finely chop the scallion, having removed the green part and the roots beforehand, along with the marjoram leaves. Heat the extra virgin olive oil in a pan, add the chopped scallion and marjoram, and fry over low heat, stirring occasionally, for a few minutes.

Then add the chopped wings and tentacles and cook over high heat for a few moments, ensuring that the water released from the squid evaporates completely.

At this point, you need to start preparing the filling. Mash the now-cold potatoes in a large bowl and add the soaked bread, the chopped squid and scallion,
the grated Parmigiano Reggiano cheese, the peeled fresh turmeric grating it directly into the bowl, the salt, the pepper, and the whole egg.

Mix thoroughly, and once all of the ingredients are combined, transfer the mixture to a disposable pastry bag. Preheat a conventional oven to 350°F (180°C), then grease the bottom of a small baking dish (that will hold 4 stuffed squid), stuff the squid to the top with the filling, and lay them side by side in the dish. Season with salt and pepper to taste and finish with a drizzle of oil. Bake in a conventional oven preheated to 350°F (180°C) for approximately 30 minutes. While the squid are baking, turn your attention to the accompanying sauce. Pour the yogurt and cream into a small bowl, add a drizzle of oil and the dill, and mix well. Once the squid are cooked, take them out of the oven and serve each baked stuffed squid with the accompanying sauce.

Cod with potatoes and olives
Ingredients:
- Cod 800 g
- Potatoes 700 g
- Black olives 200 g
- Vegetable broth 350 g
- Flour 00 100 g
- Golden onions 1
- Extra virgin olive oil 5 tbsp
- 3 bay leaves
- Salt up to taste
- Black pepper to taste

Cut the cod into rectangles, remove the bones with tweezers, then cut it into smaller pieces, into rectangles or squares.
Carefully flour the pieces of cod on both sides. Then peel the onion and cut it into slices.
Then chop it finely and pour it into a large pan where you have heated 2 and a half tablespoons of olive oil. Brown the onion and after 5 minutes add the floured cod.
Then cook it for 20 minutes over low heat, turning it from time to time so that the pieces of cod brown well on both sides. In the meantime, peel the potatoes and cut them into wedges (or if you prefer into slices about 1 cm thick), rinse them under cold water, then pat them dry with kitchen paper.
Take a large saucepan that can hold both the cod and the potatoes, then drizzle it with 2 and a half tablespoons of olive oil and add the potatoes. Turn on the medium heat and pour the vegetable broth into the pan with the potatoes. Leave to flavor for 5 minutes, then when the cod is well browned, remove it from the pan and add it to the pan with the potatoes together with its cooking juices.

Pour the black olives into the pan and add the bay leaves. Let everything cook for another 15-20 minutes, adding more vegetable broth when necessary so as not to dry the cod too much, which must remain "stewed" and create a tasty creamy sauce. Once the fire is extinguished, add salt and pepper to taste, then serve piping hot!

Sea bass in a herb salt crust
Ingredients:
- Fine salt (400 g)
- Sea bass 1 (550 g)
- Coarse salt (500 g)
- Sage 6 leaves
- Thyme 6 sprigs
- Parsley 1 bunch
- Dill 2 bunches
- Bay leaves 4
- Rosemary 3 sprigs
- Egg whites (105 g)
- Garlic 1 clove
- Lemons 1

To make the sea bass in a herb salt crust, start by scaling the fish with a scaler or the back of a knife to avoid damaging the flesh. Rinse thoroughly under running water. Pour the herbs and peeled garlic clove into the bowl of a blender. Chop the herbs and transfer them to a bowl. Alternatively, chop all the herbs using a knife. Grate the lemon zest and add to the chopped herbs.

Stuff the belly of the sea bass with a spoonful of the herb mix. Meanwhile, pour the egg whites into a bowl and beat them with a hand mixer until stiff. Gently mix in the herbs. Stir, add the fine and coarse salt a little at a time, and mix everything together.

Spread a sheet of parchment paper on a dripping pan and then lay a thin layer (about 1.5 cm) of the mixture obtained. Then place the sea bass on the bed of salt and cover it with the salt mixture, pressing it gently to make the dough adhere well.

Line a baking tray with a sheet of parchment paper and place a thin layer (about ½ inch) of the mixture on top. Next, place the sea bass on top of the bed of salt and cover with the salt mixture, pressing gently to ensure that the mixture adheres well, and making sure that the fish is entirely covered. Bake the sea bass in its herb salt crust in a conventional oven preheated to 390°F (200°C) for 30 minutes. Once the fish is cooked, remove it from the oven and leave to rest for a few moments. Then, take a small hammer or meat tenderizer, break the salt crust, fillet the fish and serve hot!

Stewed baby octopus
Ingredients:
- Clean baby octopus 1.2 kg
- Peeled tomatoes 1 kg
- Water 150g
- White wine 50 g
- Dried chilli to taste
- Garlic 1 clove
- Basil 6 leaves
- Extra virgin olive oil q.s.
- Salt up to taste

To make stewed baby octopus, first get yourself a large saucepan, pour the oil, the whole peeled garlic clove and the dried chillies into it. Leave to flavor for a few moments, then pour in the cleaned baby octopus
and let them brown for a few minutes over high heat, mixing them with the help of kitchen tongs. At this point add the white wine, let it evaporate for a couple of minutes and then add the tomatoes. Pour the 150 g of water into the bowl containing the peeled tomatoes so as to collect the remaining pulp residues and pour everything into the pot. Salt and flavor with the washed and dried basil leaves. Cover the baby octopus with the lid and cook over low heat for about 2 hours. After this time, remove the lid and continue cooking for another 30 minutes, keeping the heat low. Once cooking is complete, you can serve your baby octopus stewed very hot.

Marinated anchovies
Ingredients:
- Chopped anchovies 500 g (clean)
- Garlic 4 g
- Lemon juice 150 g
- Parsley 20 g
- Extra virgin olive oil 140 g
- Black pepper to taste
- White wine vinegar 20 g
- Salt up to taste

To prepare the marinated anchovies, start with the marinade: put the parsley in a mixer together with a clove of garlic and 40 g of olive oil and chop everything for a few seconds.

Squeeze the lemons, and collect the juice in a container together with the olive oil and season with salt and black pepper.

Mix well with the help of a hand whisk or the tines of a fork and, when the two compounds have bonded together, add the chopped parsley.

Keep stirring with the whisk, then keep the marinade aside. In the meantime, proceed to cleaning the anchovies; since these will not undergo any cooking it is very important to make sure that they have been blast chilled when buying (always choose fresh anchovies to buy in your trusted fish shop); for greater safety it is recommended to freeze for at least 96 hours at -18 degrees (already gutted) and then thaw to use in the recipe.

Arrange the well-cleaned anchovy fillets in a large container next to each other and pour the marinade you have prepared, then cover with transparent film. Leave to rest for at least 5 hours at room temperature.

After the necessary time, remove the film and pour the white wine vinegar, mix and finally, drain them slightly from the marinade and arrange the marinated anchovies on a serving plate to serve and enjoy them as an appetizer!

Stewed octopus
Ingredients:
- **Octopus 1 (clean)**
- **Tomato puree (310 g)**
- **Shallot 1**
- **Garlic 1 clove**
- **Thyme 4 sprigs**
- **Sage 2 leaves**
- **Water (1 l)**
- **Extra virgin olive oil to taste**
- **Fine salt to taste**
- **Black pepper to taste**

Peel the shallot. Slice the shallot and place in a bowl, then peel the garlic clove and transfer everything to the stove. Heat a splash of oil in a large pan and add the garlic and shallot.

Pour in the tomato puree and turn up the heat. Season with salt and add the thyme leaves, sage,
and water. Heat well until the mixture comes to a boil, then dip the octopus tentacles in three times. This will make them curl up nicely. Make sure the tentacles have taken on their distinctive curled shape, then plunge the whole octopus into the sauce. Cover with a lid and cook over medium heat for 50 minutes. To be sure it's cooked, remember to prick the octopus on the inside where the beak was located. If a fork penetrates the flesh easily, then it's cooked.

Sprinkle everything with a grind of pepper and transfer the octopus to a board, cutting it into pieces the size you prefer and serving in its sauce. Your stewed octopus is ready. Enjoy!

Fried cod
Ingredients:
- **Desalted cod 500 g**
- **Flour 00 to taste**
- **Black pepper to taste**
- **Lime to taste**
- **TO FRY**
- **Peanut oil 1 l**

To prepare the fried cod, rinse the already soaked cod again, then dry it with kitchen paper. Then start heating the oil. In the meantime, pull the skin off the cod, lifting it up starting from the tail and gently pulling it away with your hands. Run your hand over the cod pulp in one direction and the other to feel the presence of bones and remove them with kitchen tweezers. Cut the cod into strips about 3 cm thick, then divide into 2-3 more parts.
Carefully flour the pieces of cod on both sides. Once the oil has reached a temperature between 180° and 190° (to be measured with a cooking thermometer), dip a few pieces at a time, first eliminating the excess flour. It will take 3-5 minutes of cooking and only when they are well browned can you drain them.
Arrange them on a tray covered with a sheet of absorbent paper for fried foods, in order to remove the excess oil. Finish frying and season the fried cod to taste with freshly ground pepper and, if you like, a few slices of lime or lemon.

Stewed cuttlefish
Ingredients:
- Cuttlefish 1 kg (clean)
- White onions 160 g
- White wine 70 g
- Garlic 1 clove
- Parsley to taste
- Extra virgin olive oil q.s.
- Salt up to taste
- Black pepper to taste
- Peeled tomatoes 700 g

To prepare the stewed cuttlefish, start by chopping the onion. Pour the oil into a saucepan, add the onion and stew it over low heat for about 10 minutes. When the onion is wilted, add the peeled tomatoes.

Salt, pepper and cover with a lid. Lower the heat and let it cook for 20-25 minutes on a low flame, from when it starts to boil. Cut the cuttlefish into 1 cm rings.

Take another pan, pour a drizzle of oil, a clove of garlic and let it brown. Pour in the cuttlefish and brown for 2/3 minutes over high heat. When the cooking liquid has dried, add the white wine and let it evaporate completely. Then discard the garlic.

Pour the cuttlefish into the saucepan with the tomato and cook for 15-20 minutes. Taste the cuttlefish from time to time to check if it is cooked. After the cooking time, add a nice sprinkling of minced parsley and serve.

Cod Livorno style
Ingredients:
- Cod 600 g
- Potatoes 250 g
- Flour 00 100 g
- White wine 40 g
- Salt up to taste
- Black pepper to taste
- Extra virgin olive oil q.s.

FOR THE SAUCE
- Peeled tomatoes 800 g
- Golden onions 1
- Garlic 1 clove
- Salt up to taste
- Black pepper to taste
- Extra virgin olive oil q.s.

To make Livorno cod, start by preparing the sauce: peel and slice the onions, heat a drizzle of olive oil in a pan, add the whole peeled garlic clove and the onion slices. Leave to dry for 3-4 minutes over low heat, wetting with a little water, just enough so that the sauté does not dry out too much. In a bowl, mash the peeled tomatoes, then pour them into the pan with the onions. Cover with the lid and cook over medium heat for about 15 minutes. In the meantime, start cutting the cod into slices trying to obtain pieces of the same size. Carefully flour the slices of cod, then heat a drizzle of oil in a pan and place the cod, browning it on both sides for a few moments, turning it gently, salt and pepper.

Deglaze with the white wine and let it evaporate. Meanwhile the sauce will have come to cooking, now you can remove the garlic, then pour the sauce into the pan with the cod, cover with the lid and cook over low heat for about 20 minutes. If you mix, do it very gently so as not to flake the cod. Meanwhile, peel the potatoes and cut them into cubes. After 20 minutes of cooking the cod, add the potatoes, cover with the lid and continue cooking for another 20 minutes, always being careful to stir so as not to flake the cod too much.

Wash and chop the sprig of parsley, once the cod is cooked, turn off the heat and flavor with the chopped parsley. Serve your Livorno cod piping hot.

Baked sardines

Ingredients:
- Sardines 18 sardines for a total of about 250 g (clean)
- Breadcrumbs 60 g
- Extra virgin olive oil 60 g
- Parsley 1 sprig
- Thyme 1 sprig
- Garlic 1 clove
- Grated Grana Padano DOP 20 g
- Pine nuts 30 g
- Extra virgin olive oil to grease the pan 15 g

Pour the breadcrumbs, grated cheese and crushed garlic clove into a bowl.

Rinse, dry and finely chop the parsley; then add it too to the breading and flavor further with the thyme leaves; pour the 60 g of oil and mix everything until you get a uniform mixture.

At this point, take a 19x15 cm baking dish and sprinkle it with about 15 g of oil. Arrange the sardines horizontally without overlapping each other, salt (not excessively), pepper and cover with half of the previously prepared mixture.

Arrange another layer of sardines, being careful to position them vertically (opposite to before), salt and pepper and cover the entire surface with the remaining part of the breading.

Finish by decorating the surface with pine nuts. Then cook the sardines in the oven in grill mode at 200° for 8 minutes, until they are golden brown. Once cooked, serve the baked sardines still hot.

Sauteed swordfish
Ingredients:
- **Swordfish 480 g**
- **Extra virgin olive oil 300 g**
- **Oregano a few leaves**
- **Lemons 2**
- **Parsley 20 g**
- **Garlic 1 clove**
- **Salt up to taste**

To prepare the swordfish in salmoriglio, start by preparing the marinade: rinse and dry the parsley carefully, then chop it finely and keep it aside. Cut the lemon in half and squeeze out the juice which you will filter with a fine-mesh strainer: you will need to obtain about 130 g. Now pour it into a large bowl that will be used for the marinade, in which you will also add the oil, seasoning with salt and pepper.With a whisk, emulsify the ingredients until salt and pepper are completely dissolved. At this point add the chopped parsley and crush the garlic inside. Also flavored with the oregano leaves and whip the mixture vigorously again: you will have to obtain a homogeneous emulsion. At this point cut the swordfish giving the slices a thickness of about 1 cm: you will have to obtain about 4 of about 120 g each. Transfer them to the bowl with the marinade, which will have to cover them entirely, and cover them with transparent food film. Place in the fridge and leave to marinate for at least 1 hour. After the necessary time, remove the fish from the fridge, remove the film and let the swordfish fillets drip (do not throw away the marinade: you will need it later). Then place them on an already hot pan and cook the fillets for 4-5 minutes over low heat, turning them once: they should be lightly browned on each side. In the meantime, pour the marinade (salmoriglio) into a non-stick pan with high edges and cook it for about 5 minutes over low heat: in this way you will make a reduction of the marinade which will become more dense and full-bodied. At this point both the swordfish and the marinade will be ready: arrange the fish slices on a plate and accompany your swordfish in salmoriglio with a jug containing the marinade!

Black pepper to taste
Pan-fried sea bream
Ingredients:
- **Sea bream 2 pieces (clean)**
- **Extra virgin olive oil 30 g**
- **Carrots 150 g**
- **Zucchini 150 g**
- **Fresh spring onion 70 g**
- **Garlic 1 clove**
- **Thyme to taste**

Wash and peel the carrots, then trim the ends and cut them into slices about 5 mm thick. Also wash and trim the zucchini, cut them in half lengthwise and then further divide each half; finally cut them into cubes about 1 cm thick 6. Lastly, wash the spring onion, remove the base and cut it into slices about 5 mm thick. Pour the oil into a large non-stick pan, add the poached garlic clove and fry it for a couple of minutes. When the oil is flavoured, remove the garlic from the pan and place the sea bream inside, then add the carrots, the zucchini, spring onion and sprigs of thyme, salted and peppered to taste. Cover the pan with a lid and cook over medium heat for 7 minutes, then turn the sea bream with the help of 2 spatulas, being careful not to break them; cover again with the lid and cook for another 7 minutes. The cooking times, of course, can vary depending on the weight of the sea bream you will be using. The pan-fried sea bream is ready to be served!

Sicilian sardines
- Ingredients:
- Already cleaned sardines 520 g
- Bay leaf to taste

FOR THE STUFFING
- Breadcrumbs 50 g
- Raisins 25 g
- Parsley 10 g
- Pine nuts 25 g
- Anchovies in oil (the fillets) 15 g
- Sugar 15g
- Salt up to taste
- Black pepper to taste
- Extra virgin olive oil 20 g

FOR THE EMULSION
- Acacia honey 35 g
- Extra virgin olive oil 10 g
- Orange juice 35 g

To prepare the beccafico sardines as before, make sure your sardines are already clean (you will need 520 g of open sardines). Then go on to prepare the filling, first rinse and then soak the raisins in cold water for about ten minutes. Then pour a drizzle of oil into a pan, add the breadcrumbs and toast it for a couple of minutes over medium heat, stirring constantly.
In the meantime, chop the parsley and roughly chop the anchovies. Pour the breadcrumbs, drained and squeezed raisins, pine nuts, anchovies, parsley, sugar, salt and pepper into a bowl.
Mix everything together and set aside for a moment. Then grease a 20x20 cm baking dish and go on to stuff the sardines. Arrange a little stuffing on each sardine

and roll it up starting from the side of the head, to form a roll. Gradually place the sardines inside the pan, in an orderly manner, so that they are close to each other. Take the bay leaves, if they are very large divide them in half, otherwise use them whole. Then arrange the leaves between one roll and another. At this point sprinkle the surface with the leftover filling. You just have to prepare the emulsion. Pour the honey and orange juice into a small bowl and the oil. Emulsify by beating rapidly with a fork, then spread over the sardines using a spoon. Bake in a preheated static oven at 200° for about 20-25 minutes. Then take it out and serve.

Fried mixed seafood
Ingredients:
- Shrimps 12 – red (clean)
- Anchovies 12 (clean)
- Goatfish 4 (clean)
- Codfish 4 (clean)
- Squid (350 g in rings)
- Semolina(250 g)
- Fine salt to taste

FOR FRYING
- **Vegetable oil to taste**

Heat the oil in a pan until it reaches a temperature of 356- 374° F (180-190° C) (to be measured with a kitchen thermometer). In the meantime, pour the semolina into a low, wide container. When the oil has reached the right temperature, completely flour the cod. Remove the excess semolina and dip the fish one at a time in the boiling oil. Flour the goatfish and fry them together with the cod. Wait 3-4 minutes; when they are golden, drain them and transfer them to a tray lined with oil-absorbing paper. Flour the calamari and use a sieve to remove the excess flour by shaking it. Fry for a few minutes until golden and place them next to the other fish. Next flour the anchovies and remove the excess semolina. Immerse in oil. Then flour the anchovies and fry. Wait a few minutes minutes until they are golden, drain them and transfer them to a tray lined with oil-absorbing paper. Now move on to the shrimp. Flour them in the semolina, then dip them in the hot oil.
Wait about a minute and when they are golden, drain them and move them to the tray together with the other fish. Decorate with lemon slices and serve the fried mixed seafood warm.

Meat

Sicilian-style chicken
Ingredients:
- Chicken (1 kg) - in pieces
- Cherry tomatoes (150 g)
- Black olives (50 g) - pitted
- Capers in vinegar 3 tbsp
- Garlic 2 cloves
- Fresh chili pepper 2
- Wild fennel to taste
- Rose wine (300 g)
- Water (300 g)
- Extra virgin olive oil to taste
- Fine salt to taste

To make Sicilian-style chicken, wash and dry the cherry tomatoes, then cut them in half and set them aside. Remove the center of the chili peppers, cut them to extract the seeds, then slice them thinly. Heat the olive oil in a pan, add the two garlic cloves and chili peppers and brown for a couple of minutes, then add the chicken. Brown the chicken pieces 2-3 minutes per side over medium heat, then pour in the cherry tomatoes, olives, and capers,
then add the wild fennel. Blend with wine, let it evaporate, then pour in the water.
Cover the pan with a lid and continue cooking for 25 minutes over low heat. Then, add the remaining fennel and continue cooking without the lid for 15-20 minutes over medium heat, stirring occasionally. After cooking, remove the garlic cloves and adjust the salt if necessary. Serve your Sicilian-style chicken hot.

Vintage veal with tuna sauce
Ingredients:
- Round veal 500 g
- Garlic 1 clove
- Salt up to 5 g
- Black pepper to taste
- White wine 80 g
- Whole milk 150 g
- Drained tuna in oil 125 g
- Anchovies in oil 20 g
- Capers 20 g
- Boiled eggs 4
- Marsala 15 g
- Vegetable broth 40 g
- Extra virgin olive oil 40 g

To prepare the veal with tuna sauce in the old-fashioned way, start by preparing the vegetable broth. Once ready, take care of tying your piece of veal, to do this you will need some kitchen string and scissors. This will serve to keep the piece still while cooking. Season the meat with salt and pepper. At this point stack a clove of unpeeled garlic on a toothpick, it will be easier to remove it from the cooking juices later. Pour 20 g of oil into a pan that can also be used in the oven and let it heat up. Then add the meat and the garlic clove. Brown the walker over medium-high heat on all sides for 2-3 minutes. At this point add the tuna fillets, anchovies and capers. Slightly break the tuna fillets and when it is toasted and golden brown, add the white wine. Once the white wine has reduced, pour the milk slightly without going directly on the meat. At this point, transfer to a preheated oven at 180° for 7-8 minutes, then turn the meat and continue cooking for another 7-8 minutes. Remove from the oven, cover with aluminum foil and leave to cool completely at room temperature.

In the meantime prepare the hard-boiled eggs, cooking them for about 9 minutes from the boil. Once cold, shell them and keep them aside. As soon as the meat has cooled, transfer it to a cutting board and remove the garlic clove from the cooking juices; then pour the base into a mixer container
and add the hard-boiled eggs cut into slices. Start blending with an immersion mixer and add again: 20 g of oil,
the vegetable broth and the marsala. Blend everything until you get a smooth cream, adding more broth if it turns out to be too thick. Transfer to the fridge to let it cool down a bit.
Take care of the meat by removing the string and slice it thinly using a very sharp knife. Arrange all the slices of meat on a cutting board and stuff them with a teaspoon of cream, placing it in the center. Close each slice like a half moon and arrange them on a serving plate. We have chosen to add some lettuce leaves and season them with salt, oil and balsamic vinegar. The veal with tuna sauce in the ancient way is ready, you just have to taste it!

Chicken Marengo
Ingredients:
- Chicken 1 (in pieces)
- Porcini mushrooms 4
- 4 slices bread
- Garlic 1 clove
- White wine 500ml
- Lemons 1
- Parsley 1 sprig
- Medium eggs 4
- Extra virgin olive oil 50 g
- Salt up to taste
- Black pepper to taste
- Peeled tomatoes 500 g
- Scampi 4

Pass the chicken pieces in the flour; then peel the garlic clove and finely chop the parsley tuft.
Clean the mushrooms and slice them finely. Then pass the peeled tomatoes and collect the pulp in a small bowl. In a pan, heat a drizzle of oil with the peeled garlic clove; then add the chicken pieces and brown them. Salt and pepper to taste and when the chicken is well browned, pour in 100 ml of white wine. Let it evaporate before pouring the peeled tomato puree. Cook for about 20 minutes with the lid on. Then add the mushrooms to the chicken and cook for another 20 minutes. Meanwhile, clean the scampi under running water and cut the carapace. Pour the remaining white wine into a saucepan, add salt and as soon as it starts to simmer, add the scampi and cook for at least 5 minutes. Drain the scampi and add them to the chicken in a pan, then add the lemon juice, mix and a few minutes before turning off the heat, add the chopped parsley.

Pour 3 tablespoons of oil into a pan, toast the slices of bread while in another pan fry the eggs for a few minutes with another two tablespoons of oil, salting them lightly. Then transfer the chicken Marengo onto a serving plate and place the croutons on top of which you will place the eggs.

Scallops in pink
Ingredients:
- **Veal slices 400 g**
- **Whole milk to taste**
- **Mascarpone 200 g**
- **Red wine 50ml**
- **Triple tomato paste 1 tbsp**
- **Butter 30 g**
- **Extra virgin olive oil q.s.**
- **Flour 00 to taste**
- **Salt up to taste**
- **Black pepper to taste**
- **Pink peppercorns 2 tsp**

To prepare the escalopes in pink sauce, the meat must be of excellent quality and very tender. First take a cutting board, lay the slices on it and then beat them with a meat tenderizer, if the slices are very large, cut them in half so as to obtain regular portions. Flour the slices on both sides. Meanwhile, heat the oil and butter in a non-stick pan.

When the oil is hot, place the scallops in it and let them brown on both sides for a couple of minutes, until they are golden brown. Add the wine and let it evaporate.

Meanwhile, dilute the tomato paste with water or hot broth. When the wine has evaporated, add the tomato and season with salt and pepper, according to your tastes. When the tomato is well blended, add a few tablespoons of milk to dilute the cooking juices
and then add the mascarpone that you will have diluted with a drop of milk, pour the mascarpone into the pan and mix everything well, let it cook until the sauce thickens, then add the pink peppercorns. Serve the escalopes in pink covered with the mascarpone sauce.

Meat stew with onions
Ingredients:
- Celery 1 rib
- Carrots 2
- Red onions 600 gr
- Tomato puree 200 g
- 1/2 glass of red wine (about 100 ml)
- Salt to taste.
- Pepper as needed.
- Olive oil to taste
- Meat broth to taste
- Veal beef 800 gr

To prepare the meat stew with onions, start by chopping the celery and carrots that will serve as the base for the sauté. Heat a large frying pan with two tablespoons of oil, add the chopped celery and carrots and cook the sautéed mixture.
Cut the onions into thin slices and set them aside. Meanwhile, prepare the meat: cut the veal into bite-size pieces and when the sauté is ready, add the pieces of meat and brown them.
Deglaze with the red wine and add the onion slices. Continue cooking over a low heat, gradually adding the meat broth,
Finally, add the tomato puree. Cooking the stew will take about 1 hour. Once the gravy has been absorbed by the meat, season with salt and pepper. The meat and onion stew is ready when the meat is tender and the onions well cooked.

Stew Chicken
Ingredients:
- Chicken breast 800 g
- Pitted green olives 50 g
- Thyme 2 sprigs
- Rosemary 1 sprig
- Fresh chilli 1
- White onions 1
- Garlic 1 clove
- Flour 00 20 g
- Salt up to taste
- Chicken broth to taste
- Extra virgin olive oil 80 g

To prepare the chicken stew, start by removing any cartilage and fat from the chicken breast, then cut it into cubes of about 3 cm per side. Chop the chilli pepper, rosemary and thyme and keep them aside, finely chop the olives
garlic and onion and let them dry gently in the extra virgin olive oil, then when they are transparent, add the chopped rosemary, thyme, chilli pepper and olives. Leave to fry for a couple of minutes and then add the chicken, stir and fry for 10 minutes, stirring constantly.
When it is well browned, add the chicken broth to cover the cubes of meat and cook over low heat for about 40 minutes, covering the pan with a lid.
When the chicken stew is tender, add salt if necessary, add the flour through a sieve and mix to avoid the formation of lumps. Let the sauce thicken for about 5 minutes (you can add a few whole green olives to the stew if you wish), then turn off the heat and serve.

Pork loin roast
Ingredients:
- Pork loin 1 kg
- Potatoes 500 g
- White wine 1 glass
- Vegetable broth to taste
- Extra virgin olive oil 4 tbsp
- Garlic 1 clove
- Rosemary 2 tbsp
- Black pepper to taste
- Fine salt to taste
- Thyme 1 tbsp
- Sage 10 g

To prepare pork loin roast, start by taking a part of the aromatic herbs: thyme, rosemary and sage (leave the remaining part to one side); coarsely chop the herbs on a cutting board. Now place the pork loin on the cutting board and cut a flap into it using a sharp-edged knife, without entirely detaching it from the meat cut. Now open it out and place the previously chopped herbs inside; season with salt and pepper.

Close the flap and tie the roast, to hold it together and give shape to your meat cut. Run a piece of kitchen twine under and then over the meat lengthwise; be sure to tie both ends with a knot and leave a part of the twine slightly longer than the other. Run the longer piece of twine back to the opposite end and tie one last knot so that the twine does not come undone. In this way the casing will stick nicely to the meat cut. Now continue to cage the meat by running the twine up and down the sides. After running the twine around the last part, form a loop and hold it down with your fingers. Run the end of the twine through the loop a couple of times, then the meat, tighten and tie the last knot. Once you have tied the meat, you can cook it. Heat a drizzle of oil in a non-stick pan and add the pork loin roast when hot.

Brown thoroughly on all sides without burning it, to seal the pores of the meat, so that all the juices remain inside. When nice and golden, add the white wine, which will enrich the naturally sweet pork with a touch of acidity. Wait a few moments, then use a pair of tongs to place the meat cut in a baking tray; leave the baking sauce to one side.

Now thoroughly wash the potatoes and dry them with a cloth. Cut them in half and then into slices, all the same size if possible. Place them in the tray and add a little salt. You won't need to add any oil because as the pork loin cooks its casing will melt and flavor the potatoes. Bake in the oven at 355°F (180°C) for around 15 minutes. In the meantime, finely chop the aromatic herbs you saved for later, then gently crush an unpeeled garlic clove. Once the 15 minutes are up, remove the meat from the oven, add the garlic clove and the aromatic herbs.

Pour the broth into the tray, around the meat cut and place back in the oven at 355°F (180°C); you'll need a thermometer to know exactly when it is done. The temperature in the middle of the meat should be 143°-149°F (60°-65°C). Cooking times vary according to the size of the meat cut used, but it should take around 40-50 minutes. Remove the tray from the oven and place the meat alone on a cutting board.

Cover with a sheet of aluminum foil and leave the meat to rest for 3-4 minutes; according to the size of the meat cut, the temperature inside could increase by 36°-41°F (2°-5°C). In the meantime, reduce the baking sauce you left to one side on a low flame. Now untie the meat and be sure to remove all the twine.

Cut it into slices, according to where the bones are. Now place the meat and potatoes on a plate and pour the baking sauce over them. The pork loin roast is ready to be served!

Crispy chicken thighs
Ingredients:
- Chicken thighs 8
- Garlic powder 1 pinch
- Yellow mustard powder 1 pinch
- Sweet paprika 1 pinch
- Rosemary 1 sprig
- Thyme 1 sprig
- Extra virgin olive oil 30 ml
- Lemon zest 1
- Orange zest 1
- Instant flour for polenta 100 g
- Black pepper to taste
- Salt up to taste

To prepare the crispy chicken thighs, start by eliminating the fattest parts, place the thighs in a bowl and grease them with olive oil to make the breading stick better. Now dedicate yourself to the breading: chop the rosemary and thyme
and put the mince in a large bowl, add the sweet paprika, the yellow mustard powder, the lemon zest and the orange zest.
Add the yellow polenta, the garlic powder, salt and pepper and mix to mix the breading.
Pick up the chicken legs and make cuts along the length to better absorb the aromas. Pass the thighs in the breading making it adhere on all sides then lay the thighs on a tray.
Heat a pan over the heat and then place the chicken thighs, sprinkle them with a drizzle of oil and cook over a moderate heat for 20 minutes with the lid on, turning them halfway through cooking.
Your crispy chicken thighs are ready, enjoy them piping hot!

Bolognese Cutlet
Ingredients:
- Veal loin (4 slices of 200 g each) 800 g
- Breadcrumbs 200 g
- Flour 00 100 g
- Eggs 2
- Butter 50 g
- Raw ham 300 g
- Parmigiano Reggiano DOP (to be grated) 170 g
- Meat broth 250 g

FOR THE DRESSING
- Tomato puree 100 g

To prepare the Bolognese cutlet, prepare the meat broth (or vegetable broth even if the sauce will be lighter at that point); then start beating the slices of meat with a meat mallet to make them thinner (you can also use a sheet of baking paper to spread over the meat so as not to risk breaking the fibers); then prepare three low and wide containers: beat the eggs in one; in the other place the sifted flour and in the third the breadcrumbs. Dip the slices of meat one at a time, first in the flour turning it on both sides to coat it thoroughly. Then in the egg,
finally pass them in the breadcrumbs, making sure they are completely covered. For cooking you will have to adjust according to the size of the slices or the pan; we advise you to cook 1 or 2 slices at a time if you use a pan that is not very large, in order not to risk reusing the butter too many times. Then melt the butter in a pan and once melted place the slices;
Brown on one side, then flip to the other. Once they are well browned on both sides, place the slices of ham and sprinkle with grated Parmesan.
Once seasoned, sprinkle the slices with meat broth (one ladle for each cutlet) and cook with the lid on for 5-6 minutes; when they are ready

filter the cooking liquid from the pan in which you cooked the cutlet and transfer it to a saucepan. Then add 20 g of Parmesan and thicken over high heat.

You are now ready to serve: if you wish, you can garnish the serving dish with simple tomato sauce, then place the cutlet and season with the broth reduction. Your bolognese cutlet is ready to be served!

Scallops in Marsala
Ingredients:
- **Pork loin (8 slices) 400 g**
- **Marsala 100 g**
- **Vegetable broth 70 g**
- **Butter 50 g**
- **Extra virgin olive oil 40 g**
- **Flour 00 to taste**
- **Salt up to taste**
- **Black pepper to taste**

To prepare the escalopes in marsala, first place the slices of meat between two sheets of parchment paper and beat them with a meat tenderizer to crush them and stretch them at the same time until they are very thin: in this way the meat will be more tender. and less fibrous. Flour the slices and remove the excess flour.

When all the slices are floured, you can start cooking: in a large frying pan, gently melt the butter together with the oil, then raise the heat slightly and add the floured slices.

After a couple of minutes, turn them over with kitchen tongs and sear them for a few moments on the other side as well, then raise the heat and add the Marsala wine. Add salt and pepper.

At this point, pour in the vegetable broth (or water, alternatively) and continue to cook for a few more minutes, swinging the pan from time to time to create a delicious emulsion. When the cooking liquid has become creamy, plate up and serve your tasty escalopes with Marsala!

Coniglio alla Cacciatora
Ingredients:
- Pieces of rabbit 1 kg
- Peeled tomatoes 200 g
- Taggiasca olives 100 g
- Golden onions 1
- Garlic 2 cloves
- Sage 5 leaves
- Rosemary 2 sprigs
- Vegetable broth 200 g
- White wine 80 g
- Flour 00 to taste
- Extra virgin olive oil q.s.
- Salt up to taste
- Black pepper to taste

To make the rabbit cacciatore, first prepare the vegetable broth and keep it warm. Peel the onion and cut it into slices. Heat a drizzle of oil in a saucepan, then add the onion and crushed garlic cloves. Cook on low heat for a few minutes.

When the onion has softened, remove it from the pan and set it aside. In the meantime, flour the rabbit already cut into pieces and remove the excess flour. Place the floured rabbit pieces in the saucepan. Brown the rabbit by turning it on all sides, then add the aromatic herbs and the onion kept aside.

Now blend with the white wine and let the alcoholic part evaporate completely. Add the crushed tomatoes with their water and the olives.

Add salt and pepper, then pour half the broth and cook over medium-low heat for 45 minutes, with the lid on.

After this time, add the remaining broth and continue cooking for another 45 minutes, always with the lid on. Once cooked, remove the lid, raise the heat and reduce the sauce. Your rabbit cacciatore is ready to be served and enjoyed while still hot!

Apulian bowlers
Ingredients:
- **Thin slices of veal 12**
- **Bacon 12 slices**
- **Caciocavallo 150 g**
- **Parsley 2 sprigs**
- **Extra virgin olive oil q.s.**
- **Salt up to taste**
- **Garlic 1 clove**
- **Black pepper to taste**

To prepare the Apulian bowlers, start by cutting the caciocavallo into thin slices, then take the slices of meat, cover them with baking paper and with the help of a meat tenderizer beat them to make them thin. Salt and pepper the slices and begin to compose the bowls by placing a slice of bacon, a few slices of caciocavallo on each slice of meat and then season with the parsley and minced garlic.

Roll up the slices and secure them with a toothpick. Oil a baking dish that can hold all the bowlers and cook in a preheated oven at 200° for about 30 minutes, finish cooking by activating the grill for a few minutes and serve the Apulian bowlers piping hot.

Chicken breast with corn flakes
Ingredients:
- Chicken breast (4 slices) 400 g
- Corn flakes 100 g
- Spicy paprika 10 g
- Eggs 1
- Whole milk 10 g
- Salt up to taste

TO FRY
- Peanut oil to taste

Put the corn flakes in a transparent bag and chop them coarsely with a rolling pin until you get a rather fine mix.
Pour the chopped cornflakes into a baking dish, add 5 g of paprika and mix well.
In another separate pyrophile, pour the beaten egg and add the milk to make the flavor more delicate, finally add salt and mix well. At this point arrange the chicken breasts on the cutting board and sprinkle them evenly with the remaining paprika and a pinch of salt. Once finished, dip them one at a time first in the beaten egg and subsequently in the breading based on corn falkes. Place the chicken breasts in the breading, making it adhere evenly over the entire surface with your hands, and place them on a tray.
Take a large frying pan, heat the seed oil to a temperature no higher than 170-180° which must be kept constant by measuring with a kitchen thermometer; cook the chicken breasts which should be flush with the oil, first on one side and then on the other for about 5 minutes (alternatively you can use the oven and cook them in bite-sized pieces in a static oven preheated to 180° for 10 -15 minutes). When the chicken breasts are cooked and crunchy, turn off the heat and arrange them on a tray with absorbent paper.

Meatloaf
Ingredients:
- Minced veal 250 g
- Sausage 150 g
- Grana Padano PDO to grate 100 g
- Medium eggs 2
- Crumb bread 100 g
- Salt up to taste
- Black pepper to taste
- Nutmeg 1 pinch
- Garlic 1 clove
- chopped parsley 2 tbsp

TO COVER
- Veal slices (3 slices) 450 g
- Garlic 1 clove
- Rosemary 2 sprigs
- Thyme 2 sprigs
- Sage 6 leaves

FOR THE COOKING
- Extra virgin olive oil 4 tbsp
- Butter 30 g
- Meat broth 250 ml
- Salt up to taste
- Black pepper to taste

To prepare the meatloaf, put the minced meat, the skinned and crumbled sausage, the breadcrumbs reduced to fine crumbs, the Grana Padano cheese, the two eggs, the crushed garlic, the salt, the pepper, in a large bowl. ground nutmeg and chopped parsley; knead everything with your hands for about 10 minutes, mixing the ingredients well. With the compound obtained, make a cylinder about 20 cm long. On a cutting board beat the slices of meat with which you will coat the meat.

Arrange all the slices on the cutting board and place the meatloaf in the center. Wrap it up well
then tie it up with kitchen twine.

Finely chop the garlic together with the rosemary needles and thyme leaves and add the salt and pepper; sprinkle the meatloaf entirely with these ingredients, making them adhere well.

In a saucepan, melt the butter together with the oil, then brown the meatloaf on a low heat on all its sides,

add one or two ladles of meat broth, cover the pan with a lid and cook over low heat for at least an hour. During cooking, turn the meatloaf often and, if needed, add more broth; after an hour, pierce the meatloaf with a toothpick: if pink liquid comes out, let it cook for another 10-15 minutes, if instead the liquid is transparent, turn off the heat, because the meatloaf is cooked to perfection. Let the meatloaf rest in the heat for 15 minutes and in the meantime prepare the accompanying sauce, adding a spoonful of sifted flour to the cooking liquid and stirring over low heat until thickened. If you want a very velvety sauce, pass the sauce through a sieve. Remove the string from the meatloaf, cut it into slices and sprinkle with the previously obtained sauce.

Stewed rabbit

Ingredients:
- Rabbit 1 kg (in pieces)
- Extra virgin olive oil 5 tbsp
- White onions 1
- 2 bay leaves
- Sage 4 leaves
- Rosemary 2 sprigs
- Fresh chilli 1
- Garlic 2 cloves
- Tomato puree 400 g
- White wine 200ml
- Salt up to taste
- Black pepper to taste
- Vegetable broth 500 ml

Peel and chop the onion, put it in a pan together with the oil and let it dry over low heat for at least 10 minutes. Add finely chopped chilli, rosemary, sage, bay leaf and garlic, sauté for a couple of minutes,
then add the pieces of rabbit and brown them. Add the white wine which you will let evaporate, then add the tomato, salt and pepper and cover with a lid.
When needed, add some vegetable broth. When the rabbit is cooked, leave the pan uncovered until the cooking juices thicken, then add more salt if necessary and turn off the heat.

Stuffed chicken rolls
Ingredients:
- Chicken breast 400 g
- Black pepper to taste
- Salt up to taste
- Seed oil 3 tbsp
- Rosemary 8 sprigs
- Scamorza 8 slices
- Speck 8 slices

To prepare the stuffed chicken rolls, start by cleaning the chicken breasts from excessive fat or pieces of bone, cut them horizontally to obtain 4 slices and beat them with a meat mallet, wrapping them in baking paper.

Take a slice of chicken and stuff it first with 2 slices of cheese and then with two slices of speck, then roll up the slice on itself, cut the roll into slices thus obtaining small rolls that you will stop with a wooden skewer.

Flavor each roll with a sprig of rosemary. Proceed in the same way with all the other chicken slices. Now the stuffed chicken rolls are ready for cooking: heat a grill brushed with a little seed oil, cook the rolls on both sides, at least 6/7 minutes on each side until they are well grilled, finally add salt and pepper; then let them rest on a plate for a few minutes before removing the toothpick.

Alternatively, you can cook the stuffed chicken rolls in a pan or in the oven: brush a baking dish with oil and place the skewers inside, cook in a preheated oven at 180° for about 20 minutes, taking care to turn the rolls halfway through cooking.

Dessert

Amor Polenta (Polenta sponge cake)
Ingredients:
- Eggs 1
- Egg yolks 2
- Sugar 2 ½ tsp (115 g)
- Fine salt ¼ tsp (1 g)
- Vanilla bean 1
- Lemon peel 1
- Almond flour (68 g)
- Flour 00 3 tsp (45 g)
- Baking powder 1 tsp (4 g)
- Fioretto corn flour 2.5 tsp (38 g)
- Butter (125 g)

FOR THE BUTTER AND ALMOND MIX
- Butter 3 tsp (12 g)
- Almond flour 2 tbsp (13 g)

To make amor polenta, first prepare the butter and almond mix: put tablespoon (12,g) of butter and tablepoons (13 g) of almond flour in a mixer. Blend to obtain a homogeneous mixture and set aside. Then melt (125 g) of butter over very low heat and let cool. Whip the egg together with the sugar in a large bowl with electric whisks, then continue to whip the egg yolks and the seeds taken from the vanilla bean.

Add the grated rind of an untreated lemon, salt, and the almond and butter mix.

Once you have whipped the mixture, move on to the dry ingredients: pour the almond flour, baking powder, corn flour and 00 flour into a bowl, then sift it on a sheet of baking paper.

Add the sieved dry ingredients to the whipped mixture and incorporate them evenly. Pour in the melted butter and stir again gently to obtain a homogeneous and uniform mixture.

Now butter and flour a traditional 8x3 inch (20x7.5 cm) amor polenta mold and pour in the mixture. Bake it in a static oven at 330° F (165° C) for 60 minutes. Once cooked, let it cool before removing the mold, and sprinkle with powdered sugar: your amor polenta is ready to be enjoyed!

Soft ricotta and pear cake
Ingredients:
- **Pears 400 g**
- **Cow's milk ricotta 350 g**
- **Flour 00 250 g**
- **Baking powder for desserts 16 g**
- **Medium eggs 3**
- **Sugar 170 g**
- **Lemon zest 1**
- **Vanilla pod 1**

To prepare the ricotta and pear soft cake, start by peeling the pears, remove the central core and cut them into rather small cubes, put them in a bowl with very little lemon juice to prevent them from blackening. Beat the sugar with the ricotta with a whisk (or in a planetary mixer), then add the seeds of the vanilla pod. Then add the 3 eggs and continue beating the mixture,
add the grated lemon zest. Sift the flour with the baking powder and add them to the mixture, mixing with a wooden spoon until you get a smooth dough. Incorporate the diced pears
and mix them into the dough. Grease and flour a springform pan with a diameter of 24 cm, pour the cake mixture and level it well using a spatula. At this point, bake the cake at 180°C (static oven) for 50/70 minutes, until when a wooden toothpick is inserted into the center of the cake, it comes out dry. Remove the soft ricotta and pear cake from the oven, bake it cool, turn it out of the mold and sprinkle with powdered sugar before serving!

Magic ricotta cake
Ingredients:
- **Sheep ricotta 800 g**
- **Cane sugar 200 g**
- **Eggs 4**
- **Corn starch 45 g**
- **Orange zest 1**
- **Dark chocolate drops 200 g**

To prepare the magical ricotta cake, first put the sheep's ricotta to drain, so it will not release liquid during cooking. Pour the lightly beaten eggs into a large bowl, add the brown sugar.
Start working with the hand whisk. Add the orange zest and pour the ricotta a little at a time with a spoon.

Now add the cornstarch. Keep mixing with the whisk until you get a homogeneous mixture. Add the chocolate chips and mix with a spatula to blend.
Pour the mixture into a cake pan with a diameter of 20 cm lined with parchment paper or greased and floured. Level the surface with a spatula. Bake in a static oven at 170° for about 80 minutes. Once taken out of the oven, the magic ricotta cake will deflate a little, but this is normal because it does not contain flour but only a little cornstarch. When cooked, take the magic ricotta cake out of the oven and let it cool before removing it from the mould.

Oat apple crumble
Ingredients:
- Rolled oats (125 g)
- Wholegrain flour (125 g)
- Butter 1 stick (100 g)
- Muscovado sugar 4 tbsp (35 g)
- Sugar 3 tbsp (35 g)
- Fine salt 1 pinch

FOR THE FILLING
- Golden delicious apples (200 g)
- Muscovado sugar 2 tbsp (20 g)
- Cinnamon powder to taste

TO DECORATE
- Chopped hazelnuts 2 tbsp (20 g)

To make oat apple crumble, start by preparing the crumble: place the wholegrain flour, rolled oats, granulated sugar and muscovado sugar in a capacious bowl,
along with the cold and diced butter and a pinch of salt. Stir briskly with your finger tips to obtain a crumbly mixture. Leave in the refrigerator to rest for around 30 minutes.
Now prepare the filling: peel the apples, cut them in half and remove the core, then cut them into wedges and lastly, thinly slice. Place the apples in a bowl, add the muscovado sugar, the cinnamon and stir with a spoon.
Now take an 8" (20 cm) cake mold, line with parchment paper and add half of the crumble mixture: try to create an even layer by gently pressing it down with your fingers. Spread the filling over the base, leave a 0.4 inch (1 cm) space along the edge and then cover with the remaining crumble mixture.

Press the surface down with your finger tips and sprinkle with the chopped hazelnuts. Bake in a static oven preheated to 355°F (180°C) for around 35 minutes. Once baked, remove your oat apple crumble from the oven and leave it to cool thoroughly before enjoying it!

Pear and chocolate strudel
Ingredients:
- Breadcrumbs (50 g)
- Powdered ginger ¼ tsp
- Puff pastry (230 g) - (1 rectangular sheet)
- Butter 2 ¼ tbsp (40 g)
- Bartlett pears (350 g)
- Dark chocolate (75 g)
- Peeled almonds 1 tsp (25 g)
- Brown sugar 2 tbsp (30 g)
- Cinnamon powder 1 tsp

FOR THE SURFACE
- **Fresh liquid cream to taste**
- **Brown sugar to taste**

To prepare the pear and chocolate strudel, start by placing the butter in a pan. Melt it, then add the breadcrumbs and leave to brown for a few minutes, stirring all the while. As soon as it is ready, place in a bowl and leave to one side. Finely chop the almonds and the chocolate, and leave to one side. Now you can prepare the pears. Peel and tip them on both ends,
cut them into 4 pieces and remove the core. Lastly, thinly slice the pears and place them in a bowl. Add the dark chocolate
the almonds, the brown sugar, the powdered ginger and
the cinnamon. Mix everything well. Unroll the puff pastry and imagine dividing it into 3 pieces lengthwise. The filling will go on the central part; cut both side parts into slanted slices that are 0.4 in wide.

Now cover the central part, first with the toasted breadcrumbs and then with the pear and chocolate filling. One at a time, lift both side strips and place over the central part, in alternation.

This way you will achieve a cage effect. Discard any leftover pieces of dough. Lastly, brush a little cream onto the strips and sprinkle with the brown sugar.

Bake in a static oven preheated to 400F for around 20 minutes. Once baked, leave the pear and chocolate strudel to cool thoroughly before cutting into slices and enjoying it.

Carnival donuts
Ingredients:
- Flour 00 100 g
- Malt 1 tsp
- Milk 60ml
- Fresh brewer's yeast 12 g

FOR THE DOUGH OF 20-25 DONUTS
- Flour 00 500 g
- Medium eggs 6
- Sugar 200g
- Butter 100 g
- Salt 1 pinch
- Lemon zest 1
- Orange zest 1
- Vanilla pod 1
- TO SPRINKLE
- Powdered sugar to taste

TO FRY
- Seed oil to taste

To make the fried carnival donuts, start by preparing the yeast: crumble the brewer's yeast in a small bowl, add the warm milk and the malt (or, instead, the sugar), then mix to dissolve everything. Add the flour and mix the ingredients until a soft and homogeneous mixture is obtained which we will leave to rise in a bowl covered with transparent film inside the oven which is switched off but with the light on (or in a warm place) for about 30-50 minutes. Meanwhile, in the bowl of a planetary mixer (or in a normal bowl if you work by hand), put the flour, the eggs, the salt, the sugar, the grated rind of 1 lemon and 1 orange, the seeds of the vanilla pod and knead for a few minutes until obtaining an elastic and homogeneous mixture. We also combine the yeast which will have doubled its volume and knead to mix it well.

Add, a few at a time, small pieces of butter softened at room temperature and work the dough until the butter is all absorbed. Put the mixture obtained in a bowl covered with transparent film in the oven off but with the light on and let the dough rise for three hours (it should at least double its volume). After the indicated time, roll out the dough on a floured pastry board without kneading it too much and roll out the dough to a thickness of 1 cm.

With a pasta bowl, we obtain circles with a diameter of about 8 cm which we will pierce in the center with another pasta bowl with a smaller diameter (about 3 cm). Place the donuts obtained on large trays lined with parchment paper and let them rise for about 30 minutes (still in the oven off). Then fry the donuts in hot oil at 160-170° and then let them drip on absorbent kitchen paper, then sprinkle them with vanilla icing sugar or granulated sugar. Don't throw away the donut dough clippings, but fry them too!!!! Carnival fried donuts are ready to be tasted!

Lemon loaf
Ingredients:
- **Lemons 450 g**
- **Flour 00 300 g**
- **Sugar 300 g**
- **Whole milk 100 g**
- **Sunflower oil 100 g**
- **Medium eggs 3**
- **Baking powder for desserts 16 g**

To prepare the lemon loaf, first peel the lemons, then divide them in half. In all, you will need 170 g of lemon pulp.
Preheat the oven in static mode to 180° and combine all the ingredients in a mixer fitted with blades: add the instant yeast for desserts, the sugar, the flour, the lemon pulp.
Also add the seed oil, whole milk and whole eggs,
then blend everything until you get a creamy and uniform mixture. Now take a springform pan of 20 cm in diameter and butter it thoroughly, then flour it.
Pour the dough inside and cook in the preheated static oven at 180° for about 60 minutes, placing it on the low shelf. Once cooked (always do the toothpick test at the end of cooking), take the cake out of the oven and let it cool in the mould, then turn it out of the mold and sprinkle it with icing sugar. Your fragrant lemon bread is ready to be tasted!

Villager cake
Ingredients:
- **Stale bread 300 g**
- **Whole milk 1 l**
- **Medium eggs 2**
- **Macaroons 120 g**
- **Bitter cocoa powder 50 g**
- **Sugar 120g**
- **Raisins 70 g**
- **Pine nuts 50 g**
- **Oranges zest and juice 1**

To prepare the village cake, start by heating the milk (it shouldn't reach the boil). In the meantime, take the stale bread and cut it into slices, then cut it into cubes. Place the bread in a bowl.
Grate the zest of an untreated orange (then keep the orange aside, it will be used later), then pour the hot milk on the bread. Mix with a spoon and cover with transparent film; let the bread soak for half an hour. Stir occasionally, so that all the bread absorbs the milk and softens well.
Meanwhile, squeeze the orange and soak the raisins in its juice. Then in a mixer pour the amaretti and bitter cocoa,
operate the blades to reduce everything to a powder. At this point, take the now soft bread, mix with a spoon or fork to flake it further and add the bitter cocoa. Mix it with the bread; then beat the eggs in a separate bowl and pour them into the mixture. Mix with a spatula
and when they are absorbed, add the sugar too. Then pour in the pine nuts and drain the raisins well from the orange juice,
before adding it to the mixture. Mix well with a spatula to mix all the ingredients. Grease and line a 24cm diameter pan with greaseproof paper

and pour the mixture inside. Bake in a preheated static oven at 180° for 60 minutes (or at 160° for 50 minutes if you use a convection oven). Once cooked, take the cake out of the oven and let it cool down, then take it out of the mold and let it cool on a wire rack before serving.

Bicolor cake
Ingredients:
- **Flour 00 380 g**
- **Sugar 200g**
- **Eggs (4 medium) at room temperature 270 g**
- **Corn seed oil 180 g**
- **Whole milk at room temperature 180 g**
- **Vanilla pod 1**
- **Salt up to 1 pinch**
- **Baking powder for desserts 16 g**
- **Bitter cocoa powder 40 g**
- **TO DECORATE**
- **Powdered sugar to taste**

To prepare the two-tone cake, first put the eggs in a bowl together with a pinch of salt. Whip them with an electric whisk for a few seconds and as soon as the mixture becomes frothy, add the sugar and the seeds that you will have taken from the vanilla pod. Whip again for 5 minutes, until the mixture is swollen and frothy.

Add the oil and milk. Whip again for 2 minutes. Add half of the flour by sieving it and mix again with the whisk until it is absorbed. Then add the remaining flour, always sifting it and mix again with the whisk. Also add the sifted yeast and incorporate it into the rest, mixing with electric whisks. Finally mix with a spatula, then divide the dough in half, transferring it into two bowls equally. In one of the 2 bowls add the sifted cocoa and mix it into the dough with the help of an electric whisk.

Grease a 22cm cake tin. Pour half of the clear dough into the pan, spread it with a spatula, and pour all the cocoa dough over it.

Complete with the remaining light dough and if necessary smooth it gently. Bake in a preheated static oven at 170° for 50 minutes.
Always do the toothpick test before taking the cake out of the oven. Leave to cool, transfer the cake to a plate and decorate it with icing sugar. The two-tone cake is ready to be served.

Nua Cake
- Ingredients:
- Butter 250 g
- Flour 00 250 g
- Sugar 250g
- Baking powder for desserts 16 g
- Medium eggs 6
- Orange zest 1
- Salt up to taste

FOR THE CUSTARD CREAM
- Whole milk 250 ml
- Sugar 75 g
- Flour 00 25 g
- Medium yolks 3
- Orange zest 1

FOR THE CHOCOLATE CUSTARD
- Whole milk 250 ml
- Dark chocolate 60 g
- Sugar 60 g
- Flour 00 10 g
- Corn starch 10 g
- Medium yolks 3

To make the Nua cake, start by preparing the custard. Place the eggs and sugar in a bowl and whisk the mixture with an electric whisk until it becomes clear. Then add the sifted flour a little at a time, stirring with a wooden spoon. Meanwhile, pour the milk into a saucepan, add the orange zest and bring it to the boil over a moderate heat. When it is hot, pour it over the egg mixture, mix with a whisk and then transfer the cream into the saucepan and let it thicken over low heat, continuing to mix with the whisk. When the cream is thick and compact, turn off the heat, transfer it into a large, shallow bowl and cover it with cling film to let it cool.

Now take care of the chocolate custard: whip the eggs and sugar with an electric whisk to obtain a clear mixture. Incorporate the sifted flour and cornstarch, mixing with a spoon. Separately, heat the milk in a saucepan and bring it to the boil, then pour it slowly into the egg mixture.

Transfer the mixture into the saucepan, chop the dark chocolate and add it to the cream. Let the cream thicken over low heat, stirring with a whisk. When the custard is thick and compact, turn off the heat, transfer it into a bowl, cover it with cling film and let it cool.

Now proceed with the cake dough: whip the eggs with half the sugar and a pinch of salt, using an electric whisk. You have to get a clear and fluffy dough. In another bowl, soften the butter with the remaining half of the sugar, again with the help of an electric beater. to get a cream. Combine the two compounds: mix with a spatula to mix them. Incorporate the sifted flour and baking powder, flavored with grated orange zest. Pour the dough into a 26 cm diameter mold greased and lined with parchment paper. Take back the two now cold creams, distribute some mounds of custard with the help of a spoon.

Repeat the same operation for the chocolate custard and cover the entire surface of the cake. Bake at 180°C for 65 minutes in a preheated static oven. When cooked, the Nua cake will be well browned on the surface, take it out of the oven and let it cool before turning it out of the mold.

Apple and orange cake
Ingredients:
- Apples 4
- Oranges 1
- Flour 00 (380 g)
- Eggs 4
- Sugar (200 g)
- White yogurt (90 g)
- Butter (100 g) - melted
- Powdered yeast for sweets 3 ⅓ tsp (16 g)

TO GARNISH
- **Powdered sugar to taste**

To make the apple and orange cake, first melt the butter over very low heat and set aside to cool. Wash and dry the apples thoroughly, then slice them in half and remove the cores . Cut three of the four apples into thin, uneven slices without peeling them, then cut the fourth apple into more even slices, as these will be used for decoration later.

Season the uneven apple slices with the orange zest and juice, stir, and set aside.

Pour the eggs into a bowl and whip them with an electric whisk, adding the cup (200 g) of sugar a little at a time. Next, add the cooled melted butter and white yogurt, continuing to stir as you do so, to achieve a light, even mixture. Now sift in the flour through a sieve, along with the baking powder, and stir gently with a spatula. Add the orange-flavored apples to finish. Grease and flour an 8-inch (20-cm) cake pan and pour in the mixture.

Spread it with the back of a spoon 16 to get an even surface. At this point, take the apple slices that you set aside for decoration and arrange them side by side covering the whole cake.

Sprinkle the surface with granulated sugar and bake in a conventional oven preheated to 350°F (175°C) for 70 minutes, until golden brown. When it's done baking, take the apple and orange cake out of the oven and serve sprinkled with powdered sugar to taste.

Lemon sorbet
Ingredients:
- Lemon juice 75 cups (130 g)
- Egg whites 1 (30 g)
- Water 1 cup (250 g)
- Sugar 1 ¼ cup (170 g)
- Limoncello 1 ½ tbsp (30 g)

To prepare your lemon sorbet start by placing the egg white in a bowl and whisk. When the egg white is semi-whipped, you will notice as a little froth will form on the surface, sprinkle 2 tbsp of sugar over them and continue whisking all the while. As soon as the mixture becomes white and frothy it is ready: leave it to one side. Squeeze the lemons to obtain 0.75 cups of juice, filter in a fine mesh colander to remove any pulp, and place the juice in a container into which you have already added the water.
Whisk and add the remaining 0.75 cup of sugar, then gradually add the egg whites so as not to deflate the soft mixture. After thoroughly mixing the ingredients together, add the limoncello and stir some more.
Pour the mixture into the ice cream maker (follow instructions for your machine) and switch it on. As soon as the sorbet acquires a classic creamy consistency, which will take around 40 minutes, place it in glasses and serve your lemon sorbet garnished with zest.

Bread Cake
Ingredients:
- Homemade bread 400 g
- Whole milk 400 g
- Raisins 100 g
- Lemon zest 1
- Butter at room temperature 100 g
- Sugar 100g
- Breadcrumbs 30 g
- Eggs 1
- Grappa 20 g
- Pine nuts 50 g
- Flour 00 100 g
- Water to taste

To prepare the bread cake, remove the bread and the crust: you will need to obtain 300 g of breadcrumbs which you will cut into pieces and put them in a bowl to soak in the milk for about 10 minutes. Soak the raisins in water for five minutes to revive them. Meanwhile that the crumb softens, grate the peel of a lemon and butter a 22 cm cake pan with a small piece of butter of the total dose, sprinkling it with the breadcrumbs.

After ten minutes, squeeze the crumb well and add the sugar and egg, then the softened butter cut into small pieces. Mix well with a wooden spoon, to mix all the ingredients.

Add the grappa, then the drained raisins, the lemon zest, the pine nuts and finally the sifted flour.

Mix the ingredients very well until you obtain a compact and homogeneous mixture which you will transfer into the buttered cake tin. With the back of a spoon, spread it evenly and flatten the surface, bake the cake at 180 degrees for about 60 minutes: the surface should be golden. Remove from the oven and let it cool: your bread cake is ready!

Tiramisu with chocolate cream
Ingredients:
- Dark chocolate 120 g
- Yolks 6
- Sugar 100g
- Mascarpone 400 g

FOR THE BASE
- About 8 ladyfingers
- Coffee 300 g
- Sugar 20g

TO DECORATE
- Bitter cocoa powder q.b.

To prepare the chocolate tiramisu, start by melting the dark chocolate: chop it, then melt it in a bain-marie, avoiding that the water comes into contact with the chocolate (alternatively, you can melt it in the microwave several times, inserting it for 2-3 minutes , then stir and put it back in the microwave to melt it in a controlled manner). Stir to melt and once ready, transfer it to a bowl and leave to cool.
Meanwhile, separate the yolks from the whites and add the sugar to the yolks, then work with an electric whisk to make a frothy and clear mixture. With the leftover egg whites you can prepare delicious meringues or cat's tongues.
Work the mascarpone with a whisk, then add it to the egg and sugar mixture that you have whipped, mix again with a whisk to obtain a thick cream. When the chocolate has cooled, add it to the cream.

When the cream is ready, place it in the refrigerator while you continue the preparation. Prepare the coffee and pour it into a shallow, large bowl; dissolve the sugar inside (you can omit it if you prefer) and let it cool.

Divide each biscuit in half and dip it into the coffee on both sides, then place two halves at the base of the glass and pour in the chocolate mascarpone cream; you can also use a disposable sac-à-poche to create the layers of cream. Continue by sprinkling with bitter cocoa, then continue again with a layer of ladyfingers moistened with coffee and one of cream.

Once ready, you can dust again with bitter chocolate powder and serve your chocolate tiramisu!

Part 4

Appetizers, sides and snacks

Tomato bruschetta
Ingredients:
- **Homemade bread 8 slices**
- **Cluster tomatoes 500 g - ripe**
- **Basil 8 leaves**
- **Oregano to taste**
- **Extra virgin olive oil to taste**
- **Fine salt to taste**
- **Black pepper to taste**

To prepare tomato bruschetta, first wash the tomatoes, divide them in half and then cut them into cubes. Pour the cut tomatoes into a bowl and add basil leaves, previously washed and dried. Season with a pinch of oregano, salt, pepper and oil. Stir well and let the flavors blend for about 30 minutes. This step is optional, but we recommend it to enhance scents and flavors.
Meanwhile, cut the bread into slices. After the resting time, heat a grill and place the slices of bread on it. Grill them on both sides until toasted.
Now top the bread slices with your tomato salad, drizzling a little more oil. Let rest for a couple of minutes, then serve your tomato bruschettas!

Biscuits with parmesan and pecorino
Ingredients:
- Parmigiano Reggiano DOP 50 g
- Pecorino cheese 50 g
- Flour 00 130 g
- Cold butter 100 g
- Cold whole milk 30 g
- Salt up to 1 pinch
- Black pepper to taste
- FOR COVERAGE
- Parmigiano Reggiano 40 g
- Black pepper to taste

To prepare the biscuits with parmesan and pecorino, start by pouring the flour into the pitcher of a planetary mixer fitted with a leaf hook. Also add the two types of cheese, the cold butter cut into cubes, the pepper and the salt.
Activate the planetary mixer at medium speed, add the cold milk slowly, and mix until a rather compact mass is formed (if you don't have a planetary mixer, you can easily prepare this dough by hand). Transfer the dough to the work surface (preferably cold) and knead it just enough to give it the shape of a flattened loaf.
Cover it with transparent film, and let it rest in the fridge for 30 minutes. After this time, retrieve the dough and roll it out with a rolling pin on a lightly floured pastry board, until it is 3 mm thick. Using a cup of the desired shape, now form your biscuits; with these doses and with molds of 6 cm in diameter, about 14 came out!
Arrange them on a baking tray lined with baking paper and sprinkle a little Parmesan in the center of each biscuit. Complete with a grind of black pepper, and bake in a preheated static oven at 200° for 15 minutes (if you want to cook in a convection oven, you can try baking one or two biscuits to test the times and temperatures for the next ones). Bake your biscuits with parmesan and pecorino, let them cool and... enjoy them!

Stuffed friggitelli
Ingredients:
- Friggitelli 10
- Breadcrumbs 40 g
- Copper tomatoes (about 1) 180 g
- Dried tomatoes in oil 40 g
- Parmigiano Reggiano DOP to grate 30 g
- Basil to taste
- Salt up to taste
- Extra virgin olive oil q.s.

To make the stuffed friggitelli, first wash and dry the friggitelli, cut them laterally to cut out a small portion, extract the internal seeds with a teaspoon.

Wash and dry the tomato, then cut it first into slices and then into cubes. Drain the dried tomatoes and cut them into small pieces.

In a large bowl, pour the fresh tomatoes, the dried ones in oil, flavor with the grated Parmesan, the breadcrumbs
and perfume the mixture with roughly chopped basil leaves. Finally, salt the filling and stir to mix the ingredients. Now place the friggitelli on a baking tray lined with parchment paper and stuff the hollow with the filling, helping yourself with a teaspoon.

Drizzle the friggitelli with oil and cook in a preheated static oven at 180° for 20 minutes (if you prefer them very soft, you can cook them for a few more minutes). When cooked, take the stuffed friggitelli out of the oven, let them cool down and then serve them.

Potatoes and peppers
Ingredients:
- Potatoes 800 g
- Extra virgin olive oil 140ml
- Yellow peppers 300 g
- Red peppers 300 g

To prepare the potatoes and peppers, start by washing the peppers, dry them with paper towels, then cut them in half and remove the white filaments and internal seeds.
Cut the peppers into thick strips and place them in a bowl. Peel the potatoes, and cut them into wedges not too thin (1 cm).
In a large pan, put the extra virgin olive oil and let it heat up, then add the potatoes, the red peppers
and yellow peppers. Cook the vegetables and with the help of a spatula, turn gently from time to time, being careful not to flake the potatoes, add salt and continue cooking until the ingredients are well cooked and are presented with a crispy browning (about it will take about 20 minutes), remove them from the heat and serve the potatoes and peppers piping hot.

Neapolitan pasta fritters
Ingredients:
- Bucatini pasta 500 g
- Cooked ham 150 g - (for chopping into cubes)
- Frozen peas 75 g
- Garlic 1 clove
- Extra virgin olive oil to taste
- Peanut seed oil 1.5 l
- Fine salt to taste

FOR THE BÉCHAMEL SAUCE
- Flour 00 200 g
- Butter 130 g
- Whole milk 1 l
- Fine salt to taste
- Nutmeg to taste

FOR THE BATTER
- Water 325 g
- Flour 00 200 g

To make the Neapolitan pasta fritters, start with the béchamel sauce. Heat the milk in a saucepan, and in the meantime, melt the butter in a pot. As soon as the butter has melted, add the flour all at once and whisk until the mixture thickens up. Don't worry if it condenses quickly.

Next, dilute with the hot milk, pouring it in a little at a time and making sure that no lumps form. Once the mixture is well diluted, add salt and nutmeg and continue cooking until you get a nice thick cream. Transfer it to a bowl, cover with plastic wrap, and leave to cool at room temperature.

Move on to the filling Cut the ham into slices, strips, and finally ¼-inch (0.5-cm) cubes. Next, crush a clove of unpeeled garlic and put it in a frying pan together with a drizzle of oil. Allow the flavor to develop for a few minutes over medium heat, then add the ham cubes and peas. Sauté for a minute or two, season with salt, remove the garlic, and set aside . At this point, you can cook the pasta in salted boiling water; be sure to drain it when there are 2-3 minutes of cooking time left. Pour the pasta out onto a lightly greased work surface, then add a drop of oil and mix it in quickly so you don't burn yourself . Cut the pasta roughly with a knife and leave to cool. When all the ingredients are at room temperature, pour the béchamel sauce over the pasta. Mix together well with your hands and then take a handful. Make a little indentation in the middle of the pasta mixture and fill with a handful of peas and ham. Close the pasta around the filling and then press it down inside of a 3-inch (8-cm) food ring mold to form a medallion. Alternatively, you can also shape the medallions by hand.
Carefully lift the medallions using a small spatula and arrange them on a tray lined with parchment paper. Remove the ring mold and repeat the process so you get around 15 medallions. Once they're all ready, leave to cool in the fridge for at least an hour or until they've firmed up nicely.

Next, heat the oil for frying and prepare the batter. Pour the flour into a bowl and slowly add the water to it while whisking. Season with salt and continue whisking until you get a smooth batter without any lumps , and then dip the first medallion in.

Drain the excess batter and plunge into the boiling oil. You can add other medallions, too, but no more than 2 or 3 at a time. This way, the oil temperature will remain hot at 350°-375°F (180°-190°C). After 3-4 minutes, they should be nice and golden, so drain on paper towel and continue cooking the others. Now your Neapolitan pasta fritters are ready! Buon appetito!

Marinated egg plant
Ingredients:
- Eggplant 700 g
- Extra virgin olive oil 100 g
- White wine vinegar 3 tbsp
- Fresh chili pepper 1
- Garlic 1 clove
- Marjoram 2 sprigs
- Thyme 3 sprigs
- Mint 1 sprig
- Fine salt to taste

To prepare marinated eggplants, start by cleaning the eggplants: wash and dry them, then remove the stalk and cut them into slices about 5-6 mm thick. Grease a plate with oil and heat it.
Grill the eggplants on the very hot grill first on one side and then on the other and transfer them on a plate 6. When you have finished, let it cool while you prepare the sauce.
Peel the garlic, remove the core and slice thinly. Clean the chili by rubbing it between your fingers to release the seeds and then slice thinly.
Place chopped garlic and chili in a bowl. Clean and chop the fresh aromatic herbs. Also transfer these to the bowl.
Pour in oil and vinegar and mix with a fork.
Sprinkle the eggplants with the aromatic emulsion. Season with a pinch of salt, cover and let them rest in the fridge for a few hours. Enjoy your marinated eggplants.

Roman spinach
Ingredients:
- Spinach 1 kg
- Butter 100 g
- Pine nuts 80 g
- Raisins 100 g

To prepare Roman spinach, soak the raisins in a bowl of warm water for at least half an hour; in the meantime, peel the spinach and wash it under fresh running water, then drain it well. Melt the butter in a non-stick pan,
add the spinach, add salt and let them soften for a few minutes over a moderate heat, covered with a lid.
At this point, drain the raisins well, squeeze them and add them to the spinach, add the pine nuts, mix and season with salt. Saute everything for a couple of minutes and your Roman spinach is ready!

Baked Tropea onions
Ingredients:
- Tropea red onions 4
- Rosemary to taste
- Sage to taste
- Thyme to taste
- Coarse salt 5 g
- Black pepper to taste
- Extra virgin olive oil q.s.

To prepare the Tropea onions in the oven, first remove the part with the roots and peel them. Then cut them vertically so as to obtain 2 halves. Arrange the onions in a pan (also suitable for cooking in the oven), sprinkle them with a drizzle of oil and brown them over high heat for about 5 minutes, being careful to move them from time to time, leaving them with the cut side facing you. 'high, so as not to burn them. In the meantime, take the aromatic herbs
and chop them finely. Then as soon as the onions are lightly browned, remove them from the heat and sprinkle them with the freshly chopped herbs. Season with coarse salt, add a drizzle of oil and pepper. At this point, cook in a preheated static oven at 190° for about 30-35 minutes on the central shelf. Remove from the oven and serve your Tropea onions in the oven with your favorite main courses!

Sautéed cabbage
Ingredients:
- Cabbage (to be cleaned) 600 g
- Taggiasca olives 50 g
- Golden onions 50 g
- Extra virgin olive oil 3 tbsp
- Vegetable broth 100ml
- Salt up to taste
- Black pepper to taste

To prepare the cabbage in a pan, first peel the onion, chop it finely and keep it aside. Switch to the cabbage. Remove any more damaged outer leaves, wash it well under running water and cut it in half with a sharp knife.

Then cut it into strips, leaving out the hardest central part which will be thrown away. In a fairly large pan, pour the extra virgin olive oil and the onion. Let it wither over medium heat and add the cabbage.

Pour in the hot broth, cover with the lid and cook for 10 minutes, stirring several times. Remove the lid, season with salt.

Add some pepper, pour in the Taggiasca olives and continue cooking until the broth has evaporated. Serve the cabbage hot and with a generous sprinkling of pepper.

Baked peas with bacon
Ingredients:
- Peas (450 g cleaned) 2 kg
- Smoked bacon 100 g
- Water 150g
- Extra virgin olive oil q.s.
- Shallot 1
- Salt up to taste

To prepare stewed peas with bacon, first peel the peas by collecting them in a bowl, you should obtain about 450 g. Switch to the bacon: first cut it into slices.
From these you get strips. Chop the shallot and move to the stove. Heat a drizzle of oil in a pan and add the shallot.
Cook for two minutes over medium-low heat with a pinch of salt (optional), then add the bacon and cook for 3-4 minutes. Add the peas and a pinch of salt.
Pour in the water and cover with the lid and cook for about 12-13 minutes, stirring occasionally. Season with salt to taste, paying attention to the bacon which is flavoursome. Once cooking is over, switch off and serve your peas with bacon!

Eggplant Sweet & Sour
Ingredients:
- **Eggplants 780 g**
- **White wine vinegar 40 g**
- **Sugar 40 g**
- **Extra virgin olive oil 40 g**
- **Garlic 1 clove**
- **Mint (about 10 leaves) to taste**
- **Basil (about 10 leaves) to taste**
- **Salt up to taste**
- **Black pepper to taste**

To make sweet and sour eggplants, wash and dry the eggplants, then trim them and cut them into rather thick strips. Peel the garlic and slice it thinly

In a large saucepan, heat the 40 g of oil and fry the sliced garlic clove in it. Once you have sautéed the garlic, add the eggplants and cook over medium heat, stirring frequently until they are soft enough and begin to release their water (it will take about 20 minutes).

At this point, raise the heat further and add the aromatic herbs, mint and basil previously washed and delicately dried, the vinegar, sugar,

the salt and pepper. Mix everything well and let the vinegar evaporate. Lower the heat, cover with lids and cook for 10 minutes. Remove the lid, stir well and finish cooking for the last 5 minutes. Your sweet and sour eggplants are now ready to be served!

Breadcumb Potatoes
Ingredients:
- **Potatoes 1 kg**
- **Garlic 1 clove**
- **Rosemary 2 sprigs**
- **Crumb bread 50 g**
- **Breadcrumbs 20 g**
- **Sage 3 leaves**
- **Extra virgin olive oil q.s.**
- **Black pepper to taste**
- **Salt up to taste**

To make sandy potatoes, peel the potatoes and cut them into wedges then place them in a bowl with cold water to keep them from blackening. Meanwhile, finely chop the rosemary and sage and keep the mixture aside. Now take the loaf, remove the crust with a knife,
Coarsely cut the breadcrumbs and place them in a small bowl, add the breadcrumbs, the chopped aromatic herbs
and a clove of crushed garlic. Now drain the potato wedges in a colander then pour the chopped breadcrumbs and herbs on the potatoes, season with a drizzle of olive oil,
salt and pepper to taste. Mix the potato wedges and pour them into a baking tray lined with previously moistened baking paper and then well squeezed so that it adheres better to the baking tray, finally cover the potatoes with a spoonful of breadcrumbs. Cook the sandy potatoes in a static oven at 180° for 40 minutes (if a fan oven at 160° for 30 minutes) and then put them on the grill for 5 minutes. When cooked, your sandy potatoes will be golden and crunchy, take them out of the oven and let them cool before serving.

Crispy zucchini fritters

Ingredients:
- Zucchini 370 g
- Flour 00 250 g
- Cold beer 155 g
- Cold water 155 g
- Grana Padano PDO 50 g
- Salt up to taste
- Black pepper to taste

TO FRY
- Peanut oil 300 g

To prepare the crispy zucchini fritters, first pour the flour, the Grana cheese and the salt into a bowl. Mix the powders and continuing to mix, add the beer and water. You should obtain a smooth, lump-free batter.

Wash the zucchini, peel them and cut them into slices a couple of mm thick. Pour them into the freshly prepared batter and stir to mix everything.

Add the black pepper and mix again. In a large skillet, heat the oil. As soon as it has reached the temperature of 170°, using two spoons, dip a little of the mixture into the oil, so as to form the pancakes. Fry a little at a time, so as not to lower the oil temperature.

Fry for 2-3 minutes, then turn the pancakes, finish cooking for another 2-3 minutes and, with a slotted spoon, drain the pancakes on a tray with absorbent paper. Continue cooking the others and serve them still hot!

Cauliflower in a pan
Ingredients:
- Cauliflower 1.6 kg
- Extra virgin olive oil q.s.
- Garlic 3 cloves
- Salt up to taste
- Black pepper to taste
- Dried chilli to taste
- Thyme 4 sprigs
- Rosemary 2 sprigs

To prepare the cauliflower in the pan, start by cleaning the cauliflower. Eliminate the outer leaves that you can use to flavor a broth for example. Separate the florets from the core, cut the florets into small pieces. Rinse under running water.
In a pan, pour the oil, garlic, aromatic herbs and cauliflower florets. Season with salt, pepper and dried chilli, then cook over medium heat for about 10-15 minutes, stirring occasionally: the cauliflower should be golden brown. The cooking time may vary according to the size of the florets. The pan-fried cauliflower is ready to enjoy.

Zucchini salad with mint and basil
Ingredients:
- Zucchini 800 g
- Basil 4 leaves
- Mint 4 leaves
- Coarse salt 1 tbsp
- Extra virgin olive oil q.s.
- Salt up to taste
- Black pepper to taste
- Garlic 1 clove

To prepare the zucchini salad with mint and basil, start by carefully washing the zucchini under running water. Dry them with a cloth and place them on a chopping board, then clean them, removing the two ends. Then divide the zucchini in half.
Cut it in half again lengthwise and begin to obtain slices about 1.5 cm wide. Now take a large pot, fill it with water and bring to a boil. Then pour the sliced zucchini into the boiling water.
Add a spoonful of coarse salt and cook for 10 minutes. After 10 minutes, drain the zucchini with a colander and let them cool. Then transfer them to a baking dish and dress them with a drizzle of extra virgin olive oil.
Salt and pepper the zucchini to taste and add a peeled clove of garlic.
Then add the chopped mint leaves and basil leaves. Mix everything with a fork or a spoon and your mint and basil zucchini salad is ready to be served and eaten both warm and cold. If you don't serve it immediately, keep it in the fridge until it's time to consume it!

Pasta

Pasta alla vecchia bettola (Old tavern pasta)

Ingredients:

- Penne Rigate pasta (320 g)
- Datterino tomatoes (750 g)
- Liquid cream 2 tbsp (30 g)
- Vodka 1.25 tbsp (20 g)
- Garlic 1 clove
- Yellow onions 1
- Oregano 1 tsp
- Fresh chili pepper 1
- Extra virgin olive oil to taste
- Parsley to taste
- Black pepper to taste
- Fine salt to taste
- **Parmigiano Reggiano DOP cheese 3 tbsp (40 g) – grated**

To prepare pasta alla vecchia bettola (old tavern pasta), first cut the tomatoes in half , chop the garlic and cut the onion into small pieces.Take a frying pan suitable for cooking in the oven (otherwise you will have to transfer the content into another pan later), and add oil, garlic, onion, oregano and chili pepper. Stir and fry for a few minutes over moderate heat. Now blend with vodka and let it evaporate completely, then add the tomatoes, salt, and pepper. Stir and cook for a few minutes over moderate heat. At this point, bake in a static oven preheated to 350° (180° C) for 45 minutes.

Bring a pot of salted water to a boil and put the pasta in just before the tomatoes are cooked. After the cooking time has elapsed, remove the pan from the oven and transfer the seasoning into a tall, narrow glass, then reduce it to a cream with a hand blender.

Put the pan back on the stove, pour in the mixture obtained and add the cream. Stir and cook for a few minutes over moderate heat.

Drain the pasta and transfer it directly into the pan with the sauce, stir and sauté briefly, then add grated Parmesan cheese and stir again. Finally, plate and garnish with plenty of chopped parsley: pasta alla vecchia bettola (old tavern pasta) is ready to be enjoyed!

Calamarata pasta with swordfish ragù
Ingredients:
- Calamarata pasta (320 g)
- Swordfish 11 (300 g) - steaks
- Extra virgin olive oil 2 ½ tbsp (30 g)
- White wine 1 ¼ tbsp (20 g)
- Garlic 1 clove
- Parsley 3 bunches
- Black pepper to taste
- Fine salt to taste

FOR THE TOMATOES
- Cherry tomatoes (400 g)
- Extra virgin olive oil 2 ½ tbsp (30 g)
- Capers in vinegar (10 g)
- Garlic 1 clove
- Fine salt to taste
- Black pepper to taste

To make this calamarata pasta with swordfish ragu, first wash the tomatoes, dry them, and cut them in half. Heat the oil in a frying pan with a whole clove of garlic , then pour in the cherry tomatoes . Season with salt and pepper and stir to help the flavors develop, then add the capers, cover with a lid and continue cooking for 20 minutes over low heat.

In the meantime, prepare the swordfish, cutting it into slices if necessary, and removing the skin and dicing it. Heat a pan full of water, salted to taste, to cook the pasta in. In another pan, heat some oil with a whole clove of garlic, add the swordfish, and leave to brown slightly. Deglaze with the white wine, remove the garlic clove, and season with salt and pepper. The water should have come to a boil by now, so you can cook the pasta.

After 20 minutes, remove the garlic clove from the cherry tomatoes and fish. Add the diced swordfish to the sauce, and as soon as the pasta is cooked, drain it and transfer to the pan.

Sauté everything for a few moments, add the chopped parsley, and stir again. Your calamarata pasta with swordfish ragu is ready to be dished up and served!

Neapolitan pasta and beans
Ingredients:
- Mixed pasta 320 g
- Dried cannellini beans 300 g
- Pork rind 80 g
- Peeled tomatoes 400 g
- Extra virgin olive oil 80 g
- Garlic 3 cloves
- Celery 80 g
- Tomato paste 15 g
- 2 bay leaves
- Salt up to taste
- Black pepper to taste

To prepare the pasta and beans, start by soaking the beans for 6-8 hours, remember that the longer they are soaked, the faster they will cook. At this point, drain and rinse them, to remove any impurities and pour them into a large saucepan.

Cover with plenty of cold water and add the bay leaves, bringing everything to the boil. Then lower the heat a little, in order to gently cook the beans for about 15-20 minutes, just long enough to prepare the tomato sauce on the side. During cooking, some foam may emerge from the bean cooking pan: collect it with a strainer and remove it.

Meanwhile, peel the garlic cloves and set aside. Peel the celery, place it in a blender and blend it for a few seconds to obtain a very finely chopped mixture.

Pour the oil into a pan, add the cloves of garlic and the chopped celery, leave to flavor for 2-3 minutes. Pour the tomato pulp into large pieces and cook for about 15 minutes. Remove the garlic cloves, then pour the sauce obtained into the pan with the beans.

Also add the tomato paste together with the whole pork rind and cook for about 2 hours or until the beans have reached the consistency you prefer. After this time, make sure that the beans are quite soupy, remove the bay leaves, add salt and finally pour the pasta directly into the pan, taking care to stir often so as to prevent it from sticking to the bottom. Once the pasta is cooked, turn off the flame and add the ground black pepper.

Mix well and cover with a lid for 5 minutes, so that the paste absorbs all the aromas. Your Neapolitan pasta and beans is ready to be served.

Pasta alla vesuviana (Spicy pasta)
Ingredients:
- Wholegrain Spaghetti pasta (320 g)
- Fresh chili pepper 1.3 tsp (6 g)
- Peeled tomatoes (400 g)
- Black olives (40 g) - pitted
- Fior di latte mozzarella cheese (100 g)
- Salted capers 1 ½ tbsp (20 g) - rinsed
- Red onions ⅔ cup (70 g)
- Fine salt to taste
- Extra virgin olive oil to taste
- Oregano to taste – fresh

To make pasta alla vesuviana (spicy pasta), clean the red onion and slice it thinly. Also cut the fresh chilli pepper and olives into thin slices.
Carefully drain the mozzarella and cut it into small pieces. Place a pot full of salted water to boil, which will be used to cook the pasta. Pour the olive oil into a pan, add the onio and chili pepper. Let the onion stew over medium heat adding a couple of ladles of water from the pasta until the onion is soft and golden. Now pour the peeled tomatoes and crush them slightly with a wooden spoon. Then season with olives, capers and salt. Cook the sauce for about 12 minutes over low heat. In the meantime, cook the spaghetti in boiling water for the time indicated on the package. When the sauce is cooked, add the mozzarella cheese and add the fresh oregano. Drain the pasta, transfer it directly into the pan with the sauce and stir with a ladle of cooking water. Mix and serve your pasta alla vesuviana (spicy pasta) hot.

Tortellini with ham and cream
Ingredients:
- **Prosciutto cotto (300 g) - in one slice**
- **Whipping cream (400 g)**
- **Butter 3 ½ tbsp (50 g)**
- **Nutmeg 1 pinch**
- **Parmigiano Reggiano DOP cheese to taste - grated**
- **Black pepper to taste**
- **Fine salt to taste**

Slice the ham into strips, then into cubes. Melt the butter in a very large pan and brown the ham for a few seconds.

Pour in the cream and mix it all together. Sprinkle with nutmeg and season with salt and pepper to taste. Cook the tortellini pasta in a large pot with plenty of water salted to taste.

When they are cooked, drain and transfer them to the pan with the sauce. Stir briefly over low heat then serve the tortellini with ham and cream sprinkled with grated Parmesan cheese if you like!

Bavette with pesto
Ingredients:
- Linguine pasta 320 g
- Garlic ½ clove
- Coarse jump 1 pinch
- Extra virgin olive oil 100 g
- Basil 5 tbsp (50 g)
- Pecorino cheese (30 g) - (grated)
- Pine nuts 2 tbsp (15 g)
- Parmigiano Reggiano DOP cheese (70 g) - (grated)

FOR DECORATION
- Basil to taste

To prepare bavette with pesto, start with the Genoese pesto; after picking the basil leaves, remember not to wash them under running water, but clean them with a soft cloth, or place them in a bowl of cold water and rinse delicately. Now place the peeled garlic in the mortar, together with a few grains of coarse salt. Start grinding and upon obtaining a garlic cream, add the basil leaves along with a pinch of coarse salt. Crush the basil leaves against the sides of the mortar by rolling the pestle left to right and rolling the mortar in the opposite direction (right to left); continue to coax a green liquid from the basil leaves.

Now add the pine nuts and crush into a cream. Gradually add the cheese for an even creamier sauce, and then last of all, gradually add the extra virgin olive oil, stirring with the pestle all the while. Thoroughly amalgamate all the ingredients into a homogeneous sauce. Bring abundant salted water to the boil in a saucepan and cook the pasta. Now place the pesto in a large pan (remove from the heat) and temper with a little pasta cooking water.

Stir with a spatula and as soon as the pasta is ready, add it straight to the pesto;

stir to flavor the dish and lastly, serve your bavette with pesto garnished with a few basil leaves.

Fettuccine Alfredo
Ingredients:
- **Fettuccine 320g**
- **Butter (80 g)**
- **Parmigiano Reggiano DOP cheese (80 g) - grated**
- **Fine salt to taste**
- **Black pepper to taste**

Bring some salted water to the boil in a saucepan, to cook the fettuccine. Cook the fettuccine in the water which will have come to the boil by now. As the pasta cooks, it'll only take 2-3 minutes, prepare the sauce: melt the butter on a very low flame in a capacious pan, but be sure not to burn it.

Add a ladle of pasta cooking water: the starch it contains will help you create an even creamier condiment. Drain the fettuccine and place them in the pan with the butter, add another ladle of cooking water and briefly saute, stirring rapidly all the while.

Now remove from the heat and add the grated parmesan cheese; last of all, season with a pinch of salt and a generous grating of black pepper; stir once more to thoroughly coat the pasta in the sauce. Your fettuccine Alfredo are ready to be served!

Ricotta and walnut pasta
Ingredients:
- **Fusilli 320 g**
- **Ricotta 400 g**
- **Walnuts 50 g**
- **Extra virgin olive oil 20 g**
- **Nutmeg (to be grated) to taste**
- **Salt up to taste**
- **Black pepper to taste**

To prepare the ricotta and walnut pasta, start by boiling the pasta in plenty of salted water. While the fusilli are cooking, dedicate yourself to the sauce: chop the walnuts, keeping aside some whole kernels for the final decoration. Pour the oil into a large-bottomed non-stick pan.
Then add the ricotta. Heat over a very gentle heat and mix with a spatula. Then dilute the pasta cooking water with a ladle, you will need about 150 g.
Then with the hand whisk continue to mix the ingredients well to make the ricotta creamy. Season with salt and pepper.
Finally add the walnuts and mix them with the sauce, flavoring with nutmeg.
Drain the pasta directly into the pan with the sauce and mix it with the other ingredients, stirring for 1 more minute. Now the ricotta and walnut pasta is ready to be served. Garnish the dish with whole walnuts and enjoy!

Monzese-style pasta
Ingredients:
- Penne rigate 320 g
- Sausage 250 g
- Liquid fresh cream 250 g
- Saffron pistils 0.3 g
- Parmigiano Reggiano DOP to grate 60 g
- Salt up to taste
- Black pepper to taste

To prepare the Monzese pasta, boil a pot of water and add salt to the boil (it will then be used to cook the pasta); so start peeling the sausage. Cut the luganega lengthwise and remove the casing. Then cut into bite-sized pieces of a couple of centimeters, so as to be sure that the cooking is homogeneous. Heat a non-stick pan on the stove and then pour in the bites, brown them well without adding any fat, until they are completely golden brown; it will take a few minutes. Pour in the cream, season with salt and pepper and continue cooking for about ten minutes. Meanwhile, boil the penne and while the pasta is cooking, take a little cooking water and pour it into a container where you have put the saffron pistils.

Quickly dilute with a fork and then pour them into the pan so as to mix everything well. At this point the pasta will be cooked, drain it directly into the pan (set aside a little of the pasta water) and mix well to incorporate the flavours.

Turn off the heat and add the grated Parmesan, while stirring make sure the cheese melts well. If the base should become too dry, just add a little more cooking water from the pasta to dilute. Give one last sauté, add salt and pepper to taste, always with the flame off, and then your Monza pasta is ready to be served!

Norcina pasta

Ingredients:
- **Penne rigate 320 g**
- **Sausage 300 g**
- **Ricotta 200 g**
- **Onions 100 g**
- **Garlic 1 clove**
- **Parmigiano Reggiano DOP to grate 50 g**
- **Extra virgin olive oil q.s.**
- **Salt up to taste**
- **Black pepper to taste**

To prepare the Norcina pasta, peel and finely chop the onion. Slightly score the sausage, remove the casing and roughly break it up with your hands.

Pour a drizzle of oil into the pan, add the chopped onion, the garlic clove and fry over medium heat for about minutes. Add the chopped sausage to the onion and cook over a moderate heat for another 5 minutes, until golden brown. Meanwhile, put a pan full of water on the fire and add salt to the boil, it will be used to cook the pasta.

Remove the garlic and put out the fire. Cook the pasta. Pour the ricotta into the pan. Add a ladle of pasta cooking water and mix. Drain the pasta directly into the pan with the sauce and sauté over high heat for 2 minutes. Finish the preparation by adding the Parmesan, mix well and serve the pasta alla norcina piping hot!

Penne with peppers
- **Penne rigate 320 g**
- **Red peppers 275 g**
- **Yellow peppers 275 g**
- **Anchovies in oil 2**
- **Tomato puree 200 g**
- **Basil to taste**
- **Cane sugar 1 pinch**
- **White onions 80 g**
- **Salt up to taste**
- **Black pepper to taste**
- **Extra virgin olive oil q.s.**

To make the penne with peppers, peel the white onion and slice it finely, heat the olive oil in a pan with two anchovies drained from the conservation oil and the sliced onions, simmer the onion in a little water until it is soft, it will take about 10 minutes. Meanwhile, put a pot on the stove with plenty of water, to be salted when it boils: you will need it later to cook the pasta. At this point, wash the peppers under running water, remove the stalk Cut them in half and with a small knife remove the seeds and internal filaments; now cut them into strips and once the onion is well stewed add the peppers, wet them with a little water and simmer for about 15 minutes, then add the tomato puree and dampen the acidity with a pinch of cane sugar. Flavor the sauce with fresh basil leaves (keep some aside to garnish the dishes if you prefer), mix then cover with the lid and continue cooking for about 10 minutes, stirring occasionally. In the meantime, cook the pasta, taking care to cook it al dente for about 10 minutes (adjust according to the cooking time indicated on the package).

Drain the pasta directly into the pan with the pepper sauce, stir to flavor well. The penne with peppers are ready, serve them piping hot, garnishing the dish with a basil leaf!

Spaghetti poveri (Spaghetti with anchovies, olives and capers)

Ingredients:
- Spaghetti (320 g)
- Anchovies in oil (100 g)
- Red onions (80 g)
- Salted capers 4 tbsp (30 g)
- Taggiasca olives (100 g) - pitted
- Garlic 1 clove
- Fresh chili pepper 2
- Parsley to taste
- Breadcrumbs 3 tbsp (40 g)
- Extra virgin olive oil 3 tbsp (40 g)

To prepare spaghetti poveri (spaghetti with anchovies, olives and capers), start by bringing a pot of salted water to a boil to cook the pasta in. Next, prepare the sautéed vegetables: finely chop the red onion and the garlic clove. In a large frying pan, pour the extra virgin olive oil until it almost covers the bottom and add the onion and freshly chopped garlic.

Leave to fry for a few minutes, stirring occasionally to prevent the sautéed vegetables from sticking to the bottom of the pan. When the water has come to the boil, pour the pasta in and let it cook for the time indicated on the package. Rinse the capers well under running water to remove excess salt and chop them coarsely.

Then add them to the sautéed vegetable meals, stir and add the anchovies. Remove the seeds from the chili peppers, chop them coarsely,

and add them to the pan . Leave to cook over low heat, stirring frequently, until the anchovies have dissolved. If necessary, thin the sauce with a ladle of pasta cooking water. Toast the breadcrumbs: take a pan, drizzle with oil and add the breadcrumbs. Toast them by stirring until they are golden. Remove from the heat and transfer to a bowl.

Go back to the seasoning, which will be ready by now: add the taggiasca olives , mince the parsley and add it to the pan stirring to mix well.

Drain the pasta, saving some of the cooking water, and pour it into the pan with the sauce. Stir and fry the spaghetti for a minute, then add the breadcrumbs.

Add a ladle of cooking water and stir well before serving. Your spaghetti poveri (spaghetti with anchovies, olives and capers) is ready to be enjoyed!

Risotto all'amarone
Ingredients:
- **Rice 320 g**
- **Amarone red wine 350ml**
- **Parmesan to grate 60 g**
- **Shallot 50 g**
- **Butter 60 g**
- **Meat broth 1 l**
- **Salt up to taste**

To prepare the risotto with Amarone, start by finely chopping the shallot. In a casserole, melt 30 g of butter, add the shallots and let it dry with a ladle of meat broth.

Add the rice and toast it well, then pour the Amarone slowly in two or three times, waiting for the wine already poured to be well absorbed. It will take at least 5 minutes, during which you will mix with a wooden spoon.

Continue cooking the risotto over a low heat, adding the meat stock a ladle at a time. When the rice is ready, turn off the heat and stir the risotto with the remaining 30 g of butter and the grated cheese, mixing with a spoon. The Amarone risotto is ready to be served!

Spaghetti with bottarga
Ingredients:
- Spaghetti 320 g
- Anchovies (anchovies) 3
- Garlic 1 clove
- Butter (cold from the freezer) 40 g
- Tuna bottarga 40 g
- Extra virgin olive oil q.s.

To prepare pasta with bottarga you will need to have a pot with boiling unsalted water available. In a large frying pan, heat a drizzle of oil, add a whole, peeled clove of garlic and brown it. Finely chop the anchovies, pour them into the pan and let them melt over low heat. Eliminate the garlic.

Pour a ladleful of boiling water, add the raw spaghetti. Continue cooking the pasta over medium heat, adding a ladle of water at a time, as soon as the previous one has been absorbed (as for a risotto). Cooking depends on the type of spaghetti, it will certainly be longer than the time indicated on the package. Once the last ladle of water has been absorbed, add the cold freezer butter cut into small pieces and stir. Finally, grate the tuna roe to taste. Stir to flavor, serve garnished with other bottarga to taste. Spaghetti with bottarga are ready to be served.

Spaghetti all'assasina
Ingredients:
- Spaghetti 320 g
- Tomato sauce 300 g
- Garlic 1 clove
- Dried chilli 1
- Extra virgin olive oil 25 g
- Hot and salted water q.s.
- Basil to taste

To prepare spaghetti all'assassina, start by heating the leftover sauce in a saucepan prepared with sautéed onion and cooked puree for 30-40 minutes. Meanwhile, in another pan, fry a clove of garlic with a drizzle of oil for a couple of minutes. Then add the spaghetti and immediately pour hot water.

Stir for a few moments to soften the pasta and then pour a ladleful of the heated sauce. Crumble a dried chilli

and continue to wet the pasta with hot water as if you wanted to cook it again. At the end of cooking, remove the garlic and add the rest of the sauce.

Season with salt as needed and finish cooking by raising the temperature, leaving the bottom to burn to make the pasta crunchy and golden. Your spaghetti all'assassina is ready, serve it piping hot and garnish with fresh basil as desired.

Main Course

Risotto all'amarone

Ingredients:

- Rice 320 g
- Amarone red wine 350ml
- Parmesan to grate 60 g
- Shallot 50 g
- Butter 60 g
- Meat broth 1 l
- Salt up to taste

To prepare the risotto with Amarone, start by finely chopping the shallot. In a casserole, melt 30 g of butter, add the shallots and let it dry with a ladle of meat broth.

Add the rice and toast it well, then pour the Amarone slowly in two or three times, waiting for the wine already poured to be well absorbed. It will take at least 5 minutes, during which you will mix with a wooden spoon.

Continue cooking the risotto over a low heat, adding the meat stock a ladle at a time. When the rice is cooked, turn off the heat and stir the risotto with the remaining 30 g of butter and the grated cheese, mixing with a spoon. The Amarone risotto is ready to be served!

Neapolitan spaghetti omelette

Ingredients:

- Spaghetti 500 g
- Parmigiano Reggiano PDO 100 g
- Whole milk 100 g
- Eggs 8
- Salt up to taste
- Black pepper to taste
- Extra virgin olive oil q.s.

FOR THE TOMATO SAUCE

- Tomato puree 700 g
- White onions 1
- Basil to taste
- Salt up to taste
- Extra virgin olive oil q.s.

To prepare the Neapolitan-style spaghetti omelette, boil a pot of water, add salt to the boil. Then peel and chop the onion. Pour it into a saucepan in which you have heated the oil. Leave to dry for a few minutes over low heat, stirring often, then dip in the tomato puree.

Season with salt, cover with the lid and cook gently for half an hour. At the end of cooking, flavor the sauce with basil. Meanwhile, cook the spaghetti.

Once cooked, drain and pour into a bowl, cover with the sauce and mix thoroughly.

Leave to cool and in the meantime prepare the egg cream: break them in a bowl and add the grated cheese, milk, salt and pepper. Beat with a whisk to mix everything.

Pour the mixture over the pasta and mix well to mix. Pour a drizzle of oil into a pan of 30 cm in diameter (measured on the surface) with a rather high edge, heat slightly and dip everything.

Distribute the pasta evenly with the help of a spatula, then close the lid and cook over medium heat for 10 minutes. After the time, help yourself with a pizza plate (or a smooth lid) to turn the omelette upside down.

Slide it back into the pan and continue cooking on the other side for another 10 minutes without a lid. Your Neapolitan spaghetti omelette is ready, enjoy your meal!

Tomato soup

Ingredients:

- Tomatoes 1.5 kg
- Extra virgin olive oil 30 g
- Basil 5 leaves
- Garlic 1 clove
- Salt up to taste
- TO GARNISH
- Fresh liquid cream q.s.
- Basil to taste

To prepare the tomato soup, start by washing the tomatoes. Then dry them and with a small knife remove the stalk and the skin. Cut them in half and empty them of the seeds and juice. Once cleaned, chop them all up.

In a saucepan, heat the extra virgin olive oil together with a peeled clove of garlic, after a minute add the tomatoes and mix, leaving the flavors to infuse for a few minutes.

Then add the basil leaves, salt and give one last stir before covering with a lid and letting it cook, over low heat, for at least 35 minutes.

Once the time has elapsed, remove the basil and garlic, then using an immersion blender blend the tomatoes in order to obtain a smooth puree. Let it cook for another 25-30 minutes so as to let it dry and shrink a little; then turn off the heat and let it cool at room temperature.

At this point your tomato soup will be ready, we have chosen to serve it in small bowls and garnish it with fresh cream. If you want to do it too, it's really very simple, just pour a little cream on the soup and form a spiral with a spoon. Finally, give a touch of color and extra aroma to your tomato soup by adding a basil leaf and serve.

Rice potatoes and mussels

Ingredients:

- **Mussels (clean) 500 g**
- **Potatoes 500 g**
- **Garlic 1 clove**
- **Breadcrumbs 50 g**
- **Parsley 25 g**
- **Water 300 g**
- **Carnaroli rice 300 g**
- **Salt up to taste**
- **Extra virgin olive oil q.s.**
- **Black pepper to taste**
- **Parmigiano Reggiano DOP to grate 50 g**

Finely chop the garlic and add it to the breadcrumbs; then chop the parsley and add half of it to the breadcrumbs. Mix and add the extra virgin olive oil.

Peel the potatoes and cut them into wedges. Take a 23 cm square baking dish and cover the bottom with extra virgin olive oil, place the potatoes, salt and pepper and add a sprinkling of parsley.

Continue with a layer of mussels, sprinkle with Parmesan and continue adding the raw rice. Now add the liquid from the mussels that you have kept aside, taking care to pour it delicately over the whole baking dish.

Continue with another layer of potatoes, mussels and rice, add a sprinkling of parsley, salt and pepper and complete the layer with breadcrumbs. Gently add the water, from one side of the pan, until you reach just below the breading. Complete with a drizzle of oil and bake the rice, potatoes and mussels in the lowest part of the oven at 180° for 60 minutes in a static oven. The surface should be golden brown and your rice, potatoes and mussels will be ready to be enjoyed!

Split Pea Soup

- **Split peas, 250 gr**
- **Diced smoked bacon, 70 gr**
- **Onions 1 small**
- **Carrots 1 small**
- **Celery 1 rib**
- **Garlic 1 clove**
- **Extra virgin olive oil, 3 tbsp**
- **Vegetable broth, 1 lt**

To prepare the split pea soup, start by soaking the split peas in plenty of cold water and leaving them for at least 3 hours. Finely chop the carrot, celery and onion and fry them with the garlic in the extra virgin olive oil in a large saucepan. Brown them for about 10 minutes and then add the diced bacon (if you prefer you can add the bacon in a single slice) and brown well. Rinse the peas well under cold running water

and add them to the pan, stir to flavor them and then cover the peas with the hot vegetable broth. Cover the soup and cook over low heat (it should simmer slightly) until the peas are tender and begin to fall apart, about 60 minutes.

If you want, to obtain a more substantial dish, you can add pasta (ditaloni, broken spaghetti, etc.) or rice to the soup!

Acquacotta (Vegetable egg soup)

Ingredients:

- Yellow onions 700 g
- Celery 200 g
- Peeled tomatoes 800 g
- Extra virgin olive oil 120 g
- Water 200 g
- Vegetable broth 500 g
- Fine salt to taste
- Basil to taste
- Eggs 4

FOR PLATING

- Tuscan bread 4 slices - stale
- Pecorino cheese 3 ½ tbsp (50 g)
- Extra virgin olive oil to taste
- Basil to taste

To prepare the aquacotta, first prepare the vegetable broth and keep it warm. Start by peeling the onions , then cut them in half and slice them thinly. Transfer them to a bowl and move to the celery. First wash it well, then cut the stalks and leaves into fairly thin slices. Pour the oil into a pan,put over heat and add the onions and celery. Add water and salt. Mix with a wooden ladle and cook until the water has completely evaporated. Then add the peeled tomatoes and crush them gently with the ladle.Mix everything, add the hot vegetable broth, stir again and cook for about 40 minutes, possibly covering with a lid and stirring occasionally.

When the oil has surfaced, add some basil leaves and the eggs by breaking them directly into the pan. Arrange them distanced from each other. Add salt and cover with a lid.

Leave the eggs to cook for about 4-5 minutes. Meanwhile, crumble a thin slice of stale Tuscan bread in each cocotte bowl. You can crumble it with your hands and arrange it to line the bottom. Add grated pecorino cheese on top and add the soup with the ladle, making sure to take one egg for each cocotte. Garnish with a drizzle of extra virgin olive oil, a basil leaf and serve.

Risotto alla mantovana

Ingredients:

- **Rice 350 g**
- **Salami 300 g**
- **Grana Padano PDO to grate 100 g**
- **Butter 80 g**
- **Salt up to taste**

Place 600 ml of water in a thick-bottomed steel pan and bring to a boil. As soon as the water boils, lightly salt it and pour in the rice. When the water starts boiling again, cook the rice for 10-12 minutes over high heat and without a lid, shaking the pot from time to time. After 10 -12 minutes the rice should have absorbed all the water; remove it from the heat and cover the pan with the lid. Let it rest for 10 minutes during which the rice will complete its cooking.

Meanwhile, melt the butter in a pan, add the sausage that you will have skinned and shelled with a fork, and brown over a moderate heat, crumbling it with a wooden spoon and making it melt as much as possible.

After ten minutes, uncover the rice, fluff it with a fork and season it with the browned sausage, half of the grated parmesan and mix. Serve the rice immediately, sprinkling it with the remaining grated cheese.

Imperial soup

Ingredients:

- Eggs 4
- Semolina 135 g
- Parmigiano Reggiano DOP 90 g
- Butter 75 g
- Salt up to taste
- Nutmeg to taste
- Meat broth 1 l

To make the imperial soup, start by preparing the meat broth: wash and peel the vegetables and place them in a large saucepan with high sides with the oil. Flavored with peppercorns and cloves. Add the meat and cover with 3L of water, cook over medium-high heat for about 2 hours, until the broth has reduced by about half. Then add the remaining liter of water and cook for another hour over low heat. At the end of cooking, strain the broth with a fine-mesh strainer.

Keep the meat and vegetables for the boiled meat and add salt to the broth. Now take care of the dough: melt the butter in a saucepan over a low heat and set aside.

Pour the semolina and the grated Parmesan into a bowl, add the beaten eggs, the melted butter, the salt,

flavored with grated nutmeg and mix everything with a whisk to mix the ingredients.

Butter a 30x20cm pan and line it with baking paper, transfer the dough into the pan and level it on the surface with the back of a spoon to compact it as best as possible.

Bake the mixture in a preheated static oven at 180° for 35 minutes. When cooked, take the mixture out of the oven and let it cool, then turn the pan upside down onto a cutting board to unmold the loaf. Cut it into strips first and then into cubes of about 1x1 cm. Pour the hot broth into a plate, add the cubes of semolina and serve your imperial soup.

Ligurian meatloaf

Ingredients:

- **Potatoes 1.2 kg**
- **Green beans 600 g**
- **Parmigiano Reggiano DOP to grate 100 g**
- **Medium eggs 4**
- **Marjoram 2 sprigs**
- **Black pepper to taste**
- **Salt up to taste**
- **Breadcrumbs 50 g**

TO BUTTER AND GARNISH

- **Butter to taste**
- **Breadcrumbs 50 g**
- **Parmigiano Reggiano DOP to grate 50 g**

To make the Ligurian meatloaf, first wash well and then put the potatoes to boil for 40 minutes, starting with cold water; cook until they are soft by sticking them with the prongs of a fork, times may vary according to the size of the potatoes. Wash and trim the green beans, then cook them separately in a pan with water for about 25 minutes, always starting with cold water. They should be tender at the end of cooking without falling apart.

Once the green beans are ready, drain them and cut them into small pieces. In the meantime, the potatoes will also be cooked, drain them and pass them through the potato masher, collecting the puree in a large bowl. Pour the cooked green beans here as well, add the grated cheese and eggs. Flavored with marjoram leaves, then salted and peppered. Mix and keep aside.

Now butter a 30x23 cm rectangular pan and sprinkle the bottom and edge with breadcrumbs. Pour the batter into the pan, level the surface.

Now pour the grated Parmesan cheese and the breadcrumbs into a bowl, mix and distribute the mixture obtained on the surface.

The meatloaf is ready to cook: cook it in a preheated static oven at 180° for 50 minutes, then in grill mode for about 2 minutes, so as to brown the surface. Serve the Ligurian meatloaf after it has cooled slightly.

Potato and bacon pie

Ingredients:

- **Potatoes all of the same size 1 kg**
- **White onions 400 g**
- **Smoked bacon 250 g**
- **Grated Asiago 200 g**
- **Salt up to 1 pinch**
- **Black pepper 1 pinch**
- **Thyme 4 sprigs**

FOR THE BECHAMEL

- **Flour 00 30 g**
- **Butter 30 g**
- **Whole milk 500 ml**
- **Salt up to 1 pinch**
- **Nutmeg to grate q.b.**

To prepare the potato and bacon pie, start by cutting the bacon into strips then into cubes, then peel the onion and cut it into thin slices then peel the potatoes

and also cut them into 2-3 mm thin slices. As you slice the potatoes, you can dip them in a bowl with cold water so they don't blacken. Pour the bacon cubes into a non-stick pan and brown them over low heat; add the onions and let them dry over a very low heat for about 15-20 minutes together with the bacon (if the onion gets too dark, you can add one or two tablespoons of boiling water). At the end of cooking, add salt and pepper to taste and flavor with a few sprigs of thyme, leaving 1 aside to garnish the final dish. While the sauce is cooking, blanch the potato slices in lightly salted boiling water and after 3-4 minutes turn off the heat and drain them, then leave them to dry on a tray lined with kitchen paper or paper towels.

Finally prepare the béchamel: heat the milk in a saucepan, while in a saucepan melt the butter over low heat, then remove the saucepan from the heat and pour in the flour; mix immediately with a hand whisk so that no lumps are created and put it back on the low heat to toast the flour. Then pour the hot milk and keep stirring, to thicken over low heat. Once the béchamel is ready, flavor it with grated nutmeg.

Finally, grate the Asiago. Now you can compose the potato and bacon pie: take a Flemish pan (we used a 30x22 oval baking dish) and sprinkle the bottom with 1 or 2 tablespoons of béchamel sauce 1. Then arrange the first layer of potato slices,

then distribute the bacon and a handful of grated asiago. Cover again with the béchamel and repeat all the layers,

ending with a coating of béchamel. Season the surface with the fresh thyme leaves and cook the pie in a preheated static oven at 180° for 45 minutes (if ventilated at 160° for 35 minutes). Once cooked and well browned on the surface, take it out of the oven and let it cool slightly then serve it!

Farmer soup

Ingredients:

- Dried lentils 100 g
- Dried chickpeas 100 g
- Dried broad beans 100 g
- Barley 100 g
- Dried borlotti beans 50 g
- Dried red beans 50 g
- Dried cannellini beans 50 g
- Vegetable broth 1 l
- Celery 1 rib
- Carrots 1
- White onions 1
- Garlic 1 clove
- Bay leaf 1
- Extra virgin olive oil q.s.
- Salt up to taste
- Black pepper to taste

To make the farmer's soup you have to soak all the dried legumes: transfer the mixed beans, broad beans, chickpeas and lentils into a large bowl, cover the legumes with water and leave to rest overnight or about 12 hours. After the necessary time, drain the legumes and rinse them under running water.

Meanwhile, thinly slice a stick of celery, peel and chop a carrot and set the vegetables aside for the sauté.

In a pan with a high edge, place a drizzle of oil, the finely chopped onion, a whole clove of garlic and fry for 5 minutes to soften the onion.

Now add the celery coast and the minced carrot, salted pepper, pour a ladleful of hot broth, to prepare the broth, consult our Vegetable broth sheet. Continue cooking for another 5 minutes or the time necessary for the vegetables to soften and flavour. Remove the garlic clove with kitchen tongs and pour the legumes and barley into the pan. Mix well to mix the ingredients and add flavor to the sauce, pour in the hot broth until all the vegetables are covered. Flavor the soup with a bay leaf and continue cooking until the legumes and cereals are soft, occasionally stir gently with a wooden spoon so as not to flake the legumes or simply shake the pan. It will take about an hour and a half (if you use the pressure cooker, about 35 minutes will be enough). If the preparation gets too dry, dilute the soup with hot broth, which must not be dry. Your farmer's soup is ready, you can enjoy it hot or warm.

Neapolitan peppers

Ingredients:

- Red peppers 1
- Yellow peppers 1
- Bread 250 g
- Gaeta olives 80 g
- Parmigiano Reggiano DOP to grate 40 g
- Breadcrumbs 40 g
- Capers in salt 20 g
- Medium eggs 1
- Garlic 1 clove
- Parsley to taste
- Basil to taste
- Extra virgin olive oil q.s.
- Black pepper to taste

To make Neapolitan peppers, start by roasting the peppers for at least 10 minutes each in a pan, turning them occasionally. Place the peppers in a baking tray, cover them with plastic wrap for at least 15 minutes.

In the meantime, take care of the filling: cut the bread into slices, cut it into cubes and pit the Gaeta olives. In the bowl of the mixer, place the bread, the basil leaves and the parsley, Gaeta olives and carefully desalted capers. Add the whole peeled garlic clove and finally add the egg. Blend everything until you get a homogeneous and compact mixture. Add a little ground pepper if you like.

Meanwhile, recover your peppers and remove the outer skin which will come off easily in this way. Cut off the top cap and extract the internal seeds.

Now oil a baking dish, place the peppers and stuff them with the filling you prepared earlier. In a bowl mix the grated Parmesan with the breadcrumbs and spread the mixture over the peppers, drizzle with a drizzle of olive oil and flavor with ground black pepper to taste. Cook the peppers in a preheated static oven at 180° for 35 minutes. When cooked, they will be well browned on the surface. Leave to cool and then serve the Neapolitan peppers!

Saffron risotto

Ingredients:

- **Saffron pistils (approximately) 0.25 g**
- **Rice 320 g**
- **White wine 150g**
- **White onions ½**
- **Butter 25 g**
- **Meat broth (boiling) to taste**

TO CREATE

- **Butter (very cold from the fridge) 120 g**
- **Parmigiano Reggiano DOP (to be grated, very cold from the fridge) 80 g**

To prepare risotto alla Milanese you will need to have about 1 liter of classic meat broth ready, which must always be kept very hot. Peel and finely chop half a white onion. Pour 25 g of butter into a large pan, then the chopped onion. Sauté over medium heat, stirring occasionally to soften.

Once browned, you can pour the rice: the rice will absorb the butter and mix with the onion. When it is toasted and translucent, you can deglaze with the white wine. Let the alcoholic part evaporate for a few moments.

Pour in the very hot broth until it is covered and continue cooking over high heat, adding hot broth as needed. Gently dip the pistils in hot water, stir just ¾ of the way through cooking, add the saffron pistils to the soaking water: wait a few moments for them to soften, then stir: they will release their scent and colour. When there is one minute left before the rice is cooked, remove the pan from the heat, add about 120 g of butter cut into pieces, very cold from the fridge, mix.

Also pour in the grated Parmigiano Reggiano DOP, mix vigorously. Serve the Milanese risotto piping hot!

Sardinian gnocchi
Ingredients:
- Gnocchi 400 g
- Sausage 300 g
- Fresh Sardinian Pecorino 200 g
- Onions 50 g
- Extra virgin olive oil 30 g
- Tomato puree 300 g
- Salt 1 pinch

Start by preparing the sauté. Peel and finely chop the onion, then let it dry slowly in a pan, together with the oil. Meanwhile, peel the sausage.

Crumble it coarsely with your hands and add it to the sautéed onion. Brown the sausage for 15 minutes over high heat, stirring often and then add the tomato puree.

Mix again and cover with a lid, leaving to cook for about an hour; finally, if necessary, adjust the salt. When the sauce is ready, cook the gnocchi in abundant boiling water, salted to taste.

Meanwhile, grate the pecorino into a bowl and add a ladle of the pasta cooking water. Then blend with a blender, adding more water, if necessary, and always slowly until you get a smooth cream.

Drain the gnocchi and add them to the sausage sauce directly in the pan, mix and finally add the pecorino cream. Stir well to mix all the ingredients and serve!

Spelled and borlotti beans soup
Ingredients:
- Fresh borlotti beans 200 g
- Spelled 250 g
- Garlic 3 cloves
- Carrots 1
- Celery 1 rib
- Red onions 1
- Extra virgin olive oil 5 tbsp
- Sage to taste
- Water 1 l
- Salt up to taste

Peel the carrot and cut it into rather small pieces, chop the onion and finely dice the celery; place 2 cloves of garlic and 3 tablespoons of oil in the pan and cook for about 5 minutes until the onion is softened. Add the fresh borlotti beans and toast for another 5 minutes, add the sage leaves to taste, season with salt and add 1l of water, bring to the boil and then close the pot with its lid; calculate 30 minutes by lowering the heat to a minimum.

After this time, open the pot and check the cooking of the beans which must be tender; take about a third of the beans in a bowl and filter the rest through a strainer. Keep aside the cooking broth you will need for the spelled and pour the borlotti beans and vegetables into the mixer and blend until pureed; keep aside warm.

Now proceed to prepare the spelled by toasting it for about 3 minutes in a saucepan with the remaining garlic and oil over low heat. Add three ladles of the vegetable cooking broth and cook, adding a ladle of broth at a time for the time indicated on the package (about 15-18 minutes).

At the end of cooking, add the borlotti and vegetable puree and mix well, adding a little more broth if it turns out to be too thick; finally add the whole beans that you have kept aside before passing the others.

Serve with a drizzle of raw extra virgin olive oil if desired.

Aosta Valley fondue

Ingredients:
- **Fontina cheese 400 g**
- **Whole milk 400 g**
- **Yolks 4**
- **Butter 30 g**
- **Black pepper to taste**

To prepare the Valdostana fondue, first remove the external rind of the fontina cheese, then slice it thinly. Transfer the cheese into a rectangular baking dish and pour the milk on top.

Cover with cling film and leave in the fridge overnight. After the rest time in the fridge, drain the cheese from the milk through a strainer and keep the milk aside. Melt the cheese over medium heat, stirring with a wooden spoon.

At this point pour the yolks one at a time, and mix continuously. Add the cold butter and continue mixing. Pepper the Valdostana fondue to taste and mix again.

At this point, pour about 100 g of the milk kept aside, adjust the dose according to the consistency of the fondue which must not be too liquid or too compact. In total, cooking will take about 30 minutes. Once ready, pour the fondue into the typical fondue pan, sprinkle again with pepper and serve the Valdostana fondue immediately.

Rice and peas
Ingredients:
- Butter 60 g
- Onions 1
- Black pepper to taste
- Rice 350 g
- Vegetable broth 1300 ml
- Salt up to taste
- Peas 1 kg
- Extra virgin olive oil q.s.
- Bacon 50 g
- Grana Padano to grate 40 g
- Parsley 30 g

To prepare rice and peas, first prepare a light vegetable broth and leave it to cool. To see details on the preparation, look at the vegetable broth sheet. Meanwhile shell the peas, keeping the pods aside. Once all the pods are shelled, wash them well under running water, drain them well
and immerse them in the casserole with the broth, cover with a lid and let them cook for 60 minutes on a moderate heat after the return to the boil. After cooking, blend the pods with an immersion blender without removing them from the broth
until you obtain a puree, pour it into a sieve positioned over a bowl, and press the puree well with a spatula in order to eliminate the too fibrous part of the pods
collecting all the juices that will come out and keep warm. Now go on to cooking the rice: melt half the butter in a large saucepan and let the finely chopped onion wither, once the onion has browned, it will take about 10-15 minutes of cooking over low heat, add the bacon chopped and the chopped parsley. Cook for a couple of minutes and then add the peas and a spoonful of oil to flavor everything

pour two ladles of broth or hot water and mix, cooking for 5 minutes. Then add the broth obtained with the pods together with the peas, season with salt and pepper and bring to the boil. Then add the rice, add salt if necessary

and cook it al dente, stirring frequently with a wooden spoon; at the end of cooking, the consistency of rice and bisi should be that of a soup, but not excessively soupy. Turn off the heat and stir the rice with the other half of the butter and the grated cheese, if you like you can add more chopped parsley and serve the rice and peas piping hot!

Meat

Pork chops in a pan

Ingredients:

- Pork chops 4
- Peanut oil to taste
- Butter 50 g
- Garlic 2 cloves
- Sage to taste
- Thyme to taste
- Salt up to taste
- Rosemary to taste

FOR THE SIDE DISH

- Onions 200 g
- Potatoes 350 g
- Brandy ½ coffee cup
- Salt n q.b.
- Black pepper to taste

To prepare the pork chops, dab the chops well with absorbent paper, salt them abundantly and leave them aside for about ten minutes. Pour plenty of water into a pan with high edges and bring to the boil. Wash the potatoes, cut the larger ones into wedges without removing the peel.

When the water is boiling, add the cleaned potatoes and onions. Season with salt and cook for 5-8 minutes from the boil until soft, then drain and set aside. In the same pan, heat the seed oil.

Dab once again the chops that will have released a little water, then place them in the pan and leave them like this for 3-4 minutes, then turn them over to brown them on the other side as well. Once a nice crust has formed on both sides, add the butter cut into chunks.

Season with whole garlic, sprigs of thyme, rosemary and sage leaves. Coat the chops by tilting the pan and spraying them with the cooking juices. Cook for about 8-10 minutes in total (until it reaches an internal temperature of about 65° to be measured with a food thermometer).

Once cooked, move them onto a plate with the cooking liquid and the aromas. Cover with aluminum foil and let it rest for 10 minutes. In the same pan, add the potatoes and onions and let them brown for a few minutes.

Salt, pepper, blend with brandy. Once the potatoes are golden brown, serve them with the pork chops.

Stew Chicken

Ingredients:

- Chicken breast 800 g
- Pitted green olives 50 g
- Thyme 2 sprigs
- Rosemary 1 sprig
- Fresh chilli 1
- White onions 1
- Garlic 1 clove
- Flour 00 20 g
- Salt up to taste
- Chicken broth to taste
- Extra virgin olive oil 80 g

To prepare the chicken stew, start by removing any cartilage and fat from the chicken breast, then cut it into cubes of about 3 cm per side. Chop the chilli pepper, rosemary and thyme and keep them aside, finely chop the olives

garlic and onion and let them dry gently in the extra virgin olive oil, then when they are transparent, add the chopped rosemary, thyme, chilli pepper and olives. Leave to fry for a couple of minutes and then add the chicken, stir and fry for 10 minutes, stirring constantly.

When it is well browned, add the chicken broth to cover the cubes of meat and cook over low heat for about 40 minutes, covering the pan with a lid.

When the chicken stew is tender, add salt if necessary, add the flour through a sieve and mix to avoid the formation of lumps. Let the sauce thicken for about 5 minutes (you can add a few whole green olives to the stew if you wish), then turn off the heat and serve.

Chicken breast peppers and olives

Ingredients:

- Chicken breast 500 g
- Yellow peppers 230 g
- Red peppers 230 g
- Pitted Taggiasca olives 30 g
- Datterini tomatoes 250 g
- Small shallot 1
- Extra virgin olive oil q.s.
- Salt up to taste
- Sweet paprika to taste
- Marjoram to taste
- Black pepper to taste

To prepare the chicken breast with peppers and olives, first cut the chicken breast into two parts and remove the bone and fat and stringy parts. Arrange the two pieces on a baking dish and season on both sides with salt, oil and black pepper. Also season with sweet paprika and massage the chicken well. Cover with plastic wrap and leave to marinate in the fridge while you continue with the recipe. Wash the vegetables, cut the peppers in half, remove the filaments and internal seeds and cut them into strips. Cut the tomatoes in half. Also chop the shallot finely. Now take a large frying pan, pour a drizzle of oil and the shallots, stew for about 5 minutes over low heat. Add the peppers (yellow and red or just yellow by doubling the dosage), cook for about 10 minutes. Pour the cherry tomatoes. Season with salt and pepper and add the marjoram leaves and cook over low heat for about 10-15 minutes. At the end of cooking, add salt if necessary.

Take another non-stick pan. Pour a drizzle of oil and heat well. Brown the chicken breasts on both sides. Transfer the peppers and tomatoes to the pan, cover with a lid and cook for about 15-20 minutes. Checking the cooking and turning the chicken 4-5 times. The lid is used to prevent the chicken breast from drying out, if it gets dry add a little water. At the end of cooking, add the olives and the chicken breast with peppers and olives is ready to be served.

Duck in orange sauce

Ingredients:

- Duck 2.3 kg
- Orange juice 50 g
- 40g melted butter
- Grand Marnier 110 g
- Black pepper to taste
- Salt up to taste
- Thyme 3 sprigs
- Rosemary 1 sprig
- Oranges 3 slices
- White wine 30 g
- Water 20 g
- Extra virgin olive oil q.s.
- FOR THE POTATOES
- Potatoes 450 g
- Salt up to taste
- Black pepper to taste
- Rosemary 5 sprigs
- Extra virgin olive oil 35 g

FOR THE SAUCE

- Corn starch 15 g
- Sugar 60 g
- Oranges 1
- Water 20 g

To prepare the duck with orange, get a duck already cleaned of the innards, fat and possibly any feathers. Rinse it well under running water inside and out and dry it perfectly with a kitchen towel. Go on to tie it, helping yourself with an elastic string for food. This will help keep the shape of the whole duck well while cooking. In a large pan, heat the oil, place the duck and brown it over medium heat on both sides; then deglaze with the Grand Marnier and sprinkle with the cooking juices.

Meanwhile, cut the oranges into slices and when the duck is well browned, transfer it to a baking dish with fairly high edges and fill the inside with three orange slices, the thyme and rosemary. So brush the duck with 40 g of melted butter, salt it, pepper it and pour about 50 g of orange juice, the white wine and 20 g of water on the bottom of the pan. Before transferring it to the oven, cover the duck with aluminum foil which you will pierce with the prongs of a fork to facilitate cooking and not to burn the surface of your duck. Transfer to a preheated static oven at 200° and cook the duck with the help of a probe until it reaches 70° in the heart: it will take about 1 hour and 10 minutes. Also prepare the potatoes which will go in the oven separately but at the same temperature as the duck: wash them thoroughly and clean them with a kitchen cloth, then cut them into wedges, if possible equal, leaving the skin on; season them in a bowl with oil, salt and pepper. Then transfer them to a baking tray lined with baking paper and flavored with rosemary. Place in the oven together with the duck (you can place them on the lower cooking shelf of the oven); they will have to cook at the same temperature for about 30 minutes. In the meantime, make the sauce: take the orange, peel it with a potato peeler, squeeze out the juice and filter it: you will need 150 g. Then blanch the orange peels in boiling water for a few moments, then drain and cut them into very thin strips. Dedicate yourself to the sauce by dissolving the sugar together with the water over a very low heat: you will have to reach the temperature of 166° by measuring with a kitchen thermometer and at that point pour in the filtered orange juice; mix with a whisk to emulsify everything and add a few spoonfuls of the duck cooking liquid and the corn starch diluted in 20 g of water. Continue to work the sauce with the whisk until it thickens, then switch off and filter the sauce through a strainer, then add the finely sliced orange peel and set aside. Once the core temperature has been reached, take the duck out of the oven, remove the aluminum foil, brush it with the orange sauce and grill it for about 5/10 minutes (the time varies according to the power of the oven) to brown it for Well.

Once well browned, take your duck out of the oven and the potatoes that will have reached cooking, serve the duck with orange on a platter together with the potatoes and use the orange sauce to sprinkle the slices that you will serve to your guests.

Sicilian rolls

Ingredients:

- Slices of beef 1 kg
- Extra virgin olive oil q.s.
- 24 laurel leaves
- Red onions 1

INGREDIENTS FOR THE DOUGH

- Pine nuts 50 g
- Salt up to taste
- Black pepper to taste
- Raisins 50 g
- Extra virgin olive oil 50ml
- Caciocavallo 150 g
- Breadcrumbs 150 g
- Red onions 1

To prepare the Sicilian rolls, start by soaking the raisins in a bowl full of water for 10 minutes. Take the caciocavallo, chop it finely and put it in a bowl large enough to contain the other ingredients. Add the breadcrumbs, pine nuts and well-drained raisins to the cheese.

At this point, finely chop the onion and put it to dry in a non-stick pan with 3 tablespoons of olive oil. When it is ready, add it to the breadcrumbs mixture and add the remaining oil to mix the dough; season with salt and pepper. The mixture obtained must have a lumpy and non-compact consistency so that it can be easily modeled when you go to assemble the roll.

Now take care of creating the rolls: take the meat and beat it with the meat mallet, brush it with oil, place a little filling on it and roll it up on itself from the short side. At this point, divide the roll obtained in half with the help of a knife.

Prepare 24 onion slices by cutting the outer flaps into quarters and start building the first skewer (the slices obtained will have the length of the roll). Thread a bay leaf, a slice of onion, a roulade, a slice of onion and another bay leaf onto a skewer; continue to compose the skewer until you have skewered three rolls.

Following this procedure, also prepare the other skewers until you have used up all the ingredients and then brush them with oil. Heat up a grill pan over high heat and grill the skewers for 2 minutes on each side, just enough to brown them and cook the inside of the meat. The Sicilian rolls can be served as classic skewers or you can separate the bites and put them on a plate.

Roast beef

Ingredients:

- **Round beef 700 g**
- **Red wine 200 g**
- **Rosemary 1 sprig**
- **Extra virgin olive oil q.s.**

FOR THE EMULSION

- **Extra virgin olive oil 2 tbsp**
- **Garlic 1 clove**
- **Rosemary 1 sprig**
- **Salt up to taste**

To make the roast beef first finely chop the garlic and rosemary needles. Pour 2 tablespoons of oil into a small bowl, add the minced garlic and rosemary and the salt, then emulsify with a fork.

Tie the beef round with kitchen twine by inserting a sprig of rosemary, then sprinkle it with the emulsion and massage the meat with your hands to absorb it well. Leave to rest in the refrigerator for 10 minutes. After this time, place the meat in a hot, well-greased pan.

Brown the meat on all sides to seal it. When the roast is well browned, transfer it to a pan together with the cooking liquid, making sure that the bottom of the pan is well greased. Bake in a preheated static oven at 150° for about 20 minutes.

At this point sprinkle the meat with red wine and continue cooking for another 40 minutes at 150°, covering the meat with aluminum foil. A couple of times, during cooking, wet the meat, being careful not to burn yourself. Once cooked, take the roast out of the oven and let it rest for about ten minutes before removing the string. Cut your roast beef into slices and serve them with the gravy!

Sicilian chicken

Ingredients:

- **Chicken breast 850 g**
- **Eggplants 550 g**
- **Cottage cheese 50 g**
- **Peeled tomatoes 800 g**
- **Basil 5 leaves**
- **Garlic 1 clove**
- **Salt up to taste**
- **Black pepper to taste**
- **Extra virgin olive oil q.s.**
- **Flour 00 to taste**

TO FRY

- **Peanut oil to taste**

To make the Sicilian chicken, first cut the chicken breast into cubes, then flour it, then remove the excess flour by sifting with a sieve. Heat a drizzle of oil in a pan, add the floured chicken nuggets and brown them for 4-5 minutes on all sides.

Keep them aside and in the same pan add a clove of garlic and a drizzle of oil. Pour the peeled tomatoes, mash them with a fork, flavor with the basil leaves. Cover with the lid and cook over low heat for 30 minutes. Meanwhile, wash and trim the eggplants, then slice them along the long side and cut them into strips first on one side and then on the other, so as to obtain cubes of about 1 cm. Heat the seed oil in a saucepan and when it reaches 170°, dip the diced eggplants. Cook for a few minutes until they are golden brown, then drain.

Place them on a tray lined with absorbent or fried paper. After 30 minutes of cooking the sauce, remove the garlic and add the chicken nuggets, salt and pepper and cook for another 10-15 minutes over low heat without a lid. Turn off the heat and add the fried eggplants, grate the cottage cheese and mix to add flavour. Serve the Sicilian chicken piping hot.

Roman lamb

Ingredients:

- **Lambs ribs 450 g**
- **Extra virgin olive oil 3 tbsp**
- **Salt up to taste**
- **Black pepper to taste**
- **Rosemary 1 sprig**
- **Lemons 1**

Arrange the ribs in a baking dish, salt and pepper to taste on both sides, grease them with oil, flavored with minced garlic

and fresh rosemary. Leave the ribs thus seasoned to marinate in the fridge for about 30 minutes. After the marinating time they will be ready for cooking. Heat a cast iron plate and cook the ribs over high heat for about 4 minutes per side. When the ribs are cooked, serve your baby lamb very hot, accompanying it with a few slices of lemon.

Meat stew with onions

Ingredients:

- Celery 1 rib
- Carrots 2
- Red onions 600 gr
- Tomato puree 200 g
- 1/2 glass of red wine (about 100 ml)
- Salt to taste.
- Pepper as needed.
- Olive oil to taste
- Meat broth to taste
- Veal beef 800 gr

To prepare the meat stew with onions, start by chopping the celery and carrots that will serve as the base for the sauté. Heat a large frying pan with two tablespoons of oil, add the chopped celery and carrots and cook the sautéed mixture.

Cut the onions into thin slices and set them aside. Meanwhile, prepare the meat: cut the veal into bite-size pieces and when the sauté is ready, add the pieces of meat and brown them.

Deglaze with the red wine and add the onion slices. Continue cooking over a low heat, gradually adding the meat broth,

Finally, add the tomato puree. Cooking the stew will take about 1 hour. Once the gravy has been absorbed by the meat, season with salt and pepper. The meat and onion stew is ready when the meat is tender and the onions well cooked.

Arrosticini

Ingredients:

- **Sheep the pulp 800 g**
- **Extra virgin olive oil 30 g**
- **Rosemary 1 sprig**
- **Salt up to 4 g**

To prepare the arrosticini, start by taking the meat. With the help of a sharp-bladed knife, remove the fattest parts of the meat. Next, cut the meat into strips and then into 1cm thick cubes.

Once you have obtained the cubes of meat, thread them onto the skewers. Repeat the procedure for all the arrosticini. Now heat a cast iron grill well and oil it lightly so as to easily turn the arrosticini while cooking.

Then place the arrosticini on the hot grill.

Cooking should take approximately 1 minute per side. Cook the arrosticini on both sides until you notice a light crust. Add salt and garnish the dish with your arrosticini with rosemary and cherry tomatoes. Your arrosticini are now ready to be enjoyed!

Pizzaiola chicken

Ingredients:

- **Chicken breast 640 g**
- **Pickled capers 20 g**
- **Tomato puree 450 g**
- **Mozzarella 180 g**
- **Garlic 1 clove**
- **Basil 6 leaves**
- **Oregano to taste**
- **Salt up to taste**
- **Black pepper to taste**
- **Extra virgin olive oil q.s.**

To make the chicken pizzaiola first clean your breasts, remove the central part of the bones, the excess fat, and cut it to obtain 4 slices.

Also cut the mozzarella into slices, let it drain in a colander, so that it loses a little excess whey. Crush a clove of garlic and brown it in a non-stick pan with a drizzle of oil. Brown the chicken breasts for about 3 minutes per side, over high heat so that they take on a little colour. Remove the garlic clove and season with salt and pepper.

After browning, remove the breasts and keep them aside. In the same pan pour the capers and the tomato sauce which you will cook for about 5 minutes. At this point put your chicken breasts back in the pan and cook the chicken by cooking for about 10 minutes with a lid.

Once cooked, add the basil leaves broken with your hands, place the mozzarella on the breasts and add the oregano, put the lid back on and cook for a few minutes on a low flame, long enough for the mozzarella to melt a little. Your pizzaiola chicken breasts are ready to enjoy.

Sicilian roast

Ingredients:

- Ground beef 100 g
- Pecorino to grate 20 g
- Round beef) 600 g
- Breadcrumbs 30 g

FOR THE STUFFING

- Boiled eggs 3
- Lard 30 g
- Caciocavallo 40 g
- Extra virgin olive oil q.s.
- Mortadella 50 g

FOR THE SAUCE

- Onions 1
- Carrots 1
- Celery 1 rib
- Extra virgin olive oil q.s.
- Salt up to taste
- Black pepper to taste
- Red wine 50ml
- Tomato puree 500 g
- Triple tomato paste 1 tbsp

Start by hardening the eggs in a saucepan full of water, then take the slice of beef and beat it well with a meat tenderizer, to ensure that the thickness is uniform. Cut the mortadella, the lard and caciocavallo into strips of about half a cm, then set aside. In a large bowl, combine the minced meat and the grated cheese and the breadcrumbs, then mix well with your hands. Season with salt and pepper, then place the mixture on the slice of beef, taking care to spread it well and to leave about 2 cm of border on each side, to prevent the filling from coming out when you go to roll the meat.

Now place, alternating them, the lard, mortadella and caciocavallo, then place the hard-boiled eggs, previously cooled and shelled, in the centre.

Close by rolling up the meat on itself; use kitchen twine to seal it.

Brown the meat in a pan with a little oil, taking care to sear it well on all sides. In the meantime, prepare the chopped celery, onion and carrot and fry it in a non-stick pan with two tablespoons of extra virgin olive oil for a few minutes over low heat. Once browned, add it to the sautéed mixture, continuing cooking over medium heat; after a couple of minutes add the red wine. Then add the tomato puree, a spoonful of triple tomato concentrate, salt and pepper. Cover with a lid and cook over low heat for 60 minutes, turning occasionally to cook evenly. After this time, check that it is ready by piercing it with a fork: the meat must be tender.

Turn off the heat, remove the meat and lay it on a cutting board to remove the string and cut into slices. Serve on a platter, accompanying it with its gravy.

Sausage and provolone pork loin rolls

Ingredients:

- Pork loin (650 g) - (single piece or thin slices)
- Sausage (290 g)
- Provolone cheese (175 g)
- Marsala wine (70 g)
- Porcini mushrooms (30 g) - dried
- Whipping cream (40 g)
- Garlic 1 clove
- Butter 1 ½ tsp (20 g)
- Extra virgin olive oil to taste
- Sage to taste
- Rosemary to taste
- Water to taste
- Fine salt to taste
- Black pepper to taste

FOR FLOURING

- Flour 00 to taste

To prepare the sausage and provolone pork loin rolls, start by rinsing the porcini mushrooms thoroughly, before soaking them for 10-15 minutes in warm water so that they rehydrate. Cut 6 slices from the loin and tenderize them with a meat tenderizer.

Keeping the skin on the sausage, cut it into 6 pieces of around 4 inches (9 cm) in length, or the same width as the meat slices. Next, cut 12 pretty thin slices of provolone. Season the slices with salt and pepper, lay the sausage on top and cover with a couple of slices of provolone. Roll the whole thing up and fasten with kitchen string.

Dredge the rolls in the flour and set aside for a moment. Pour a drizzle of oil and the butter into a frying pan. Allow it to melt, then add the herbs and spices: the sage, the rosemary, and the whole clove of garlic, peeled.

Place the rolls in the pan and brown them, turning often, over medium heat until the meat is well sealed on all sides. Season with salt and pepper to taste, then drain the mushrooms well and add to the rolls.

Add the Marsala wine , and as soon as the alcohol has evaporated (this will only take a few moments), pour in the light cream.

Cover with a lid and cook over low heat for around 20 minutes. Add a little water at a time, if necessary, to prevent the cooking liquid from becoming too thick. Once cooked, everything should be creamy. Serve your sausage and provolone pork loin rolls piping hot.

Ischia rabbit

Ingredients:

- **Rabbit in pieces 1,5 kg**
- **Copper tomatoes 300 g**
- **Garlic 1 clove**
- **Extra virgin olive oil 50 g**
- **White wine 60 g**
- **Salt up to taste**
- **Black pepper to taste**
- **Basil 3 leaves**

To prepare the Ischia rabbit, start by rinsing the tomatoes under fresh water, then dry them and cut them in half. Cut and remove the top of the tomato.

Then cut them into slices and then into cubes, collect them in a small bowl. Then take a pan, pour the oil and the garlic, sauté over low heat for a few moments and when the garlic is golden but not burnt, remove it and add the pieces of rabbit washed and dried with kitchen paper. Brown the meat for 4-5 minutes, turning the pieces on all sides for even browning. Then pour in the white wine, a little at a time, turning the pieces of meat while pouring in the wine. Bring to a boil over medium heat, and when the wine has completely evaporated, add the diced tomatoes, season with salt and pepper and cook for about 30 minutes with the lid on, stirring and turning the pieces of meat from time to time. Finally, add the basil leaves broken up by hand and turn off the heat. The sauce must be thick and shiny; your Ischia rabbit is ready to be served piping hot!

Baked chicken breast with tomato and mozzarella

Ingredients:

- **Chicken breast 500 g**
- **Datterini tomatoes 250 g**
- **Mozzarella 250 g**
- **Rosemary 4 g**
- **Black pepper to taste**
- **Extra virgin olive oil q.s.**
- **Salt up to taste**
- **Garlic 2 cloves**
- **Basil 4 leaves**

To make the baked chicken breast with tomato and mozzarella, first finely chop the rosemary. Divide the chicken breast in half, place it in a bowl and season it with rosemary, salt and pepper and season with the olive oil, massage the meat well with the herbs, cover with plastic wrap and keep aside.

Now wash and cut the cherry tomatoes in half. Pour a drizzle of olive oil into a pan suitable for cooking in the oven, add two cloves of garlic and let it infuse for a couple of minutes. Then add the tomatoes.

Flavor with the basil leaves and cook over low heat for 10 minutes. After this time, remove the garlic cloves and add the chicken breast.

Cover with aluminum foil and transfer to a preheated oven for 25 minutes at 200°C. In the meantime cut the mozzarella into slices and leave to drain in a colander so that it loses its whey.

After 25 minutes, remove the aluminum foil and cook for another 10 minutes. Take the chicken out of the oven, place the mozzarella slices on top of the breasts and bake again for about 5 minutes in grill mode at 240°C, just long enough for the mozzarella to melt. Serve the baked chicken breast with tomato and mozzarella piping hot and stringy.

Fish

Drunk octopus

Ingredients:

- 1 kg octopus (clean)
- Garlic 3 cloves
- 1/2 liter red wine
- A few bay leaves
- Fresh chilli 1
- Extra virgin olive oil 6 tbsp
- Chopped parsley 3 tbsp
- Salt to taste.

Cut the octopus into pieces no larger than a walnut. Pour the oil into a saucepan and put the whole garlic cloves to brown, add the bay leaves, the chilli pepper cut into small pieces.

Now add the octopus in pieces and sauté it for a few moments, then add the red wine, a little chopped parsley, bring back to the boil and lower the heat; cover with a lid and cook for at least 40/50 minutes depending on the hardness of the octopus itself. If the sauce becomes too thick, add a few tablespoons of water. A few moments before removing the drunken octopus from the heat, add a generous handful of chopped parsley, season with salt and leave to cool for a few minutes.

Fisherman's clams

Ingredients:

- **Clams 1.2 kg (clean)**
- **Parsley to chop 1 tuft**
- **White wine 100ml**
- **Extra virgin olive oil 4 tbsp**
- **Salt up to taste**
- **Garlic 2 cloves**

Put 4 tablespoons of extra virgin olive oil in a pan and fry the garlic cloves, peeled and crushed. Drain the clams and add them to the pan, pour over the wine and continue cooking over medium heat for a couple of minutes until the wine has completely evaporated.

Cover with the lid and cook for another 2 minutes. When all the clams are well open, add a sprinkling of chopped parsley, sauté them a couple of times and your seafood clams will be ready to be served!

Fried cod

Ingredients:

- **Cod 500 g**
- **Flour 00 to taste**
- **Black pepper to taste**
- **Lime to taste**

TO FRY

- **Peanut oil 1 l**

Start heating the oil. In the meantime, remove the skin from the cod. Run your hand over the cod pulp in one direction and the other to feel the presence of bones and remove them with kitchen tweezers. Cut the cod into strips about 3 cm thick, then divide into 2-3 more parts.

Carefully flour the pieces of cod on both sides. Once the oil has reached a temperature between 180° and 190° (to be measured with a kitchen thermometer), dip a few pieces at a time, first eliminating the excess flour. You can help yourself with a kitchen spider so you don't burn yourself. Depending on the thickness, it will take 3-5 minutes to cook and only when they are golden brown can you drain them.

Arrange them on a tray covered with a sheet of absorbent paper for fried foods, in order to remove the excess oil. Finish frying and season the fried cod to taste with freshly ground pepper and, if you like, a few slices of lime or lemon.

Surmullets at Livornese

Ingredients:

- **Mullets 8 (clean)**
- **Peeled tomatoes 450 g**
- **Garlic 1 clove**
- **Extra virgin olive oil 50 g**
- **Parsley to taste**
- **Salt up to taste**
- **Black pepper to taste**

Pour the oil into a pan, add the crushed garlic and about 2 tablespoons of chopped parsley. Let the sautéed lightly dry for 2-3 minutes, stirring frequently, then add the peeled tomatoes.

Stir with a spatula to mix the ingredients and let the sauce cook for 7-8 minutes. Add salt and pepper and add the red mullets without overlapping them. At this point the mullets will not be turned or moved, to facilitate cooking and keep them moist, sprinkle them with a little sauce and cover them with a lid. Continue cooking for 10-15 minutes (depending on the size of the fish; to check doneness, try with a fork to see if the flesh of the red mullet detaches from the central spine easily, an indication that they are ready!) and sprinkle them again with a spoon of chopped parsley . At this point, all you have to do is serve your Livorno-style mullet while still hot.

Neapolitan mussel soup

Ingredients:

- Mussels 1,5 kg (clean)
- Octopus 1 kg (clean)
- Prawns 150 g (clean)
- Peeled tomatoes 600 g
- Garlic 2 cloves
- Salt up to 1 g
- Cuttlefish 300 g (clean)
- Extra virgin olive oil 60 g
- Black pepper to taste
- Parsley 10 g
- White wine 40ml

FOR THE CROUTONS

- **Baguettes 1**
- **Extra virgin olive oil 30 ml**

Cut the cuttlefish in half along the longest side and then cut them into strips. Cook the octopus in a saucepan for 40 minutes. Before draining it, pierce the meat with the prongs of a fork to check that it is the right time to remove it from the heat.

When it's ready, drain the octopus with the help of a slotted spoon and let it cool. Then transfer it to a cutting board and cut the tentacles into small pieces. Brown a clove of garlic with a drizzle of oil in a non-stick pan.

When the garlic is well browned, remove it with kitchen tongs and pour in the mussels; add the white wine and cook covering with a lid, letting them open spontaneously: it will take about 5 minutes. After this time, check all the mussels: those that have not opened will be thrown away.

Turn off the heat, drain them, reserving the cooking liquid. Separate the empty shells from the full ones, placing the latter in a container. Place a large saucepan on the fire with the poached garlic and a drizzle of oil. Brown the garlic and, when it is golden brown, remove it from the pot.

Add the cuttlefish, seasoning with salt and pepper to taste, the prawns and cook over low heat for 2 minutes, stirring with a spatula. Then add the cleaned octopus and mussels, pouring in all the cooking liquid from the latter.

Add the peeled tomatoes and cook for another 10-15 minutes until the sauce is reduced. In the meantime, prepare the croutons: cut the baguette into 3-4 cm thick slices, place the slices on a baking tray lined with baking paper and drizzle a drizzle of olive oil on each crouton.

Place under the grill for 4-5 minutes and, when the croutons are golden brown and crunchy, take them out of the oven. A few moments before the end of cooking, finish by adding the chopped fresh parsley: your Neapolitan mussel soup is ready; you just have to serve it, accompanying it with the crunchy and tasty croutons you have prepared.

Squid with peas

Ingredients:

- **Squid (clean) 800 g**
- **Frozen peas (or fresh) 400 g**
- **Fresh spring onion 1**
- **Dry white wine 100 g**
- **Garlic 1 clove**
- **Extra virgin olive oil q.s.**
- **Salt up to taste**

Rinse the squid several times under running water and finally cut them into slices about 2 cm wide.

Peel and finely chop the spring onion. Heat a drizzle of oil in a pan, add the spring onion and let it soften, then add the peas, salt and cook for about 10 minutes over medium-low heat.

Meanwhile, pour the squid into another pan with another round of oil and the garlic clove. Deglaze with the white wine and cook for about 10 minutes over medium-low heat, then remove the garlic from the pan.

At this point, add the peas, add a drizzle of oil and cook for another 10 minutes. Season with salt, if necessary, and serve your squid with peas accompanied with slices of toasted bread!

Plaice fillet Sorrento style

Ingredients:

- **Plaice (4 fillets) 250 g**
- **Garlic 1 clove**
- **Tomato puree 400 g**
- **Pitted black olives 30 g**
- **Extra virgin olive oil 25 g**
- **Oregano 3 sprigs**
- **Salt up to taste**
- **Black pepper to taste**
- **Flour 00 20 g**
- **Basil 5 leaves**

To prepare the Sorrentine plaice fillet, cut the black olives into rounds and place a non-stick pan on the heat with the oil and garlic clove. Pour the tomato puree, sliced olives, season with salt and pepper. Cook for minutes over low heat, stirring occasionally with a spatula.

In the meantime, take care of the plaice fillets. Chop the oregano, pour the flour distributing it on a tray, add the chopped oregano, salt and pepper and mix everything with a teaspoon.

Pass the fillets in the flour, pressing well with your fingers so that the breading adheres well to both sides, then put a pan with the oil on the heat; when the oil is hot, brown the fillets for 2 minutes on each side, turning them on both sides with kitchen tongs for uniform cooking. Once ready, put out the fire, then place the still hot fillets in the tomato and olive sauce that you have previously prepared. Cook for 2 minutes and finish by adding a few basil leaves: your Sorrento-style plaice fillet is ready to be served and enjoyed.

Tuna and ricotta meatballs with peppers

Ingredients:

- **Tuna in oil 320 g**
- **Cottage cheese 180 g**
- **Eggs 1**
- **Grana Padano 25 g**
- **Breadcrumbs 20 g**
- **Salt up to taste**
- **Black pepper to taste**
- **Thyme to taste**
- **Marjoram to taste**

FOR THE SIDELINE OF PEPPERS

- **Red peppers 350 g**
- **Yellow peppers 350 g**
- **Pitted black olives 12**
- **Extra virgin olive oil 30 g**
- **Salt up to taste**
- **Garlic 1/2 clove**
- **Thyme to taste**

To prepare the tuna and ricotta meatballs with peppers, start by washing and drying the two peppers; then place them on a baking sheet and bake them for about 30-40 minutes at 250°, turning them from time to time until the skin is well browned. Once toasted, close them in a plastic bag, or in a bowl covered with transparent film for about 15 minutes.

After the indicated time, remove the peppers from the bag and remove the skin which will come off rather easily. Once peeled, remove the seeds and internal filaments from the peppers, then cut them into strips. Place the peppers in a bowl and season them with the chopped thyme, salt, crushed garlic, extra virgin olive oil and finally the pitted black olives cut into slices. Mix the ingredients and let it rest.

In the meantime, prepare the mixture for the meatballs: pour the tuna into a bowl, add the ricotta, the chopped thyme and marjoram and the previously beaten egg.

Then add the grated cheese, breadcrumbs, salt and pepper. Mix everything with a ladle and finish kneading with your hands until you get a uniform mixture.

At this point, take 50 gram portions of dough and form slightly flattened meatballs. Roll them in breadcrumbs and fry in very hot oil.

Cook for about 6 minutes, browning them well on both sides. Place the meatballs to drain on absorbent kitchen paper and serve while still hot, accompanying them with the peppers.

Pan-fried sea bream fillets and potatoes

Ingredients:

- Sea bream 1
- Potatoes (500g)
- Extra virgin olive oil to taste
- Fine salt to taste
- Black pepper to taste
- Garlic 1 clove
- Rosemary 1 sprig
- Thyme 1 sprig

To prepare pan-fried sea bream fillets and potatoes, start by thoroughly washing the potatoes; cut them into roughly 0.2 inch slices, without peeling. Place them in a bowl and season with salt, black pepper and oil.

Add the peeled garlic clove too, along with the thyme and rosemary sprigs. Place the potatoes in a large pan and cook on a medium to low flame for around 30 minutes. Try not to turn them over to avoid breaking them up: sauté them only. Clean the sea bream in the meantime. Gut and descale the fish using the special tool, or a knife, using the blunt side.

Place the sea bream on a cutting board and cut the first fillet using a knife. Turn the fish over and cut the other fillet out. Trim both fillets to remove the part under the belly.

Use special tweezers to remove any spines too. Once the potatoes are soft and have browned, place them in a container and leave them to one side.

Place a drizzle of oil in the same pan you used to cook the potatoes and place the sea bream fillets in the middle. Cook for around 10 minutes on a low flame and gently turn the fillets over half way into the cooking time. Add salt and pepper to taste.

Add the potatoes when the fillets are done. Heat them up and serve your pan-fried sea bream and potatoes!

Cod with potatoes and olives

Ingredients:

- **Cod 800 g**
- **Potatoes 700 g**
- **Black olives 200 g**
- **Vegetable broth 350 g**
- **Flour 00 100 g**
- **Golden onions 1**
- **Extra virgin olive oil 5 tbsp**
- **3 bay leaves**
- **Salt up to taste**
- **Black pepper to taste**

Drain the cod well, dab it with a clean cloth, cut it into rectangles, remove the bones with tweezers, then cut it into smaller pieces, into rectangles or squares.

Carefully flour the pieces of cod on both sides. Then peel the onion and cut it into slices.

Then chop it finely and pour it into a large pan where you have heated 2 and a half tablespoons of olive oil. Brown the onion and after 5 minutes add the floured cod.

Then cook it for 20 minutes over low heat, turning it from time to time so that the pieces of cod brown well on both sides. In the meantime, peel the potatoes and cut them into wedges (or if you prefer into slices about 1 cm thick), rinse them under cold water, then pat them dry with kitchen paper.

Take a large saucepan that can hold both the cod and the potatoes, then drizzle it with 2 and a half tablespoons of olive oil and add the potatoes. Turn on the medium heat and pour the vegetable broth into the pan with the potatoes. Leave to flavor for 5 minutes, then when the cod is well browned, remove it from the pan and add it to the pan with the potatoes together with its cooking juices.

Pour the black olives into the pan and add the bay leaves. Let everything cook for another 15-20 minutes, adding more vegetable broth when necessary so as not to dry the cod too much, which must remain "stewed" and create a tasty creamy sauce. Once the fire is extinguished, add salt and pepper to taste, then serve piping hot!

Anchovies pizzaiola

Ingredients:

- **Anchovies (500 g)**
- **Cherry tomatoes 200 g**
- **Dried oregano 2 tsp**
- **Extra virgin olive oil 50 g**
- **Garlic 1 clove**
- **Salt up to taste**
- **Black pepper to taste**

Wash the cherry tomatoes and cut them into 4 parts and keep them aside ready for use. Then in a greased pan with 25 g of extra virgin olive oil arrange the anchovy fillets along the length of the pan, then the chopped tomatoes and dried oregano.

Season with salt and pepper and squeeze out some garlic, or chop it with a knife, and then start over by arranging the anchovies again, this time arranging them in the opposite direction to the previous one.

Then cover again with cherry tomatoes, salt, pepper and oregano and sprinkle the surface with the remaining extra virgin olive oil. Place the pan on a dripping pan and cook in a preheated static oven at 220° for 20 minutes, let it rest for a few minutes to let it settle and finally serve the anchovies alla pizzaiola still piping hot!

Ligurian-style sea bass

Ingredients:

- Sea bass fillets 4 (clean)
- Extra virgin olive oil 30 g
- Garlic 1 clove
- Pitted Taggiasca olives 50 g
- Pine nuts 20 g
- Thyme 2 sprigs
- Salt up to taste
- Black pepper to taste

Put a pan on the fire with the oil and a clove of garlic,

let it infuse well, and place the sea bass fillets inside the pan with the skin facing downwards. Cook for 2 minutes over medium heat, taking care to turn them with a spatula halfway through cooking, do this operation very delicately so as not to break the sea bass. At this point also pour the olives, remove the garlic with kitchen tongs.

Salt and pepper and flavor the sea bass fillets with the fresh thyme leaves. Turn off the heat and separately in another pan toast the pine nuts for 2-3 minutes over medium heat. Serve the Ligurian sea bass fillet with olives and garnish with toasted pine nuts!

Mackerel in a pan

Ingredients:

- Mackerel (550 g) - (cleaned fillets)
- Cherry tomatoes (250 g)
- Tomato puree 3 tbsp (50 g)
- Raisins 2 tbsp (30 g)
- Pine nuts 3 tbsp (20 g)
- Salted capers 10 (10 g) - (desalted)
- Black olives 8 - (pitted)
- Garlic 1 clove
- Parsley 1 bunch
- Oregano to taste
- Dry white wine (70 g)
- Extra virgin olive oil to taste
- Fine salt to taste

To make the mackerel in a pan, first chop the parsley and cut the cherry tomatoes in half. In a large pan with a drizzle of oil, put the parsley and the garlic clove, peeled and cut in half. Cover with the lid and let it dry for a minute over medium heat, then add the cherry tomatoes. Add salt and cook for 5 minutes over high heat, always with the lid on.

Pour the sauce and continue cooking for another 7 minutes, over high heat with the lid. Now add the raisins and the pine nuts.

Also add the coarsely chopped olives and the desalted capers. Stir and leave to flavor for a couple of minutes over high heat. At this point, lower the heat and place the mackerel fillets, then pour the white wine. Gently mix to cover the fish with the sauce and flavor with oregano.

Cover with the lid and cook for 10 minutes over medium-low heat. Finally remove the lid and reduce the sauce for 5 minutes over high heat. Serve your mackerel in a pan immediately!

Baked stuffed squid

Ingredients:

- Squid 1 (600g)
- Potatoes (200g)
- Breads (90g)
- Whole milk (90g)
- Fresh scallion 1
- Parmigiano Reggiano DOP cheese 1 ½ tbsp (10 g)
- Marjoram to taste
- Fresh turmeric 1 ¼ tbsp (9 g)
- Eggs 1
- Extra virgin olive oil ¾ tbsp (10 g)
- Fine salt to taste
- Black pepper

FOR THE ACCOMPANYING SAUCE

- Natural plain yogurt ½ cup (130 g)
- Whipping cream 2 tsp (10 g)
- Dill to taste
- Extra virgin olive oil to taste

To prepare the stuffed squid, start with the potatoes. Place them in a saucepan with cold water and cook for around 20-30 minutes from boiling (you can speed up the cooking process by using a pressure cooker). Once they're ready (make sure they can be pierced easily with a fork), allow them to cool, then peel and set aside. Next, remove the crust from the bread, cut the bread into chunks , and soak the chunks in the milk.

Clean the squid by removing the head and the side "wings" with a knife. Rinse the squid thoroughly, both outside and inside 6, to remove any impurities.

Chop up the wings and the tentacles, and finely chop the scallion, having removed the green part and the roots beforehand, along with the marjoram leaves. Heat the extra virgin olive oil in a pan, add the chopped scallion and marjoram, and fry over low heat, stirring occasionally, for a few minutes.

Then add the chopped wings and tentacles and cook over high heat for a few moments, ensuring that the water released from the squid evaporates completely.

At this point, you need to start preparing the filling. Mash the now-cold potatoes in a large bowl and add the soaked bread, the chopped squid and scallion, the grated Parmigiano Reggiano cheese, the peeled fresh turmeric grating it directly into the bowl, the salt, the pepper, and the whole egg.

Mix thoroughly, and once all of the ingredients are combined, transfer the mixture to a disposable pastry bag. Preheat a conventional oven to 350°F (180°C), then grease the bottom of a small baking dish (that will hold 4 stuffed squid), stuff the squid to the top with the filling, and lay them side by side in the dish. Season with salt and pepper to taste and finish with a drizzle of oil. Bake in a conventional oven preheated to 350°F (180°C) for approximately 30 minutes. While the squid are baking, turn your attention to the accompanying sauce. Pour the yogurt and cream into a small bowl, add a drizzle of oil and the dill, and mix well. Once the squid are cooked, take them out of the oven and serve each baked stuffed squid with the accompanying sauce.

Busara's Scamps

Ingredients:

- **Scampi 1 kg**
- **Peeled tomatoes 300 g**
- **Dry white wine 50ml**
- **Breadcrumbs 20 g**
- **Garlic 1 clove**
- **Parsley to chop 2 tbsp**
- **Fresh chilli 1**
- **Extra virgin olive oil q.s.**
- **Salt up to taste**

To prepare the scampi alla busara, first wash the scampi well under cold running water. With a sharp knife or scissors, make a vertical cut on the back or belly, in order to facilitate the extraction of the pulp once cooked. If you prefer, you can also leave them whole. In a large frying pan, brown a clove of garlic in extra virgin olive oil; also add the whole fresh chilli pepper. You can pierce both the garlic and the chilli pepper with a toothpick, to make it easier to remove them after cooking. When the garlic is golden, add the breadcrumbs, which will serve to thicken the tomato pulp, and mix quickly to prevent it from burning. Immediately after, add the scampi, better not to overlap them to make the cooking uniform, blend with the white wine. Let it evaporate for a couple of minutes then add salt and add the peeled tomatoes cut into small pieces, give it a stir and cover the pan with a lid. Let it cook like this for about 15 minutes. Meanwhile, finely chop the parsley and, when cooked, sprinkle it on the scampi.

Before serving the scampi alla busara, remove the chilli pepper and the clove of garlic: your scampi alla busara are ready!

Mediterranean sea bream

Ingredients:

- **Sea bream 2 pieces (clean)**
- **Extra virgin olive oil 30 g**
- **Salt up to taste**
- **Black pepper to taste**
- **Garlic 2 cloves**
- **Pitted black olives 100 g**
- **Cherry tomatoes 200 g**
- **Thyme to taste**
- **Salted capers 1 tbsp**

Stuff each sea bream with the herbs: the sprigs of fresh thyme, 1 peeled garlic clove each and finally salt and pepper.

Take a baking dish, drizzle the bottom with olive oil, place the two stuffed sea bream 8, then wash the cherry tomatoes and cut them in half, distribute them in the dish around the two sea breams, then rinse the capers thoroughly under running water to remove the excess salt and add them to the sea breams, also add the pitted black olives, scented with a couple of sprigs of fresh thyme and drizzle the sea breams with a drizzle of olive oil; season last with salt. Now cook the Mediterranean sea bream in a preheated static oven at 200° for 25-30 minutes. When cooked, take the Mediterranean sea bream out of the oven and serve it with the cherry tomatoes and olives!

Dessert

Veronese cake

Ingredients:

- **Flour 00 170 g**
- **Sugar 150g**
- **Butter 100 g**
- **Macaroons 100 g**
- **Almonds 100 g**
- **Eggs (about 3 medium) 168 g**
- **Baking powder for cakes 8 g**
- **Salt up to 1 pinch**
- **Almond flavor (sweet) 1 tsp**
- **Puff pastry (1 roll) 230 g**
- **Powdered sugar to taste**

To prepare the Verona cake, start by melting the butter over a very low heat and let it cool. Then blend the almonds in a mixer with a little sugar taken from the total dose. Also crumble the amaretti with your hands in a small bowl.

Using an electric mixer, beat the eggs with the remaining sugar until you get a light, frothy mixture. Slowly pour in the now warmed melted butter, almonds crumbled and worked with sugar, flour, baking powder, the crumbled amaretti biscuits, the sweet almond flavoring and the pinch of salt.

Work with the whisk to obtain a homogeneous mixture. Line a 20 cm diameter cake tin with a high edge with parchment paper and arrange the pastry inside so that it protrudes slightly from the edge. Pour the mixture, fold the edges inwards and bake in a preheated static oven at 180° for about 60 minutes.

If the cake should darken on the surface, you can move it to the lowest shelf of the oven or cover it with aluminum foil until the end of cooking. Once cooked, take it out of the oven, let it cool completely before unmolding it. The cake can be served by decorating with icing sugar as desired.

Red wine cake

Ingredients:

- Red wine 150ml
- Flour 00 250 g
- Medium eggs 4
- Butter at room temperature 250 g
- Sugar 250 g
- Ground cinnamon 1 tsp
- Ground cloves 1/2 tsp
- Bitter cocoa powder 20 g
- Dark chocolate 150 g
- Baking powder for desserts 16 g
- TO DECORATE
- Liquid fresh cream 200 g
- Icing sugar 20 g
- Vanilla pod seeds of 1/2 pod

To prepare the red wine cake, cut the butter at room temperature into cubes and place it in a food processor fitted with blades; add the sugar and work everything until you get a cream. Divide the yolks from the whites (keep the whites, as they will be used later) and gradually add the yolks to the mixture; mix them well, then pour in the cinnamon and cloves in powder.

Also add the bitter cocoa and then the red wine. Mix until you get a cream with a uniform color and at this point transfer the dough into a bowl; pour the sifted flour mixed with the yeast and mix well with a spatula to avoid the formation of lumps.

In a bowl, whip the egg whites that you have kept aside with an electric mixer; when the egg whites are whipped, gently add them to the mixture with the spatula in three stages, stirring from bottom to top to prevent the mixture from disassembling. Then with a knife cut the dark chocolate very finely, and add it to the dough you have obtained. Grease and line a 22 cm diameter cake tin with parchment paper and pour the mixture into it, leveling it well with the spatula.

Bake in a preheated static oven at 150° for 90 minutes (or in a convection oven at 130° for 80 minutes); to check the cooking, do the test with a toothpick: if, inserting it, it comes out dry, it means that the cake is ready; otherwise, continue cooking for a few minutes. Once ready, take the cake out of the oven and unmold it, placing it on a wire rack to cool. Just before serving, prepare the decorations: cut the vanilla pod lengthwise and then remove the internal seeds with a small knife. Pour the liquid fresh cream into a cold bowl and whip it together with the icing sugar with an electric mixer, taking care to use the cold whisks (you can place the bowl and whisks in the fridge for a few minutes before using them): in this way you will to whip the cream more easily.

Add the vanilla seeds and continue with the whips. When the cream is ready, place the red wine cake, which will have cooled down by now, on a serving plate; finally, with a sac-à-few with a knurled nozzle, decorate it with the cream you have prepared and finally serve. For a more refined final touch, you can also add a whole vanilla bean and a couple of cinnamon sticks to the decoration.

Cake 3 ingredients

Ingredients:

- **Dark chocolate (55%) 450 g**
- **Butter (at room temperature) 220 g**
- **Eggs (about 5 medium at room temperature) 245 g**

TO DECORATE

- **Liquid fresh cream 150 g**
- **Berries to taste**

To make the 3-ingredient cake, first of all finely chop the 55% dark chocolate with a knife (if you use a higher percentage, you will have to adjust the amount of butter and eggs to compensate for the fat), put it to melt in a saucepan in a bain-marie, add the butter cut into pieces. Stir with a spatula to promote dissolution and mix the ingredients well. Once ready, let it cool for about 5 minutes. Meanwhile, pour the eggs into a bowl and whisk them with an electric whisk, they must be light and frothy, it will take about 5 minutes. Now slowly pour the warmed melted chocolate into the bowl with the whipped eggs, as you pour the chocolate, mix the mixture from the bottom up so as to obtain a well-blended mixture. Line the bottom of a 20 cm diameter cake tin, to do this, cut out the shape on a sheet of parchment paper, then butter the bottom of the mold and adhere the sheet of parchment paper. Pour the batter into the pan and level the surface with a spatula. Now place the pan on a dripping pan and pour water at room temperature to cover half of the mold. Bake for 5 minutes in a static preheated oven at 210° on the central shelf, then cover with aluminum foil and continue cooking for another 15 minutes. When cooked, take the cake out of the oven and let it cool at room temperature for a couple of hours. Then place in the fridge to harden for at least 1 hour. After this time you can unmold the cake: gently pass the blade of a knife along the entire edge of the cake, then turn it upside down on a serving plate. Now proceed with the decoration: in a very cold bowl, beat the liquid fresh cream with an electric mixer until it is well whipped. At this point, spread the surface with the cream, creating a wavy pattern and garnish with red fruits of your choice.

Coffee chocolate salami

Ingredients:

- **Dark chocolate 250 g**
- **Dry biscuits 250 g**
- **Coffee 70 g**
- **Icing sugar 75 g**
- **Softened butter 30 g**
- **Bitter cocoa powder 10 g**

TO DUST

- **Powdered sugar to taste**

To make the coffee chocolate salami, first prepare the coffee: you will need 70 g. Chop the dark chocolate with a knife and melt it in a bain-marie or in the microwave, then coarsely crumble the biscuits with your hands.

Put the softened butter in a bowl, add the icing sugar and mix well with a whisk. At this point, pour in the warmed melted chocolate, the coffee at room temperature and the bitter cocoa and mix everything with a whisk. Finally add the crumbled biscuits and fold them into the mixture with a spatula. Pour the compound obtained on a sheet of parchment paper and shape it with your hands in order to give it an elongated shape, then roll up the parchment paper until it is completely wrapped and twist the ends to seal it. Place the roll in the refrigerator and let it harden for at least 2 hours.

After the cooling time, remove the parchment paper and sprinkle with icing sugar. Your coffee chocolate salami is ready to be served!

Coffee sorbet

Ingredients:

- **Coffee (250g)**
- **Sugar (350g)**
- **Water 2 cups (450g)**
- **Heavy cream (150g) - (room temperature)**

TO GARNISH

- **Heavy Cream (150g)**
- **Unsweetened cocoa powder to taste**

To make the coffee sorbet, start by preparing the coffee in a moka pot, without adding any sugar. Then, pour the water, the coffee you've prepared, and the granulated sugar into a large pot. Bring to a boil over medium heat, stirring with a whisk.

When the mixture has come to a boil, turn off the heat and pour in the heavy cream, always stirring with the whisk, and allow to cool. Next, pour the mixture into a bowl (metal is better) and place in the freezer for around 6 hours. We recommend taking the sorbet out of the freezer every two hours and stirring it with the whisk.

After these steps, you'll get the compact consistency typical of sorbet; however, since not all freezers are the same, if it's still too soft, we advise leaving the sorbet in the freezer for longer. Once it's ready, store the sorbet in the freezer and pour the heavy cream for the garnish into a bowl and whip it to stiff peaks using a hand mixer.

Take some dessert glasses and fill them with the coffee sorbet using a spoon, then garnish with a dollop of whipped cream and a sprinkling of cocoa powder. The coffee sorbet is ready to go!

Neapolitan biscuits

Ingredients:

- **Flour 00 500 g**
- **Sugar 300 g**
- **Water 250g**
- **Nutmeg 5g**
- **Cinnamon 5g**
- **Almond grain 150 g**
- **Bitter cocoa powder 30 g**
- **Orange zest 1**
- **Ammonia for cakes 3 g**

  FOR COVERAGE

- **Dark chocolate 500 g**

To prepare the Neapolitan biscuits, start by pouring the flour, the chopped almonds and the sugar into a bowl. Then sift the cocoa powder, nutmeg, cinnamon and ammonia. Finally, grate the orange zest and mix everything well. Slowly pour the water at room temperature paying attention to the necessary quantity: in fact, the dough may need a slightly lower or higher quantity. While pouring the water, knead with the other hand. As soon as you have obtained a homogeneous mixture, you can transfer it to the pastry board.

Work it by hand until all the ingredients are well blended. Wrap the dough in parchment paper and leave it to rest in the refrigerator for at least an hour. After this time, roll out the dough with a rolling pin between two sheets of parchment paper and you get a surface about 7-8 mm thick. From this, cut out about 20 rhombuses whose sides measure 7 cm. As you get the shapes, transfer them onto a baking tray lined with parchment paper, spacing them apart.

Arrange 8 diamonds at a time on the dripping pan and put into the various batches: cook in a hot oven at 180° for about 18 minutes. Once cooked, let them cool completely on a wire rack before glazing them. Coarsely chop the dark chocolate and let it melt in a bain-marie while stirring to prevent it from burning.

If you prefer, you can dip the biscuits directly into the melted chocolate and then let them harden on the parchment paper. Otherwise, for an even more beautiful result to look at, you can cover one part first by holding the biscuits by the tip and sprinkling them with chocolate with the help of a spoon. Arrange on a wire rack, with a sheet of parchment paper underneath, and leave to dry in a cool place until the chocolate has completely set.

Then turn the biscuits onto a sheet of parchment paper and place them on the wire rack. Go back to melting the chocolate and cover the other side as well. Let the chocolate harden again in a cool place. Your Neapolitan biscuits are ready, you just have to taste them!

Pignolata with honey

Ingredients:

- **Flour type 00 300 g**
- **Eggs 2 whole plus 1 yolk**
- **Butter 30 g**
- **Granulated sugar 20 g**
- **Grappa 20 g**
- **Lemons the zest of 1**
- **Salt 1 pinch**
- **TO FRY**
- **Seed oil 600 g**

TO GARNISH

- **Wildflower honey 160 g**

To make the Pignolata with honey, pour the sifted flour into a bowl, then add the soft butter cut into small pieces, the salt granulated sugar, then flavored with the grated rind of an untreated lemon and grappa.

Finally add the two whole eggs and the yolk. Start kneading vigorously by hand to mix the ingredients then transfer the dough onto a floured surface continue to knead until you obtain a compact dough which you can shape into a loaf. Wrap the dough obtained in plastic wrap and leave it in the refrigerator to harden for at least 2 hours. After the rest time, pick up the dough and with a tarot divide it into 1 cm wide pieces.

Roll each piece to obtain loaves, from these cut small pieces of 1 cm.

Now you can proceed with the cooking, heat the seed oil in a pan until it reaches about 170°C, this is the ideal temperature to obtain perfect frying, it is advisable to have a food thermometer to be able to monitor accurately. With a slotted spoon, dip a few morsels into the oil at a time, so as not to lower the oil temperature. Fry for about 3-4 minutes then drain the bites and place them on a tray lined with absorbent paper to dry the excess oil.

Collect the pignolata in a bowl and pour over the honey when the bites are still hot, stir to mix the honey, transfer the honey pignolata onto a serving plate!

Traditional tiramisu

Ingredients:

- **Ladyfingers 300 g**
- **Coffee at room temperature 200 g**
- **Mascarpone 300 g**
- **Sugar 180g**
- **Egg whites (about 4) 120 g**
- **Yolks (about 4) 80 g**
- **Water 30 g**

TO DECORATE

- **Bitter cocoa powder q.s.**

In a saucepan, pour 80 g of sugar with 30 g of water. Heat the syrup over low heat and using a cooking thermometer keep the temperature under control, which must reach 118°.

When you have reached the indicated temperature, start beating the egg yolks with an electric mixer and slowly pour the syrup onto the egg yolks, keeping the whisk in action. Continue beating until the mixture is creamy.

Now add the mascarpone to the yolks with a whisk or a spatula. Keep the mixture aside and pour the egg whites into another bowl. Start whipping them, making sure the whisks are clean.

As soon as the egg whites are white and frothy, add the remaining 100 g of sugar and continue beating until you obtain a firm and firm consistency. Add one third of the whipped egg whites to the egg yolks and mascarpone mixture and mix vigorously with the spatula.

Finish adding the remaining egg whites and mix gently from top to bottom until you get a smooth cream. At this point, soak the ladyfingers, one at a time, in the coffee at room temperature.

Gradually place them inside a 25x19 cm baking dish, in an orderly manner, so as to cover the entire surface. Now pour half of the cream and level it to completely cover the ladyfingers.

Arrange another layer of ladyfingers soaked in coffee, as done previously. Add the remaining cream and level the surface. Place in the refrigerator for at least an hour.

When serving, sprinkle the tiramisu with bitter cocoa, covering it entirely. The traditional tiramisu is ready to be cut and tasted.

Hug donut

Ingredients:

- **Flour 00 140 g**
- **Sugar 190 g**
- **Melted butter 170 g**
- **Eggs (about 4 medium) at room temperature 220 g**
- **Potato starch 60 g**
- **Fresh liquid cream at room temperature 30 g**
- **Bitter cocoa powder 20 g**
- **Baking powder for desserts 12 g**

To prepare the hug donut, first leave both the eggs and the cream at room temperature, then melt the butter in a saucepan and let it cool. Pour the sugar and eggs into a bowl. Beat them for a couple of minutes with an electric mixer at medium speed, the time necessary for the mixture to begin to swell slightly. Then work for another minute, always at the same speed, pouring in the melted and warmed butter.

Now it's the turn of the powders: turn off the whisks, place a strainer in the bowl and pour in the flour, starch and baking powder. Sift carefully and mix again with a whisk.

When the powders are well incorporated into the mixture, turn off the mixer and divide the mixture into two different bowls. In one of the two sift the cocoa, then add the cream and mix thoroughly with a hand whisk or spatula. First pour the dark dough on half of a 24 cm mold already buttered forming a semicircle, then pour the light one too and complete the circle.

Your dessert is ready to be cooked in a preheated oven at 180°, pre-set in static mode, for about 40 minutes. After making sure that the dessert is cooked with the toothpick test, let your hug donut cool down before turning it out of the mold and serving it!

Nut crunch

Ingredients:

- Peeled almonds (80 g)
- Whole peeled hazelnuts 7 tbsp (70 g)
- Pistachios 5 tbsp (50 g) - shelled
- Pine nuts 3 tbsp (30 g)
- Walnut kernels ⅔ cup (70 g)
- Sesame seeds 2 tbsp
- Sugar 1 cup (350 g)
- Water 3 tbsp
- Lemon juice 1 tsp

FOR THE MOLD

- **Vegetable oil to taste**

To prepare nut crunch, start by chopping the nuts: place the pine nuts, pistachios, almonds and hazelnuts on an oven tray, spread them over the entire surface and bake in a conventional oven preheated to 355°F (180°C) for 5 minutes. Once toasted, place the nuts on a cutting board, add the walnut kernels too and coarsely chop with a knife. Place the chopped nuts in a bowl, add the sesame seeds, and stir. Now make the caramel: place the water and sugar in a saucepan, add the lemon juice, stir with a spoon and dissolve the mixture on a medium flame: it will take around 20 minutes. Take a square 8" (20 cm) bottomless mold and place it on an oven tray lined with parchment paper.

Grease the inner edge of the mold with oil. In the meantime the syrup will have turned into the right consistency: it should be amber in color and bubbles will start to surface. Now add the nuts and stir to amalgamate; leave to cook for another 2/3 minutes. Pour the mixture into the mold, spread it evenly using a wood spoon. Leave it to cool at room temperature for around 10 minutes (it will still be soft and malleable). Once the resting time is up, before removing the mold, run the blade of a knife along the entire edge so that it will be easier to remove the mixture from the mold.

Tip the nut crunch over onto a cutting board, remove the parchment paper, cut it into 8 pieces of equal size and leave to rest until the bars take on a compact and hardened consistency. Place the nut crunch on a serving dish; it is now ready to be enjoyed!

Mantovana cake

- **Flour 00 175 g**
- **Butter 175 g**
- **Sugar 175g**
- **Yolks 4**
- **Eggs 1**
- **Peeled almonds 50 g**
- **Baking powder for desserts 5 g**
- **TO BUTTER**
- **Butter to taste**

To prepare the Mantovana cake, place the butter cut into pieces, softened at room temperature, and the sugar in a bowl. Whip the two ingredients with the whisk of an electric mixer, or with the whisk of a planetary mixer, until you obtain a frothy mixture. Now add the whole egg and continue to work the mixture to incorporate it.

Then add the yolks, one at a time, waiting for the previous one to be absorbed before adding the next. To obtain a homogeneous mixture it is important that the eggs are at room temperature; if after adding the eggs the mixture tends to separate, do not worry because by adding the flour you will get the right consistency. Sift the flour together with the yeast and add the powders, all at once, to the mixture, continuing to work with the whisk to mix all the ingredients well and obtain a frothy and homogeneous mixture. Line a 26cm cake tin with parchment paper.

Chop the almonds into pieces with a knife; Pour the mixture into the pan and level it evenly with the back of a spoon.

Sprinkle the surface with the almonds in pieces until it is completely covered; bake in a preheated oven at 180° for 30 minutes (if a convection oven at 160° for 20-25 minutes). Before removing it from the oven, do the toothpick test: if it is not yet cooked, continue cooking by covering the surface with aluminum foil and continue until the end of the set minutes. Remove from the oven, let it cool and serve your Mantovana cake! You can sprinkle it with powdered sugar or granulated sugar if you like!

Carnival Tortelli

Ingredients:

- Whole milk 210 g
- Butter 100 g
- Flour 00 300 g
- Sugar 100g
- Lemon zest 1
- Eggs 4
- Yolks 2
- Baking powder for cakes 8 g
- Salt up to 1 pinch

TO FRY

- Peanut oil to taste

TO SPRINKLE

- Sugar to taste

To prepare the Carnival tortelli, pour the milk into a pan, add the butter, sugar, grated lemon zest and salt. Bring the mixture to the boil, stirring with a wooden spoon.

When it has reached a boil, remove the pan from the heat and pour in the sifted flour together with the baking powder and mix vigorously. Then put the pan back on low heat and keep stirring for 2-3 minutes until the mixture is smooth. Transfer the mixture into a bowl and leave to cool.

When it has cooled, add one egg at a time to the mixture, mixing well until the egg is completely absorbed, then proceed in the same way with the other eggs, being careful not to add the next egg if the previous one is not has been fully incorporated; at the end you will have to obtain a smooth and fluid compound. Pour some seed oil into a pan with high edges and bring it to a temperature of 160°-170°. The tortelli will have to fry slowly so as not to suddenly darken while keeping the inside raw, therefore, before frying one, do a test with very little batter: it will have to brown slowly. When the oil is ready, scoop out a quantity of dough the size of a walnut with a spoon.

With another spoon, slide the dough into the oil, turn the tortello to make it brown and puff up equally over the entire surface. Once golden, drain the tortelli with a slotted spoon.

Place the tortelli on a tray lined with paper towels to dry the excess oil, then roll them in the caster sugar. Your Carnival tortelli are ready to be enjoyed!

Genoa Cake

Ingredients:

- **Butter at room temperature 85 g**
- **Sugar 100g**
- **Eggs 1**
- **Flour 00 300 g**
- **Salt up to 1 g**
- **Raisins 230 g**
- **Candied orange 80 g**
- **Pine nuts 20 g**
- **Whole milk 80 g**
- **Baking powder for desserts 10 g**

To prepare the Genoa cake, start by cutting candied orange into cubes. Now move on to the butter at room temperature which you will cut into pieces. Then take a planetary mixer in which to add the butter and sugar, the sifted flour and the baking powder. Add the salt and the egg and start kneading at medium speed. While kneading, slowly add the milk at room temperature. When it is absorbed, stop the mixer for a moment and add the orange and raisins, previously rinsed under running water and dried.

Finally pour the pine nuts. Run the mixer again for about 10 seconds at medium speed to mix the ingredients well. Then transfer the dough to a pastry board and compact the dough with your hands. Give it a rounded shape. At this point, lightly press the upper part of the dough with your hands to flatten it slightly. Slide your hands along the edges of the dough so as to adjust them and give a disc shape. Then place it on a baking tray lined with parchment paper.

With a sharp blade, make a diamond decoration on the surface. You can now bake in a preheated static oven at 180°C for 45-50 minutes (or in a preheated convection oven at 160°C for around 35-40 minutes). Once the cooking time has elapsed, remove from the oven and let it rest for a few minutes before bringing this Christmas delight to the table!

Cream puff

Ingredients:

- Flour 00 125 g
- Icing sugar 45 g
- Extra virgin olive oil 35 ml
- Eggs 1
- Baking powder for desserts 4 g
- FOR THE CUSTARD CREAM
- Whole milk 250 ml
- Sugar 75 g
- Flour 00 25 g
- Yolks 3
- Vanilla pod ½
- TO GARNISH
- **Crushed hazelnuts q.b.**

To prepare the puffs, start with the shortcrust pastry: arrange the flour, sugar and baking powder on a pastry board (or in a bowl). Mix the powders together, form a fountain in the center and add the eggs inside; break them up with a fork and beat them, trying to incorporate the flour; then add the extra virgin olive oil and knead with your hands, until you get a smooth and compact dough. Wrap it in plastic wrap and let it rest in the refrigerator for at least an hour.

After the resting time, take the pastry back and roll it out with a rolling pin into a very thin sheet, about half a cm thick, and with a pastry ring with a diameter of 5.5 cm, make circles. You will get about 32 circles. Place the discs on a baking tray, covered with parchment paper, well spaced from each other and bake them in a static oven, already hot, at 160° for 10 minutes (if a convection oven at 140° for 6-7 minutes). Diskettes must remain clear; take them out and let them cool. Meanwhile, prepare the custard: heat the milk in a saucepan with half a vanilla bean and its seeds; beat the egg yolk and sugar in a bowl with a whisk, then add the flour. With tongs, remove the berry and pour the heated milk onto the mixture, mixing with a whisk. Return the mixture to the heat and stir continuously until the cream thickens. Transfer the custard into a bowl and let it cool by keeping it in contact with a sheet of plastic wrap.

Once cold, transfer the cream into a sac-à-few with a star nozzle and start composing the confectioners: take a disk of pastry, fill it with a tuft of cream and place another disk of pastry on top of the cream, pressing lightly to compact the cake and to let the cream come out slightly.

Place the chopped hazelnuts on a saucer and decorate the edges of the cream puffs. Keep the cream puffs in the fridge until serving and before serving, sprinkle them with plenty of icing sugar.

Made in the USA
Las Vegas, NV
08 September 2023